Dan Soka
Adult Prob.
792-8291
24 Jan 71

BEHAVIOR THERAPY & BEYOND

**McGraw-Hill Series
in Psychology**

Consulting Editors

Norman Garmezy

Richard L. Solomon

Lyle V. Jones

Harold W. Stevenson

BEHAVIOR THERAPY & BEYOND

Arnold A. Lazarus, Ph.D.

Department of Psychology
Yale University

McGraw-Hill Book Company

New York   St. Louis   San Francisco   Düsseldorf   Johannesburg
Kuala Lumpur   London   Mexico   Montreal   New Delhi
Panama   Rio de Janeiro   Singapore   Sydney   Toronto

Behavior Therapy and Beyond

Library of Congress Catalog Card Number 70-143444

07-036800-7

1 2 3 4 5 6 7 8 9 0   MAMM   7 9 8 7 6 5 4 3 2 1

*This book was set in Bodoni Book by Monotype Com-
position Company, Inc., and printed on permanent
paper and bound by The Maple Press Company. The
designer was Marsha Cohen; the drawings were done
by John Cordes, J. & R. Technical Services, Inc. The
editors were Walter Maytham and Paula Henson.
Sally Ellyson supervised production.*

Silent truth cannot withstand error aided by continued propaganda.

Orville Wright

Die Natur scheint Alles auf Individualität angelegt zu haben.

Goethe

Science is commonly considered to give men control over nature, but in the psychological field there is no "generalized mind" to be controlled. There are only single, concrete minds, each one of which presents problems peculiar to itself.

Gordon W. Allport

To Daphne, Linda, and Cliff

CONTENTS

PREFACE

Preparation of this book, which is written entirely from the standpoint of a *clinician*, was prompted by my students, who insisted that some of the procedures I use go beyond conventional "behavior therapy." I had thought of calling the book *Beyond Behavior Therapy*, but it was pointed out that this would imply a decisive break with behavior therapy. In fact I draw very heavily upon this discipline, while also employing techniques which do not easily fit within this framework at present. Hopefully, behavior therapy will soon expand sufficiently for every method outlined in this book to be considered well within its boundaries. The intent, therefore, is not so much to depart from behavior therapy as to expand its legitimate base of operations.

Many trainees who were acquainted with my writings expressed some surprise after observing me with patients. Although my previous publications had stressed such features as interpersonal considerations and other "nonspecific" factors, the extent to which these aspects often dominate my therapeutic interactions had not been sufficiently emphasized. This book will try to spell out some specific and general aspects of treatment which my trainees and I have found successful.

The reason for employing techniques beyond those described by, say, Wolpe and Lazarus (1966) or Wolpe (1969) is simply that these methods alone are, in my present judgment, often insufficient to produce durable results (Lazarus, 1969). And the reason why not all the additional procedures were clearly apparent in my previous writings was due to the false selectivity of my own perceptions. Often, my interest and attention were so firmly riveted to behavior therapy that I translated nearly everything I did into post hoc S-R terms. At other times I erroneously failed to recognize the additional procedures I employed as anything more than incidental activity. Most of my trainees as well as several of my experienced colleagues have led me to reconsider what seems important (and unimportant) for achieving durable clinical results.

The intent throughout this book is to caution therapists and would-be therapists not to forget the obvious fact that every individual is unique, and to tailor his therapy accordingly. The term suggested by Dr. Barton Singer which best seems to describe this approach is *personalistic psychotherapy*. It takes special cognizance of individual differences. Lasting improvement seldom follows any approach in which patients are coerced into abandoning their deviant responses by methods decided in advance by the therapist. It was pointed out by Hoch (1955), Solovey and Milechnin (1958), Goldstein (1962), and Conn (1968) that people enter therapy with certain expectations, and that the effectiveness of the therapy is closely linked with these expectations. If the therapist's attitude and approach differ markedly from the patient's "ideal picture" of a psychology practitioner, positive results are unlikely to ensue. If the methods and techniques employed are not in accord with the patient's ideas about the procedures to which he would like to respond and which he would wish to have applied in his case, a therapeutic impasse is likely to be the net result. The present orientation, represented by this book, may be described as an antipanacea approach. It is not for or against "insight," nor for or against "deconditioning." It is concerned with the combination of techniques which seems likely to be most beneficial to the people who ask for help.

The emphasis of the volume is upon *techniques* rather than upon theories. As an ever-increasing number of therapeutic systems mushroom into existence, it becomes impossible to keep pace with the field. Theorists who try to integrate assumptions from divergent systems often end up embracing incompatible notions. Those who identify exclusively with one or two schools of thought often find that their devotion eventually leads to diminishing returns. But those clinicians who are willing to employ any technique that has been shown to be effective empirically, regardless of its point of origin, manage to extract the active ingredients from a vast array of different systems.

Methods of therapy are often effective for reasons which are at variance with the views of their inventors or discoverers. *Technical eclecticism* (Lazarus, 1967) does not imply a random melange of techniques taken haphazardly out of the air. It is an approach which urges therapists to experiment with empirically useful methods instead of using their theories as a priori predictors of what will and will not succeed in therapy (Eysenck, 1957, p. 271). The rationale behind the methods described in this book is predicated upon London's (1964) observation that: "However interesting, plausible, and appealing a theory may be, it is techniques, not theories, that are actually used on people. Study of the effects of psychotherapy, therefore, is always the study of the effectiveness of techniques [p. 33]."

I have included in this book improved and refined versions of many of the techniques previously developed and employed by "behavior therapists" and "behavior modifiers" to which I have added several new procedures. The methods and their effects are amenable to replication, verification, or disproof, and as such, should have some appeal for experimentally minded clinicians. By and large, this book is intended for practitioners and students who are interested in effective psychotherapy. It is also conceivable that certain patients may find bibliotherapeutic value in some of the chapters and case histories.

Various parts of the manuscript were discussed with colleagues and students at several seminars, workshops, lectures, and clinical meetings. Numerous friends and associates read several chapters and made constructive criticisms. Others read the entire manuscript and made additional helpful comments. I am especially grateful to Arnold and Carole Abramovitz, David Braff, Phil Friedman, Norman Garmezy, Barry Miller, and Terry Wilson.

I wish to express special thanks to Jerry Davison for helping me with Chapter 10.

I would also like to thank Mrs. Lynne Kugler for typing the manuscript.

Arnold A. Lazarus

CHAPTER 1
BEHAVIOR THERAPY AND CLINICAL PROBLEMS A CRITICAL OVERVIEW

Now that behavior therapy is rapidly gaining in popularity, it is time to take careful stock of the field and possibly expose some fallacies in the hopes of salvaging those elements which, in the hands of astute clinicians, can be therapeutically useful. Behavior therapy has at last achieved "front-page glamour" and has been labeled "revolutionary" in several national newspapers and international periodicals. This is unfortunate. The methods of behavior therapy are extremely effective when applied to carefully selected cases by informed practitioners. But when procedures overstep the boundaries of their legitimate terrain, ridicule and disparagement are most likely to ensue. Far from being a panacea, the methods are then held to have no merit whatsoever, and the proverbial baby gets thrown out with the bath water. This has often been the fate of methods based on suggestion and hypnosis. The history of hypnosis shows that each total eclipse was always preceded by an extremely bright and broadly focused spotlight of intense respectability and overacceptance. And so it is with behavior therapy which, having withstood extreme criticism from hostile skeptics, can be destroyed by the extravagant claims of its overly enthusiastic proponents.

Origins of the "Behavior Therapy" Concept

For the record, it should be noted that starting in 1953, B. F. Skinner, Harry C. Solomon, Ogden R. Lindsley, and Malcolm E. Richards, under contract with the Office of Naval Research, U.S. Navy, conducted research "to determine the applicability of operant conditioning techniques to the experimental analysis of psychotic patients." This research was conducted in the Laboratory for Behavior Research at the Metropolitan State Hospital, Waltham, Massachusetts, and was referred to as "Studies in Behavior Therapy." On the basis of the mimeographed status reports of these operant conditioning studies of psychotic behavior, Wolpe (1968a) gives credit to Skinner and Lindsley for introducing the term *behavior therapy.*

   The first time the terms *behavior therapy* and *behavior therapist* appeared in a scientific journal was when I endeavored to point out the need for adding objective, laboratory-derived therapeutic tools to more orthodox psychotherapeutic techniques (Lazarus, 1958). My use of the term behavior therapy was quite independent of Skinner et al., 1953, and conceptualized the role of behavior therapists entirely different from their application of operant conditioning principles to psychotic patients. For me, behavior therapy has always been a useful psychotherapeutic adjunct. "Where necessary, the behaviorist or objective psychotherapist employs all the usual psychotherapeutic techniques, such as support, guidance, insight, catharsis, interpretation, environmental manipulation, etc., but in addition ... the behavior therapist applies objective techniques which are designed to inhibit specific neurotic patterns" (Lazarus, 1958).

   About a year after my 1958 paper appeared, Eysenck (1959) independently used the term *behavior therapy* to denote a decisive break with psychoanalytic thought in which he held that neurotic responses are simply acquired on the basis of classical conditioning. He then edited two books on behavior therapy in relatively quick succession (Eysenck, 1960, 1964) and is therefore responsible for disseminating the widespread notion that behavior therapy only treats symptoms because if you "get rid of the symptom . . . you have eliminated the neurosis [Eysenck, 1959; 1960, p. 9]." Thus, Eysenck (1960, p. ix) argued that "psychotherapy itself, when shorn of its inessential and irrelevant parts, can usefully be considered as a minor part of behavior therapy."

Yates (1970) has argued that behavior theraphy developed (in theory and approach, if not in name) at the Maudsley Hospital under Dr. M. B. Shapiro during 1950 to 1955, and was essentially a method in which individual patients were investigated as experimental problems in their own right. Shapiro's behavior therapists were (and perhaps remain) opposed to the development of standardized techniques of behavioral treatment. Behavior therapy, in this setting, was essentially construed as an attempt to establish the interaction of theories derived from experimental psychology with empirical data obtained from controlled studies on the individual patient. Yates is emphatic that Shapiro's approach was by no means limited to "learning theory," but encompassed the entire field of experimental psychology and related disciplines such as physiology and neurophysiology. The reports of H. G. Jones (1956) and Yates (1958) are typical of this behavior therapy approach.

Although the first written report limited the term *behavior therapy* to operant conditioning, while the first published report conceptualized behavior therapy as a useful psychotherapeutic adjunct, popular usage (or misusage, depending on one's viewpoint) now links the term *behavior therapy* mainly with the genesis and treatment of unadaptive anxiety responses within a counterconditioning framework (Wolpe, 1968b). While Wolpeans are permitted to use operant conditioning and modeling techniques, the devotees of these latter methods usually avoid the term *therapy* and refer to themselves as *behavior modifiers* (e.g., Ullmann & Krasner, 1965, 1969).

The Relevance of Learning Principles to Behavior Therapy

The standard definition is that behavior therapy "denotes the use of experimentally established principles of learning for the purpose of changing unadaptive behavior" (Wolpe, 1968b, p. 557). Just what are these so-called "experimentally established principles of learning"? Do they apply to human beings as well as to animals? Although parallels may be drawn between the unadaptive behavior of animals and human beings, suffice it to say that even at the animal level, a basic statement such as "stronger reinforcers will produce stronger conditioning" is theory rather than fact. Some established principles of learning may exist in animal laboratories, but insofar as their relevance for human behavior is concerned, there are, to say the least, many debatable points of issue (Breger & McGaugh, 1965; Wike, 1966). Thus, Eysenck's (1968, p. 376) insistence that behavior therapy denotes "methods of treatment which are derived from modern learning theory" amounts to little more than a beguiling slogan. In fact Bambeck (1968) has shown many logical inconsistencies and gaps in the theories and meta-theories of Tolman, Guthrie, Hull, and early Skinner, and has seriously challenged, if not disproved, the validity of many methatheoretical axioms and postulates in "Modern Learning Theory."

While there is considerable evidence in support of the hypothesis that neurotic behavior is mainly a function of *learning* (rather than the product of lesions, biochemical imbalance, or genetic endowment) it should not be forgotten that this is but a hypothesis. Yet Wolpe treats this hypothesis as an established fact. He points out that behavior therapy is mainly applicable to overcoming unadaptive forms of behavior which *owe their existence* to learning, and then adds: "Pre-eminent among them are the neuroses" (Wolpe, 1968b, p. 557). Eysenck (1963) is more cautious and refers to the *belief* that "behavioral disorders of the most divergent type are essentially learned responses, and that modern learning theory (in its widest sense) has much to teach us regarding the acquisition and extinction of such responses." Apart from the fact that Eysenck employs "modern learning theory" in a very narrow sense (cf. Breger & McGaugh, 1965), we might well inquire what the widest sense of modern learning theory might include.

In their book *Theories of Learning*, Hilgard and Bower (1966) discuss Tolman's sign learning, Gestalt theory, Freud's psychodynamics, and information processing, in addition to the learning theories of Guthrie, Hull, Pavlov, and Skinner. In terms of learning theory in its widest sense, the statement that neurotic behavior is acquired or learned becomes quite meaningless and trite. There appear to be different types of learning and different levels of learning (e.g., cognitive versus affective) that may one day be shown to obey different "laws" and that would presumably lead to different processes of "unlearning." Even in many simple learning situations it is usually unclear whether movements, habits, responses, and/or expectancies have in fact been learned. In complex learning situations (such as psychotherapy), these elements merge and are inclined to become extremely intricate. What is learned? How is it learned? Where, when, and why is it learned? As Smith (1965, p. 138) points out, even Rank's birth trauma theory is a hypothesis about learning. "It asserts that a single traumatic experience, a single experience providing an increase in excitation to the nervous system, one moreover that apparently results in no adaptive behavior but just "panic" and one that often occurs very early in life, will make a sufficient impression that it will continue to influence behavior for years, decades, after its occurrence."

Wolpe (1958, 1968b) has continued to use the term *conditioning* as a synonym for all kinds of learning. English and English (1958, pp. 107–108) refer to this practice as "theory-begging" and argue that "the term conditioning is best reserved for those forms of learning that bear *close resemblance* to the experimental design of conditioning." There are relatively few behavior therapy techniques that bear a close resemblance to the conditioning paradigm. Even in a learning situation as precise as "aversive conditioning," Carlin and Armstrong (1968) found data to support their contention that "factors other than conditioning may account for the behavioral changes in aversive conditioning therapy paradigms." Several decades ago, Jersild and Holmes (1935) referred to conditioning as "a decided oversimplification of what occurs in daily life." Suffice it to say that when Alexander (1963) wrote about "the beginnings of a most promising integration of psychoanalytic theory with learning theory," the type of "learning theory" he had in mind bore very little resemblance to mechanistic conditioning approaches. The danger lies in a premature elevation of learning principles into unwarranted scientific truths and the ascription of the general term of "modern learning theory" to what in reality are best described as "modern learning theories." For an excellent review of the nature of learning in traditional and behavioral psychotherapy, the reader is referred to Murray and Jacobson (1971).

The Animal Game

Some approaches to behavior therapy may be said to constitute a game. The name of the game could be: "Let us never lose sight of the fact that man is an animal." A more detailed title would be: "Let us deny that human beings have a cerebral cortex and let us reduce man to a hypothalamic, subcortical creature dominated by a primitive autonomic nervous system." Hence Wolpe (1964) gives the name "behavior therapy" to "the conditioning methods of therapy of human neuroses that have been developed on the basis of experiences with experimental neuroses," and he holds that "human neuroses are like those of animals *in all essential respects* (Wolpe, 1968b, p. 559)." When confronted by people intent on self-destruction, torn asunder by conflicting loyalties, crippled by too high a level of aspiration, unhappily married because of false romantic ideals, or beset by feelings of guilt and inferiority on the basis of complex theological beliefs, I fail to appreciate the clinical significance of Wolpe's (1958) neurotic cats and sometimes wish that life and therapy were really as simple as he would have us believe. Certainly for those who insist upon animal analogues, Harlow's neurotic monkeys would be a better animal analogue of human neuroses (e.g., Harlow, 1962; Griffen & Harlow, 1966).

There would be little argument if behavior therapy was considered a most useful objective psychotherapeutic adjunct, extremely valuable whenever clear-cut maladaptive approach or avoidance responses are evident. But Wolpe (1968b, p. 557) emphasizes that behavior therapy is no mere supplement to other systems of therapy, but in fact challenges these systems "and bids fair to replace them." Indeed, methods based on principles of extinction, counterconditioning, positive and negative reinforcement, and aversive conditioning or punishment, are sometimes the most rapid, if not the only available, means of overcoming certain phobias, compulsions, tics, addictions, speech problems, cases of enuresis and encopresis, and various sexual disorders such as fetishism, transvestism, and even selected cases of homosexuality. Hence, it probably behooves clinicians of diverse theoretical persuasions to master several behavior therapy techniques. But in my estimation, the twenty or so behavioral techniques described by Wolpe (1969) represent a useful *starting point* for increased clinical effectiveness rather than a complete system which can put an end to 90 percent of the world's neurotic suffering. Although many of Wolpe's theoretical shortcomings are stressed throughout this chapter, it is by no means intended to be a comprehensive critique of his work. This would require a detailed discussion of his theory of emotions and a lengthy discourse on the inadequecy of his model of the etiology of neurotic behavior. To delve into these issues here would constitute a digression from the main thrust of this book. A review article in a scientific journal would seem to constitute a better medium for the evaluation of such problems.

Behavior Therapy as an Objective Psychotherapeutic Adjunct

My own view of behavior therapy has always been that it adds objective laboratory-derived therapeutic tools to more orthodox procedures (Lazarus, 1958). I have stressed that "conditioning techniques are in fact additional to many of the methods in conventional use" (Lazarus, 1963). Wolpe (1963) espoused a similar view when he considered behavior therapy a special segment of psychotherapy and defined it as "the class of psychotherapeutic practices in which behavior is deployed in a manner designed directly to bring about change in specific habits." This is a reasonable definition because it permits definite qualifying clauses. Behavior therapy would *not* include those cases in which behavior is deployed in a manner designed *indirectly* to bring about change in nonspecific habits (e.g., the use of drugs and shock treatment). Nor would it include methods, whether direct or indirect, to bring about change in nonspecific habits (e.g., the therapist's empathic understanding for reducing loneliness and self-abnegation). In other words, the definition tacitly acknowledged that there was more to psychotherapy than the direct modification of specific habits. Behavior therapy would be operative whenever the methods being employed and the problems being treated did not stretch Wolpe's analogies with cats beyond the point of credulity.

Behavior Therapy: Narrow-band or Broad-spectrum

I once successfully treated a child who was afraid of riding in automobiles by providing him with chocolate and tasty snacks in a manner similar to Wolpe's frightened cats (Lazarus, 1959). This case did not call for anything more elaborate or complicated. More complex procedures immediately present theoretical difficulties. Weitzman (1967) cautions against the formation of analogies that obscure differences of "profound significance between the systematic desensitizations of cats and men." He emphasizes that the many images, symbolic materials, ideas, and cognitive-affective interchanges that occur during desensitization "stretches the analogy to Wolpe's procedure with the cats rather thin." Nevertheless, when applying desensitization one is clearly engaging in behavior therapy whether or not desensitization really works on the basis of conditioning principles or for psychodynamic reasons. The same is true when teaching a mother to ignore her child's deviant behaviors and to reward his prosocial responses. But when trying to unravel the complex expectancies in a dyadic marital struggle in which the respective partners misperceive each other's roles and are each vying for leadership, one is apparently no longer necessarily engaged in behavior therapy, although one is involved in a clinical procedure that behavior therapists might often be called upon to administer (Lazarus, 1968c).

When expressing the virtues of personal integrity as opposed to hypocritical modes of social intercourse, therapists will be hard-pressed to justify their actions in S-R terms. The same is true when faced with moral issues involving divorce, sexual practices, business ventures, and other such daily or indeed *hourly* therapeutic topics. The practicing clinician will find that those who impugn intuition, wisdom, and the necessity for clinical experience per se, mercifully do not engage in therapy themselves, or unmercifully create even more intractable problems for those unfortunate patients who turn to them for help.

Eysenck (1965, p. 157) should be commended for stressing that in addition to a knowledge of "learning theory," therapists require "a very special ability to understand the difficulties and troubles of the neurotic, and to devise ways and means of getting them out of these difficulties." Eysenck's reference to "a very special ability" is probably related to what Rogers, Truax, Carkhuff, Berenson, Bergin, et al. call "high levels of facilitative conditions" such as empathy, respect, genuineness, and concreteness, about which there is a wealth of research data (Truax & Carkhuff, 1967; Carkhuff & Berenson, 1967). Whether or not these facilitative abilities are inborn or can be learned is not as relevant as the fact that they can only be put to effective clinical use by persons who have had sufficient therapeutic contact with patients to know exactly how and when to display them. In short, several behavior therapists now acknowledge the fact that more varied and complex inter-actional processes other than reciprocal inhibition and operant condi-tioning permeate their interviews and contaminate or facilitate the application of their specific techniques. To cite but one example, Leiten-berg, Agras, Barlow, and Oliveau (1969) ran controlled studies which "pose certain problems for reciprocal inhibition conceptions, and suggest that the effects of systematic desensitization cannot be attributed solely to the variables of a graded hierarchy plus relaxation." They showed that the patient's cognitive set, derived from therapeutically oriented instructions, plays a significant role.

Disease or Disordered Habits: A False Dichotomy?

Even the recent writings of Eysenck (1968) and Wolpe (1968b) suggest that clinicians must either choose the "disease model" of psychoanalysis with its emphasis on putative repressed complexes, or adhere to the "learning model" of behavior therapy which reduces the most complex human problems to malconditioned habits. Other writers also stress this false dichotomy. Sloane and Payne (1966) state that "there are two current approaches to psychotherapy as a means of modifying unde-sirable behavior." They then distinguish between the "medical model" which stresses "insight," and the behavioral approach which applies "principles of psychological learning theory to the amelioration of the presenting behavior." If therapists only had to choose between two broad approaches to psychotherapy, how simple life would be. In 1959, Harper outlined thirty-six separate approaches to psychotherapy that covered a range of medical, nonmedical, hydraulic, learning, and other models. Since then, I have become acquainted with at least another twenty separate and distinct systems of therapy based upon a variety of different models. There are undoubtedly dozens more with which I am not familiar. Yet Eysenck (1968, p. 364) seems to draw a neat dichot-omy between (1) "*psychotherapy* which is defined so as to include all types of interpretative, dynamic, or even Rogerian systems," and (2) "psychological systems involving re-education, conditioning, or behavior therapy." Is there no overlap or common ground? It would be difficult to categorize each of the following systems as either predominantly psychodynamic or reeducative: reality therapy, tactilization, integrity therapy, general semantics, Gestalt therapy, hypnosynthesis, rational-emotive therapy, autogenic training, Morita therapy, assumptions-centered therapy, fixed role therapy, marathon and group encounters, bioenergetic analysis, and eidetic psychotherapy, to mention but a few of the numerous psychological approaches other than the well-known Freudian, Jungian, Adlerian, neoanalytic, or behavioristic methods. Who would care to separate these and the many other systems into "disease" and "learning" models or to discern possible mergings between the two? But this Herculean labor would serve no useful function because the separation into disease and learning models is based upon an oversimplification and distortion of the enormous range of psychological modes of intervention. The available choices go far beyond "insight versus action," or "psychoanalysis versus behavior therapy." It might be noted en passant that Rachman (1968, p. xi) who adheres rigidly to a conditioning and learning model of neuroses in general and phobias in particular, still writes about "the prognosis for phobic *ill-nesses*" (italics inserted). This might be due to the fact that Rachman follows Wolpe's medical model (e.g., he employs neurological constructs rather than social-psychological concepts) when describing behavior (cf. Ullmann & Krasner, 1969).

Little Hans, Little Albert, or Neither?

In his book *Fact and Fiction in Psychology*, Eysenck (1965) has a chapter entitled "Little Hans or Little Albert?" Freud's (1909) paper, "An Analysis of a Phobia in a Five-Year-Old Boy," is commonly referred to as the "case of little Hans" and is supposed to be paradigmatic of psychoanalysis in general (Eysenck, 1965, p. 106). Little Hans was afraid of going into the streets and was especially afraid that a horse would bite him. Freud resorted to the familiar circuitous construct of the Oedipus complex, castration anxiety, repression, projection, etc., to "explain" Little Hans's fears. On the other hand, Little Albert was an eleven-month-old child whom Watson and Rayner (1920) rendered fearful of furry objects by striking an iron bar, very loudly, whenever Albert reached out toward and touched a laboratory-reared white rat.

Prior to the experiment, the infant was evidently quite fond of white rats and used to play with them frequently and fearlessly. After relatively few trials of Watson and Rayner's aversive training, Little Albert would whimper and try to crawl away from rats, and showed similar avoidance reactions, along a generalization gradient, to other furry animals and objects. Little Albert is held to be paradigmatic of behavior therapy in general, and the genesis of phobias in particular (Rachman, 1968).

Nevertheless, of significance to the present discussion is the well-known selectivity of perception. Freud considered Hans's phobia a product of the boy's repressed libidinal and aggressive wishes. To a family therapist (Strean, 1967) "Hans's phobia was the displayed expression of family conflict and held the family together, preserving its equilibrium. When Hans, the family member with the presenting problem, improved, the parents' marriage soon after dissolved." In this context, the marriage relationship should have been the focus of therapeutic attention. The behavioral interpretation of Hans's phobia finds evidence of various preconditioning experiences and a final precipitant when a horse-drawn bus fell down and Hans became very frightened (Wolpe & Rachman, 1960).

The numerous writings of Eysenck, Wolpe, Rachman, et al. lead one to suppose that a choice must be made between the theories of Watson and Freud (e.g., Eysenck & Rachman, 1965). The prevailing notion is that one either resorts to complex intrapsychic explanations of behavior, or one "considers neurotic symptoms as simple, learned habits" (Kugelmass, 1968, p. viii). You are either a Freudian or a Behaviorist, a neo-Freudian or a neo-Behaviorist. The representatives of Freud are supposed to view all phobias as overt manifestations of unconscious conflicts, such as castration anxiety and repressed hostility, in which mechanisms such as displacement and the condensation of symbols take place and form a protective cathexis which defends the ego against painful id impulses. In contrast to this, behavior therapists maintain that "phobias develop through a process of conditioning (Rachman, 1968, p. 27)." We have already commented on this false dichotomy by pointing out how many systems of therapy owe no allegiance or support either to Watson (or Pavlov) or to Freud. The choice is not between Little Hans or Little Albert. We may reject both models; the first for being too complex and abstruse, and the second for being simplistic and too mechanistic (except in accounting for traumatic neuroses, which will be discussed more fully later on). A simple illustration should be sufficient to capture the essence of what may be called "a functional approach to unadaptive behaviors."

The Functional Model

Let us assume that a therapist is consulted by a patient complaining of a phobia of pens and pencils. The straw-man psychoanalyst, Dr. Hans, would say, "Your fear of pens and pencils is the overt manifestation of unconscious processes. The objects you fear are obviously phallic symbols and are indicative of your disturbed sexual functioning. After years of intensive analysis you might appreciate the full meaning and purpose of your displaced anxiety, and thereby resolve it by acquiring insight into the relevant unconscious dynamics." The (not so) straw-man behavior therapist, Dr. Albert, would say, "Your phobic reactions are nothing but maladaptive conditioned responses, bad habits, acquired in frightening or painful situations. All we have to do is desensitize you to pens and pencils and we will have eliminated your neurosis."

The functional approach rejects both the psychoanalytic and the behavioristic conception of symptom formation. It accepts that under laboratory conditions and traumatic life experiences, conditioned emotional reactions to neutral objects and situations may persist, but it holds that most patients seeking relief from emotional suffering acquire their fears and other tensions quite differently. In the example above, one would ask, "What functions do pens and pencils perform? For what are they empolyed?" The answer, of course, is that they are mainly used for writing and for drawing. If we knew the patient to be a writer or an artist who was no longer able to work because of his affliction, we might assume that his phobia of pens and pencils was the objective reflection of an avoidance gradient stemming from central tensions and misgivings in his work situation. Therapy would then focus mainly on overcoming his fears and inadequacies about work. If no such obvious functional connection was evident, we would inquire, "In what way does your fear of pens and pencils interfere with your life?" While searching for possible central dimensions, we would endeavor to pinpoint the development of the presenting problem. When did it start? What was going on at the time? Was it sudden or gradual? Did anything happen to make it better or worse? In short, the person's *interpersonal relationships* would be thoroughly investigated. There are some well-functioning and happily adjusted human beings with monosymptomatic phobias, but they are very much the exception rather than the rule. Family interactions usually provide the breeding ground for maladaptive behavior, and it is therefore within family relationships that therapists should seek for most causes and cures.

Phobias and Conditioning: Evidence from 100 Clinical Cases

On examining the records of 100 patients of mine whose presenting complaints included specific irrational fears, there were only *two* cases who recalled having undergone traumatic experiences which were clearly associated with the object of their fears. More than half the people reported never actually having encountered their feared objects and situations. In this sample, Rachman's (1968, p. 31) contention that "stimuli develop phobic qualities when they are associated temporally and spatially with a fear-producing state of affairs" is certainly not upheld. He might reason that these patients had acquired their fears "by second, third or tenth remove (p. 37)," but this fails to shed any further clinical light on the subject.

Consider the case of Mr. S., who was incapacitated by his excessive fear of chemical solvents. What was the primary conditioned response which led, through higher-order conditioning, to Mr. S.'s excessive fear of contamination? It all began ten years previously when he had been ridiculed in school. How do we proceed with a conditioning model from ridicule to fears of contamination by chemical solvents? If only the ridicule had occurred during a lecture on chemistry, or in temporal contiguity with a bunsen burner, some kind of case for conditioning could be made. But Mr. S. had been ridiculed for misquoting Shakespeare—a fact which diminished neither his interest in nor his enthusiasm for literature, plays and poetry in general, and the works of Shakespeare in particular.

Perhaps Mr. S. developed his fears vicariously, on the basis of modeling or imitation. But neither his parents, his siblings, nor any of his friends or associates suffered from a similar affliction. Elsewhere, Rachman (1968, p. 39) mentions en passant that phobias "can also be acquired as the result of exposure to conflict." Now there was little doubt that Mr. S. was in a state of conflict, but two facts should be stressed in this regard. The nature of his conflicts bore no discernible resemblance to the types of ambivalent stimuli employed in conditioning experiments, nor did they resemble the unconscious forces which psychoanalysts so readily infer.

There was not the remotest hint that his contamination phobia was the terminal manifestation of unconscious incestuous desires or similar psychosexual displacements. While working with Mr. S., it became clear that his fears were related to his feelings of personal unworthiness and to his uncertainties about strong religious beliefs he had held in the past. An overcritical mother, who had displaced antipathies from husband to son, played a prominent role. Perhaps the most parsimonious manner in which his problems could be conceptualized would be in terms of numerous irrational expectancies and uncertainties. But the procrustean maneuvers required to fit his problems within the confines of a conditioning model, would so truncate their original form as to render them unrecognizable.

Out of the 100 cases surveyed, fourteen were severely claustrophobic. The conditioning theory of phobias asserts that they usually develop after many exposures to traumatic or subtraumatic experiences. The repeated-subtraumatic-experience hypothesis seemed to fit only one of the claustrophobic patients, a twenty-six-year-old housewife who recalled having had several pillow fights with her brother when they were young children, and having "nearly been smothered several times." She also accidentally locked herself in a closet when about seven years of age and had to remain there for almost a half hour before someone heard her banging and screaming. At age fifteen she had been trapped in an elevator for more than an hour. She married at age twenty-two and developed claustrophobia a year later "after my husband and I had a terrible fight and he put his hand over my mouth and I felt that I couldn't breathe ... and thought that he was going to suffocate me to death." In this instance, a fairly strong case could be made for a conditioning explanation of the patient's fear of confined spaces, but I would still argue that the precipitating incident had more to do with her attitudes toward her husband in general than towards his traumatic act of "suffocation" in particular. Is it merely coincidental that the patient's claustrophobia made it impossible for her to attend symphony concerts and visit the theatre and that her husband was an avid lover of music and plays? She would urge him to attend concerts and plays without her, but never failed to make him feel guilty whenever he did so. One might well inquire whether the patient's claustrophobia was a conditioned avoidance reaction and/or a transactional marital game (Berne, 1964).

This is not to deny that people are capable of forming persistent avoidance reactions on the basis of situational or direct conditioning experiences. One of the patients traced her car phobia to a severe automobile accident. A detailed behavior analysis failed to reveal any other significant factor. Similarly, a lady with a bird phobia traced the origin of her fears to incidents which had occurred during her childhood. She was once trapped in an aviary which was a very frightening experience; and, at a later time, a belligerent budgerigar had pecked her hand and drawn blood. There was no evidence that her fear of birds symbolized something deeper. Nor was there any hint that her phobia served any secondary function. Straightforward desensitization therapy was necessary and sufficient to rid these patients of their unadaptive fears. There is no definite data on whether or not cases of this kind are seen clinically more than 2 percent of the time, but whatever the final figure, it will probably be less than 5 percent of the cases that seek help from psychologists and psychiatrists. Marks (1969, p. 105) states that "phobic states are found in less than 3 percent of psychiatric outpatients."

Does this imply that 95 to 98 percent of patients require treatment that promotes insight into repressed complexes and other unconscious processes? Not at all. It does, however, demand unlearning or relearning of basic interpersonal as well as situational sources of anxiety. And it certainly calls for the realization that cognitive, affective, and overt response patterns are not separate units but interactive processes which constitute *behavior* in its broadest sense (Ellis, 1962).

The Evaluation of Behavior Therapy

Claims for the superiority of behavior therapy are based upon numerous case studies (e.g., Ullmann & Krasner, 1965) and several uncontrolled clinical reports (e.g., Lazarus, 1963; Wolpe, 1958; Wolpe & Lazarus, 1966). A number of controlled comparative outcome studies are also often cited (e.g., Lazarus, 1961; Paul, 1966; Lang, Lazovik, & Reynolds, 1965) but most of these dealt with people who were solicited for treatment and did not request it of their own accord. It is cogent to argue that relatively unitary fears obtained from questionnaires handed to students who are then invited to have free treatment, differ from psychiatric patients who seek out therapists and actively ask for help. Good comparative studies among psychiatric patients have usually been limited to specific symptoms such as enuresis, tics, thumb-sucking, or asthma (e.g., Moore, 1965). In short, despite Wolpe's (1958) oft-cited claim of a 90 percent recovery rate, there are still no acceptable data which would entitle anyone to make claims for the overall superiority of behavior therapy. The trend in fact seems to point to the conclusion that behavior therapists are guilty of oversimplification and that "behavior therapy might ultimately prove suitable for only a limited number of specific conditions" (Sloane & Payne, 1966). Hence, the present emphasis is on the need to proceed *beyond behavior therapy* or to expand the scope of behavioral approaches.

In the literature numerous cases are reported (including some of my work) in which behavior therapy produced rapid change and neither relapse nor symptom substitution was present several years after treatment (Eysenck, 1960, 1964; Ullmann & Krasner, 1965). A detailed and more systematic follow-up inquiry of 112 cases, randomly selected, leads me to a very different conclusion, however, concerning the durability of behavior therapy.

Past patients were interviewed personally or were contacted by telephone. Where this was not feasible, they were sent the follow-up questionnaire (below) which urged them to be totally honest in their replies:

Follow-up Questionnaire

To: _____   *From* Arnold Lazarus

We last saw each other approximately _____ months ago. I would like to have a fairly clear idea of how you have been feeling and what you have been doing, especially with regard to your reason(s) for having consulted me.

When people are asked to give follow-up information, they often answer in a socially acceptable way, and try to please their ex-therapist by leaving him with a good impression. Many people are so reluctant to report developments which, they feel, might disappoint their therapist (e.g., relapses, new problems, or other unhappy occurrences) that they distort the truth. I cannot overemphasize that negative reports are just as important as positive ones. A clinician cannot assess his work or improve his methods unless he receives honest feedback.

Please be as frank as possible. Let me thank you for the care with which you fill out this questionnaire. I look forward to hearing from you as soon as possible. A stamped, self-addressed envelope is enclosed for your convenience.

1. Your main reasons for consulting me were:

2. Please comment as to how you are coping with regard to the above.

3. If there have been significant improvements or setbacks, please tell me what you attribute them to.

4. Have you developed any new symptoms or problems? If "yes," please elaborate.

5. How do you think we could have proceeded in therapy to make things *better* for you?

6. Have you consulted a psychologist, psychiatrist, and/or a physician during the past six months? Please elaborate, if relevant.

7. Has there been any favorable or unfavorable change in your general life situation (e.g., new friends, change of job, death in family) which you feel has had an effect on your adjustment?

8. In the past six months have you taken any drugs (especially tranquilizers or energizers or aspirins)?

9. Do you have any new interests, sports, hobbies, or social activities?

10. Please *underline* the words which you feel best describe my personality:
    Warm, disorganized, sympathetic, friendly, dishonest, rigid, critical, formal, sensitive, inconsistent, gentle, indifferent, spontaneous, systematic, open, informal, unsystematic, considerate, cold, well-orga-

nized, aloof, flexible, secretive, interested, unfriendly, honest, kind. Any other:

11. Has anyone in your family required psychotherapy or developed emotional problems or received medical attention in the last six months?

12. Please add any information that you think might be of assistance in this follow-up.

Some interesting trends emerged. Less than 5 percent failed to answer the questionnaire. Only the most tenuous indications of "symptom substitution" were present in five or six cases, but forty-one (about 36 percent) had relapsed anywhere from one week to six years after therapy. The reasons for relapse were obscure in some cases, but most relapses followed new stress-producing situations which had not, or could not, be foreseen during therapy. It should be emphasized that the nature of these stress-producing situations usually consisted of life patterns involving new responsibilities at work or at home, the disapproved marriage of a son or daughter, disappointment in love or friendship, and rarely involved traumatic events such as the death of loved ones, bodily injury, or other major upheavals.

On the other hand, certain patients pointed out very emphatically that they had maintained their therapeutic improvements in the face of inimical circumstances. Referral to the case notes of these individuals revealed that their improvements were often contingent upon the apparent adoption of a different outlook and philosophy of life and increased self-esteem in addition to an increased range of interpersonal and behavioral skills, presumably as a result of therapy.

Thirty patients who had maintained their improvement had at least one close family member who had entered therapy since the termination of their own course of treatment. This may support the notion of many family therapists that one member of a household may sometimes improve to the detriment of others in the home.

There was a good deal of variation in response to the question: "How do you think we could have proceeded in therapy to make things *better* for you?" Some people felt that they should have been seen more often than once a week; others stated that longer intervals between sessions would have been better for them. Some wanted more examples drawn from my own personal experience; others would have preferred less self-disclosure on my behalf. Several people felt that therapy would have been more helpful if I had involved more of their family members. Others wished that I had left their spouses, parents, or siblings out of therapy. This simply bears out that there are few valid general therapeutic rules. What one patient finds especially helpful another considers distinctly harmful.

On the adjective checklist the words that were used to describe me more often than any others were *sensitive, gentle,* and *honest.* Just how well these adjectives correlate with the Truax triad (accurate empathy, nonpossessive warmth, and authenticity or genuineness) is open to conjecture (cf. Truax & Carkhuff, 1967).

A case history might add substance to the many issues raised up to this point. The case illustrates the usual range of behavior therapy practices (that often led to therapeutic failures in terms of follow-ups) as well as the specific life changes above and beyond conventional behavior therapy techniques (that seemed to yield more durable follow-up results).

The Charitable Lady

Mrs. D., aged thirty-five, was housebound by anxiety. If she ventured further than her front porch she became faint, panicky, and shaky. Her condition started when she was twenty-nine years old, and followed an incident when her husband was falsely accused of stabbing a fellow worker. At the time, she and her husband were employed by wholesale merchants; she as a private secretary and he as a division manager. Her husband was dismissed and she resigned. They both obtained new employment the very next day, but on her way to work, Mrs. D. was suddenly overcome by anticipatory anxiety that reached panic proportions. She turned back, went home, and found herself anxious and panicky whenever she left her home thereafter. Her anxiety was less severe when accompanied by her husband, but even then, she was, at best, extremely uncomfortable when out of her own house.

This pattern continued for about two years and became much worse when she was forced to go out of town to attend her mother's funeral. Despite heavy sedation she felt acutely anxious, and upon returning home refused to leave the premises at all. One of her neighbors, a psychiatrist, treated her at home for approximately 1½ years. He discussed her dependency needs with her and also spent time interpreting her dreams. He described her as "a passive-dependent personality who ... had regressed to a pre-oedipal level of fixation," and felt that "prognosis was poor." In describing his handling of the case, the psychiatrist referred to Freud's (1919) paper in which the need to expose patients to their fearful experiences had been emphasized; he outlined how he had constantly encouraged Mrs. D. to leave the house, and how he gently coerced her to accompany him on longer and longer walks.

His treatment seemed to have helped her to function as she had before her mother's demise. She could again venture away from home, with varying degrees of discomfort, only when accompanied by her husband. She never went out without him.

Mrs. D. Receives Behavior Therapy. Mrs. D. consulted me at the insistence of one of my former patients whom she had befriended. The first therapeutic objective was to enable her to come for her visits accompanied by someone other than her husband. This was simply achieved by hypnotizing her and asking her to picture herself accomplishing this feat without undue disturbance. During the course of extensive history-taking, the patient and her escort were encouraged to take public transportation to and from the clinic instead of driving by car.

Next, she was again hypnotized and told that by *thinking* the words "calm, no panic" over and over, she would in fact succeed in reducing or tempering anxiety attacks when necessary. Under hypnosis, she was also repeatedly asked to picture herself traveling unaccompanied to and from the clinic. She was seen twice weekly. Subsequent to her sixteenth session, less than two months after her initial consultation, she was able to come for her appointments alone.

There was evidence that her husband was subtly attempting to undermine her progress, and I stressed the fact that he had encouraged (if not somehow provoked) her extreme dependency. The husband was interviewed and admitted, after some initial denials, that he had felt a sense of security in knowing that his wife was always at home and was so dependent on him. He then expressed the fear that if she was mobile and self-sufficient, she would leave him for another man. It then transpired that this fear was a product of his own sexual ineptitude. Mr.

and Mrs. D. were then seen together several times and were given didactic instructions for increasing their range of sexual practices and enjoyment. Several discussions were devoted to ways and means of improving their relationship in general.

Various hypochondriacal fears in Mrs. D. were dealt with by simple hypnotic desensitization. Under hypnosis she would be relaxed and told to imagine various aches, pains, and other aspects of bodily discomfort which bothered her, e.g., dizziness and palpitations. As each physical symptom was mentioned, she was instructed to think of several benign explanations. Other anxiety-provoking situations dealt with by desensitization included crowded places such as restaurants, movies, shops, and center city streets.

She was at all times encouraged to stand up for her rights, and difficult areas in this regard were dealt with by *behavior rehearsal*. It became easier for her to contemplate standing up to her father, for instance, after enacting several role-playing sequences.

After a total of thirty-eight sessions (about five months after commencing behavior therapy) Mrs. D. enjoyed taking long walks alone and was able to go shopping, visiting, and traveling without distress.

The Effects of Mrs. D.'s Exposure to Behavior Therapy. The foregoing represents a fairly typical sequence of techniques and strategies commonly employed by behavior therapists and especially by broad-spectrum behavior therapists (Lazarus 1965a, 1966). Important changes had accrued above and beyond Mrs. D.'s capacity to venture out of her home. Her marriage relationship in general and her sexual experiences in particular were more gratifying. She was no longer hypochondriacal and socially submissive. Furthermore, her husband confirmed that she showed renewed interest in life (in place of her previous self-preoccupation) and took pride in her home and her cooking and enjoyed a wider range of social outlets. In assessing Mrs. D.'s therapeutic gains over the five months of treatment, who could dispute that impressive and significant improvements were evident? *Nevertheless, according to my latest follow-up information, the relapse rate in cases that responded to behavior therapy no less dramatically and gratifyingly than Mrs. D., turned out to be disappointingly high.*

Omitted from the case report thus far is the fact that Mrs. D. had faith and confidence in my therapeutic skills and found procedures such as hypnosis and desensitization very compatible with her passive dependent needs. She found active therapy much more congenial and inspirational than the interpretative methods employed by her psychiatrist-neighbor. People with the same problem as Mrs. D. but with different needs and expectancies could be predicted to respond less favorably to the same procedures and would, in fact, require substantially different modes of treatment. Returning to the contention that behavior therapy and even broad-spectrum behavior therapy, as applied in the case of Mrs. D., is often insufficient to produce durable outcomes, we must ask *what lies beyond?*

Taking Mrs. D. Beyond Behavior Therapy. Must we fall prey to that semimystical notion which holds that "something deeper" has to be unearthed? Are there some hidden underlying unconscious forces that have to be discharged? Emphatically not. As already mentioned, those patients who maintained their improvements usually acquired increased self-esteem in addition to their more obvious behavioral gains. Let us relate this again specifically to Mrs. D.

Although she was delighted by her newfound ability to remain anxiety-free while traveling and engaging in the niceties of social interaction, she continued to view herself as a worthless person who was contributing nothing of value to society. She referred to herself as "the height of mediocrity" and added, "I'm not especially intelligent, good-looking, well-educated, or knowledgeable. . . . I'm kind of blah!" Using a variation of the view that self-worth should not be based upon extrinsic virtues (Ellis, 1962), I elaborated on the theme that she was exceedingly kind, compassionate, considerate, honest, and sensitive, and that these rare qualities should combine to produce a positive self-concept. I also emphasized that happiness is a birthright and that one did not have to earn it. These discussions resulted in what Mrs. D. called a "temporary ego boost," but did not alter her feelings of uselessness. She stated, "Call it my early conditioning if you will, but I need to feel worthwhile and useful. . . . You say I have all these wonderful qualities, but what good are they if you don't *do* something with them?" Numerous discussions centered on the pernicious effects of overcompetitive strivings; man's inhumanity and indifference to man; and the fact that the world is filled to capacity with good-looking, athletic, intelligent, and well-educated people who function like efficient computers and radiate little, if any, warmth and love to those around them. The logic of these discussions led Mrs. D. to conclude that, "If you want to *feel* useful, you have to *be* useful."

It was over two months before I heard from Mrs. D. again. At that time she reported that she had founded an organization which would eventually distribute basic essentials, such as food and clothing, to as many impoverished Americans as possible. She began in a modest way by soliciting goods from friends and strangers. Considerable time was spent contacting needy families and establishing centers in other communities. The contrast between the fearful Mrs. D. who could not venture beyond her front porch, now pounding on strange doors in strange neighborhoods while pursuing her worthy cause, affords a thought-provoking spectacle. The organization, of which Mrs. D. is the president and founder, has since spread to many areas of the United States and has already fed and clothed thousands of needy persons.

In a follow-up interview one year later, Mrs. D. was asked to put aside modesty and to stress the fundamental facts. She confided that she viewed herself as "eminently worthwhile," and pointed out that "thanks to the fact that I exist and care, thousands of people now derive benefit." Her husband was no less delighted and referred to the therapeutic outcome as "miraculous."

The case of Mrs. D. provides a somewhat poignant illustration of behavior therapy and beyond. It should be noted that the way in which Mrs. D. achieved her sense of well-being and personal worth was compatible with her own needs and is not to be regarded as a general prototype. In proceeding beyond behavior therapy, the attempt is made to help each patient find his own way of achieving a gratifying *modus vivendi*.

On Science and Psychotherapy

Early in 1964, several psychologists and psychiatrists of various persuasions observed me treating three patients behind a one-way mirror at the Veterans Administration Hospital in Palo Alto, California. These patients had proved refractory to conventional psychotherapy, and one of them, a young woman with anorexia nervosa and compulsive vomiting, presented a problem of considerable clinical urgency. After several months of behavior therapy, she was eating normally, had gained weight, and was discharged from the hospital. Improvement in the other two patients, though less dramatic, was also quite apparent. My colleagues who had observed the entire course of treatment were asked whether they considered the proceedings symptomatic rather than fundamental, and, above all, whether they could specify the processes to which the therapeutic gains could be ascribed.

On the first issue, all agreed that the therapy had been fundamental rather than superficial. But no agreement could be reached concerning the reasons for the undisputed gains. My own views, at that time, leaned heavily upon notions of counterconditioning and extinction. The views of my colleagues, however, were as different from my own as they were from one another's! Opinions were as diverse as (1) The methods facilitated your being introjected as a benevolent authority figure, thus effecting a change in libidinal cathexes; (2) the effective therapeutic forces had nothing to do with conditioning but centered around several peak experiences which permitted a new and different "being" to fill certain existential voids; and (3) the real basis of the therapy was a purely didactic process in which clear labels were attached to nebulous emotions. These are not verbatim statements but represent a few typical trends among the many ideas which were offered.

The variety of theoretical opinions generated some heated arguments. It was obvious that the many theoretical positions adopted could not all be correct. But it was possible that every theoretical explanation, including my own, could be false. The above-mentioned interactions led me to regard post hoc theorizing with disdain. Why do so many psychotherapists who view themselves as "scientists" behave with the same defensive fervor that we ordinarily associate with religious fanaticism?

Theories are essentially a set of speculations that seem to explain empirical facts. A sound and accurate psychological theory should give a practitioner confidence in what he is doing and why he is doing it. A good theory of human behavior should generate more effective methods of treatment. Yet many psychological theories, like most religious taboos, prevent practitioners from engaging in helpful activities. For instance, Freudian theory deflects attention from overt behavior toward "inner dynamics," yet the observable phenomena of manifest behavior are often extremely important in their own right. Thus, psychoanalysis has not proved noticeably helpful in the treatment of alcoholism and other addictions, or in the treatment of tics, stuttering, phobias, and compulsive disorders which usually require direct attention *both* to the disruptive behavior and the underlying attitudes (Walton & Mather, 1963).

On the other hand, many Skinnerians deemphasize cognitive variables and other internal events, and focus attention upon behavior and its consequences, thereby relegating fantasy and other subjective experience to a subordinate, if not irrelevant, position. A person riddled with guilt, self-doubts, and self-defeating attitudes is unlikely to derive much benefit from any therapy which ignores introspective material. Another self-limiting situation is a patient appealing to a nondirective therapist for advice, instruction, or specific guidance, and receiving only a noncommittal echo of his own perplexity and despair.

There are numerous reasons why so many psychotherapists defend their theories with a religious crusading fervor instead of adopting a detached and impartial attitude, but perhaps the most obvious reason is that the rigors of science dash false hopes and destroy wishful thoughts. Science does not deal in absolutes or in unassailable truths. In fact, scientists do not set out to prove their theories; they seek only to strengthen them. It demands courage from a practicing therapist to admit that his theories are, at best, partly true. Adherence to scientific principles demands a constant and vigorous search for data that can weaken or at least compromise one's theories. Can a practicing therapist adhere to the canons of scientific reserve and still be clinically effective? Or must he endorse some theoretical position with sufficient faith and ardor to spill forth in the guise of conviction and confidence in the clinical situation? A therapist who exudes abundant self-confidence, based upon the conviction that he has all the answers, can probably be of immeasurable benefit to passive-dependent individuals. But he is likely to antagonize those thinking individuals who realize that psychology is still very far from its ultimate goal—understanding the reasons for all forms of behavior.

Tremendous headway in psychotherapy would follow a determined and consistent effort to separate techniques from theories. Therapists are too intent to attach a label to their activities instead of spelling out precisely what operations they perform with various patients. Typically, a therapeutic gain which a Freudian will attribute to increased "emotional insight," another therapist will ascribe to the inadvertent application of "reciprocal inhibition." Debates about these issues lead to sterile polemics because a vague neurological construct such as *reciprocal inhibition* has few explanatory advantages over a term such as *emotional insight*. But even those who avoid inferred constructs in their explanation of behavior change may often arrive at questionable conclusions. An obvious instance may be cited.

The director of an operant conditioning ward had plotted graphs depicting each patient's daily progress in which the close tie-up between behavior change and various reinforcement contingencies seemed indisputable. He had singled out the chart of an especially recalcitrant case and was proudly proving how newfound cooperative behavior in the patient had followed a simple "deprivation schedule." The patient had been denied all privileges (including food) for forty-eight hours. Upon examining the graph, it was clearly evident that immediately after the deprivation procedure there was a dramatic upward curve in a pattern that had previously been extremely erratic. A heated discussion then ensued concerning the ethics of depriving a patient of food for more than two days, whereupon the ward attendant argued irrelevantly that the patient had eaten very little when finally given a plate of food. It then transpired that during this postdeprivation meal, a telephone call from the patient's family was relayed bearing the good news that a younger brother presumed killed in Viet Nam was in fact safe and well. Could this have had a bearing on the patient's behavior? The director of the ward remained adamant that the good tidings had little, if anything, to do with the patient's subsequent upsurge of cooperative behavior. He insisted that the patient's behavior change was entirely due to the deprivation. The point is, of course, that two variables were confounded and that the therapist's theoretical leanings tended to create an important "blind spot." When explaining theories (as opposed to administering techniques), therapists enter the domain of science and should be cognizant of their responsibilities. This example is by no means intended to impugn the operant approach per se but only to highlight an error that unsophisticated operant conditioners frequently commit.

Scientific method typically proceeds along the intricate and delicate progression from hypothesis formation to hypothesis testing via careful controlled experimentation. Theories which arise are then subjected to further rigorous and extensive tests to confirm or disconfirm their structure and content. But this path is riddled with pitfalls and innumerable hazards. Even an expert can adhere to the rules, follow the signs, exercise great caution, and still come to grief.

Hypothesis generation presupposes a certain inventiveness or creativity. This innovative flair, however, must be kept within strict bounds. Any hypothesis, no matter how plausible or ingenious, for which critical experiments cannot be devised has limited utility. If the measuring instruments of today are unable to assess the potential merit or demerit of a given assumption, it must be discarded or shelved. Thus, any hunch is immediately met with the question: "How can we design an experiment, or series of experiments, that will test this notion?" If no plausible way can be discovered, the hypothesis or hunch is declared beyond the boundaries of science. Scientific method, then, implies very strict adherence to a narrow path which is deliberately and intentionally delimited. Only special kinds of hypotheses are permitted (those which can be tested) and the process of experimentation permits no latitude whatsoever (eliminate bias; watch out for artifacts; keep every contaminating variable under strict control).

Long ago, Skinner (1938, p. 44) declared introspective data or covert behavior too private for inclusion into the realm of scientific inquiry and stressed that psychological concepts should be "defined in terms of immediate observation." But while operant conditioners can predict and control many classes of behavior, their *explanation* of behavior can proceed no further than the identification of reinforcement contingencies. Both extremes—behavioristic and mentalistic—should be avoided. Compare the notion that behavior is a function of its consequences, in which overt behavior is the only respectable domain of scientific investigation with its opposite; namely, the notion that overt behavior is but the visible ripple of an unfathomably deep unconscious maelstrom. Scientifically minded persons might justifiably sneer at unprovable statements such as Segal's (1964, p. 2) contention that "a hungry, raging infant, screaming and kicking, phantasies that he is actually attacking the breast, tearing and destroying it, and experiences his own screams which tear him and hurt him as the torn breast attacking him in his own inside." But it is equally imprudent to declare the entire realm of fantasy (at least in adults) beyond scientific inquiry. Another way of putting it is that the thoughts (thinking behavior) which precede and accompany observable or measurable responses are often no more, or no less, significant than the manifest behavior. A recent paper by Hebb (1968) may go far toward making *imagery* a legitimate and respectable subject for scientific inquiry. The same applies to Richardson's (1969) recent book.

As stressed above, hypothesis generation calls for an innovative capacity to articulate creative hunches that can be experimentally confirmed or disconfirmed. It is in the latter field of endeavor—hypothesis testing—that the opportunities for error are rampant. Apart from obvious features such as experimenter bias, poor sampling, inadequate control, statistical artifacts, and subtle but significant chance factors, researchers are faced with a host of other confounding and contaminating variables. The literature is replete with examples of how even simple animal studies are subject to innumerable degrees of confusion. One impressive story in this area concerns a most fastidious experimenter who was studying maze learning in laboratory rats. He had gone to great lengths to breed rats from identical strains, to subject them to identical conditions of rearing in which every aspect of their environment from temperature, moisture, illumination, handling, to feeding, etc., was meticulously controlled. The design and execution of the experimental procedure seemed to allow no room for error, but disparate findings emerged and were finally attributed to the fact that on some occasions the experimenter wore a white coat, whereas at other times he would run subjects in ordinary apparel. There is no point in dwelling on the fact that when working with human subjects, the opportunities for permitting uncontrolled and uncontrollable factors to bias experimental processes and outcomes is almost unlimited.

Another caveat for psychotherapists concerns what might be called "the effect-cause fallacy." For example, after furnishing evidence that certain deconditioning techniques can modify unadaptive avoidance behavior in cats and in humans, Wolpe (1958, 1969) argued that the same conditioning model was therefore applicable when accounting for the acquisition of unadaptive avoidance behavior. Davison (1968) has emphasized that "from evidence regarding efficacy in changing behavior, one cannot claim to have demonstrated that the problem evolved in an analogous fashion." Wolpe's (1956) reasoning is that since techniques based on conditioning and learning can overcome various types of unadaptive avoidance behavior, these unadaptive behaviors must, in turn, have been acquired by conditioning and learning. This is like saying that because aspirin can reduce or eliminate headaches, the latter are caused by a lack of aspirin in the bloodstream (Rimland, 1964).

Although numerous notions about the genesis of abnormal behavior have been proffered, we are provided with very few hard facts. Everybody knows that conflicts, traumata, deprivation, and mishandling play an important etiological role. But, regrettably, much-needed specific facts tend to get absorbed by the miasmal theories which surround them. If we can persuade psychotherapists to separate what they do from why they think it works, progress should ensue. We will then have a technology which can probably be developed into a science.

CHAPTER 2
TOWARD A FLEXIBLE, OR PERSONALISTIC SYSTEM OF PSYCHOTHERAPY

"Nothing is working out. My wife left me and I'm about to lose my job. I drink too much and I smoke too much. I'm a nervous wreck. For no good reason, I break out into sweats, tremble inside, and feel dizzy and tight in the head. Sometimes I think about killing myself. I'm getting nowhere. I don't even know who I am most of the time. Sometimes I get a weird feeling as if I'm watching myself doing things. At other times, my heart beats so fast that I get more and more frightened. I thought there was something wrong with my heart but my doctor said it checked out fine. But sometimes I wonder about that, especially when I have pains in the chest."

The above is not an uncommon clinical syndrome. The tendency in psychiatric circles would be to label it "anxiety hysteria" or perhaps "incipient psychosis," with or without additional tags like "minor melancholia," "depersonalization," "hyperventilation," or "hypochondriasis." But diagnostic labels give little indication of antecedent factors and provide equally few clues about therapeutic management. Besides, it is difficult to find close agreement among independent raters regardless of their respective diagnostic skills. Few would disagree, however, that irrespective of the right or wrong diagnostic label, it would be desirable to enable this unfortunate individual to "find himself" and to effect a genuinely happy marriage coupled with gratification from his work, fulfillment from life, and lasting freedom from the symptoms which plague him. How is this to be achieved? Should he be psychoanalyzed, psychosynthesized, leukotomized, hypnotized, tranquilized, or hospitalized? Despite the frequent lip service that is paid to individual differences, many psychotherapists tend to generalize, if not universalize, in a manner that is totally unsupported by the facts. Some therapists believe that people must solve their own problems and that any active intervention on the part of the therapist will inevitably prove antitherapeutic. These clinicians studiously avoid offering any advice, guidance, or even reassurance. At the opposite pole, other therapists feel that since they are "experts in living" and since psychotherapy is predominantly a reeducative experience, they can only earn their keep by actively manipulating, shaping, and reinforcing their patients' behavior.

Is there a "best" or "correct" way of achieving serenity in place of turmoil, and happiness instead of misery? Wedded by faith to a theory, some therapists insist that their way is really the only way of proceeding in psychotherapy. Thus, I have had colleagues inform me that in their estimation, "No cure is complete unless the patient has gained full insight into his incestuous wishes," or "Any treatment which does not include the vigorous expression of hate and anger is, at best, half-baked" and "Unless the entire family unit is brought in for readjustment, therapy is bound to be one-sided and incomplete." More recently, I have been informed that, "Any course of treatment which fails to include systematic desensitization is bound to leave the patient hypersensitive to innocuous stimuli."

The explicit assumption throughout this book is that the saying, "one man's meat is another man's poison" is particularly applicable to the field of psychotherapy. Another explicit assumption is that the "best" therapy is that which works for the individual. Consequently, it is considered extremely important to match each individual patient to the particular therapy and therapist appropriate for him. In this regard, the most essential ingredients for an effective psychotherapist are *flexibility* and *versatility*. This implies an ability to play many roles and to use many techniques in order to fit the therapy to the needs and idiosyncrasies of each patient. By contrast, therapists with pet theories or specially favored techniques usually manage, in their own minds at least, to fit their patients' problems within the confines of their particular brand of treatment.

For example, the fact that problem-focused interviews often succeed in breaking down vague and abstruse clinical problems into areas of specific hypersensitivity, has led some therapists (e.g., Wolpe, 1964; 1969a) to believe that nearly all complex neuroses are merely clusters of phobialike responses. This rigid and oversimplified view of human functioning has the danger of omitting important conceptual problems which require treatment in their own right and at their own level (Lazarus, 1968c). Consider the following clinical excerpt, by no means atypical, in which a problem-focused interview proceeded from simple phobia to complex problem in living.

The "Bridge Phobia"

Patient:	I have a fear of crossing bridges.
Therapist:	Do you have any other fears or difficulties?
Patient:	Only the complications arising from my fear of bridges.
Therapist:	Well, in what way has it affected your life?
Patient:	I had to quit an excellent job in Berkeley.
Therapist:	Where do you live?
Patient:	San Francisco.
Therapist:	So why didn't you move to Berkeley?
Patient:	I prefer living in the city.
Therapist:	To get to this institute, you had to cross the Golden Gate.

Patient: Yes, I was seeing a doctor in San Francisco. He tried to desensitize me but it didn't help so he said I should see you because you know more about this kind of treatment. It's not so bad when I have my wife and kids with me. But even then, the Golden Gate, which is about one mile long, is my upper limit. I was wondering whether you ever consult in the city?

Therapist: No. But tell me, how long have you had this problem?

Patient: Oh, about four years, I'd say. It just happened suddenly. I was coming home from work and the Bay Bridge was awfully slow. I just suddenly panicked for no reason at all. I mean, nothing like this had ever happened to me before. I felt that I would crash into the other cars. Once I even had a feeling that the bridge would cave in.

Therapist: Let's get back to that first panic experience about four years ago. You said that you were coming home from work. Had anything happened at work?

Patient: Nothing unusual.

Therapist: Were you happy at work?

Patient: Sure! Huh! I was even due for promotion.

Therapist: What would that have entailed?

Patient: An extra $3,000 a year.

Therapist: I mean in the way of having to do different work.

Patient: Well, I would have been a supervisor. I would have had more than fifty men working under me.

Therapist: How did you feel about that?

Patient: What do you mean?

Therapist: I mean how did you feel about the added responsibility? Did you feel that you were up to it, that you could cope with it?

Patient: Gee! My wife was expecting our first kid. We both welcomed the extra money.

Therapist: So round about the time that you were about to become a father, you were to be promoted to supervisor. So you would face two new and challenging roles. You'd be a daddy at home and also big daddy at work. And this was when you began to panic on the bridge, and I guess you never did wind up as a supervisor.

Patient: No. I had to ask for a transfer to the city.

Therapist: Now, please think very carefully about this question. Have you ever been involved in any accident on or near a bridge, or have you ever witnessed any serious accident on or near a bridge?

Patient: Not that I can think of.

Therapist: Do you still work for the same company?

Patient: No. I got a better offer, more money, from another company in the city. I've been with them for almost 1½ years now.

Therapist: Are you earning more money or less money than you would have gotten in Berkeley?

Patient: About the same. But prices have gone up so it adds up to less.

Therapist: If you hadn't developed the bridge phobia and had become foreman in Berkeley at $3,000 more, where do you think you would be today?

Patient: Still in Berkeley.

Therapist: Still supervisor? More money?

Patient: Oh hell! Who knows? (laughs) Maybe I would have been vice-president.

Therapist: And what would that have entailed?

Patient: I'm only kidding. But actually it could have happened.

Therapy in this case was deflected away from his bridge phobia toward unraveling a history in which the patient, the youngest of five siblings, tended to accept his mother's evaluation that, unlike his brilliant older brothers, he would never amount to anything. Desensitization was in fact employed, but not in relation to bridges. A hierarchy of his mother's real or imagined pejorative statements was constructed, and the patient was immunized to these hurtful allegations. He was also trained in assertive behavior. As he gained confidence in his own capabilities, his bridge phobia vanished as suddenly as it had appeared.

Perhaps it can be argued that the patient's bridge phobia developed through a process of conditioning, which Rachman (1968, p. 27) regards as the basis of all phobias. A behaviorist with whom I discussed the case contended that the man was apprehensive about his future and that his anxieties *just happened by chance* to erupt while traveling on a bridge. He added that bridges thereupon became invested with high anxiety potential and that the patient's avoidance of bridges blocked the extinction of his fears. But what was he really avoiding? Bridges per se? And was the first anxiety attack on the bridge fortuitous? Did not his bridge phobia serve the function of preventing the full impact of his own uncertainties and shortcomings vis-à-vis his work, competence, obligations, and achievements? Why did the phobia disappear as soon as these basic anxieties were overcome? These questions reflect the inadequacies of peripheral S-R theories of learning as touched on in Chapter 1.

Finding the Appropriate Therapist and Therapy

A large percentage of patients are most obligingly suggestible. Those who end up in the hands of Freudian therapists provide "evidence," especially during their dreams, of infantile sexuality; while Jungian analysands end up convincing their analysts of the existence of a racial unconscious. Patients who consult Wolpeans are almost invariably phobic and hypersensitive. In other words, when a therapist has a strong theoretical bias, no matter in what direction, he will inadvertently influence his patients to react in a manner which "proves" his own theoretical assumptions. This even holds true for very farfetched notions. For instance, a mystic and his clients with whom I was acquainted claimed that they each independently perceived the origin of their diffi-

culties in acts performed during previous lives, and that these dis-
coveries were independent of any overt suggestions from their "guru."
The studies on verbal conditioning (Krasner, 1958; Krasner & Ullmann,
1965)—and more especially Truax's (1966) demonstration of the way
in which a client-centered therapist like Carl Rogers unconsciously
shaped and influenced, via selective reinforcement, his patients' perceptions—show how powerfully these subtle cues can influence behavior.

The trouble is that even therapists who lack any obvious charis-
matic qualities, but who are nonetheless capable of mobilizing some
feelings of optimism in some of their patients, are likely to receive
enough intermittent positive reinforcement to keep them behind their
desks. These factors probably account for the proliferation of today's
systems and schools of psychotherapy. The pundits of each system have
vigorously lauded their own approach while denigrating all others. But
claims for the overall superiority of any one system of psychotherapy—
including behavior therapy—have not been scientifically verified. Even
if one particular brand of therapy was shown to be superior to all
others, it still might not cater to those individuals whose rehabilitation
called for the use of certain methods practiced only by the generally less
successful schools of therapy. For example, certain people may have
such overriding needs to have their dreams interpreted or to sit in an
orgone box that only sincere practitioners of these cults will make any
headway with them (but not necessarily for reasons ascribed by the
practitioners).

In line with the foregoing, those who practice psychotherapy,
be they psychiatrists, psychologists, social workers, ministers of religion,
teachers, nurses, counselors, or intelligent laymen, should be trained to
(1) rapidly identify the patient's basic problems, (2) determine the
seemingly best way *for that individual* of dispelling these problems,
and (3) skillfully apply the necessary procedures or make the appropriate outside referral(s). This is obvious and straightforward enough,
but unfortunately a good deal of psychotherapy practiced today seldom
follows this logical sequence. Instead, problem identification is likely
to depend almost exclusively upon the orientation of the therapist. We
have already alluded to the one-sided views of some (not all) psychoanalysts, nondirective therapists, operant conditioners, and family therapists. The tendency to grasp a segment of the truth and to magnify it
into the whole truth is not confined to the aforementioned camps.

In the light of all the contradictory theories and methods, just how should the sincere and dedicated clinician proceed? He cannot afford to suspend all action and judgment until advances in neurophysiology, biochemistry, and genetics provide many of the answers he so desperately needs today. Nor can he confine himself to the drawing boards of experimental psychology because the practicing clinician still has derived precious little therapeutic ammunition from laboratory studies. He can, however, draw upon several established principles and place his own findings and practices within a broad theoretical framework while constantly searching for new empirical data to increase his therapeutic effectiveness and test the soundness of his theories. Much of this book will be devoted to stepwise descriptions of methods and techniques, because in the hands of compassionate, candid, and flexible clinicians, the skillful application of appropriate techniques will often determine the difference between therapeutic failure and success. An explicit assumption is that genuine rapport and a good therapeutic relationship are usually necessary but often insufficient for profound and durable behavior change.

The points being stressed may be said to constitute a truly "personalistic psychotherapy." While taking cognizance of general principles [e.g., the Truax & Carkhuff (1967) findings that effective therapists display accurate empathy, warmth, and genuineness], one should remain on the lookout for individual exceptions to these general rules—e.g., those cases who react adversely to warmth or empathy and require a distant, impartial, and businesslike interaction. As already mentioned, within this framework *flexibility* and *versatility* are the key ingredients of efficient and effective therapeutic interaction. Yates (1970, p. 380) in his scholarly book on the academics of behavior therapy stresses that "each abnormality of behavior represents a new problem so that each patient must be considered as a subject of experimental investigation in his own right."

Nearly all therapists must have seen cases who remained refractory to their own valiant psychotherapeutic efforts, and who derived no benefit from colleagues of similar or even different persuasions, but whose emotional suffering came to a sudden and oftentimes dramatic end upon discovering a chiropractor, or some other such person who manipulated their spine, or perhaps irrigated their colon, or prescribed some herbal mixtures. Our diagnostic interviews should enable us to determine whether the case under consideration is more likely to derive benefit from a brief spell of relaxation rather than a protracted regime of assertive training; whether prolonged free association would help more than rapid desensitization; or if a series of seances, some sessions with a Ouija board, or a course of yoga, or any combination of the foregoing plus several other procedures would be the answer.

This does not imply a random trial-and-error procedure where the "flexible clinician" prescribes anything from mineral baths to phenothiazines as his whims dictate. Well-conceived guiding principles and general theories about human behavior should enable the clinician to decide when and why certain therapists and therapies are to be favored. Let us consider some obvious cases in point:

Example One: The Therapist's Age and Appearance

Therapist: Mrs. Miller?

Patient: Yes?

Therapist: Hi! I'm Arnold Lazarus. Good to see you. Would you like to sit in that armchair or do you prefer this one over here?

Patient: This one will be just fine.

Therapist: Did you have any difficulty in finding this office?

Patient: No, your directions were very clear.

Therapist: Oh, good. Well, let me just take down some formal details and then we can look into your problems.

Patient: So you're Dr. Lazarus.

Therapist: Why do you say it like that?

Patient: Oh, I don't know. It's just that I expected you to look different. Umm! (laughs) You don't look like a psychologist.

Therapist: How do you think a psychologist should look?

Patient: (Laughs) Oh, I know it sounds stupid, but I

expected to find a little old man with a gray beard.

Therapist: (Joking) Well, did you notice my gray hairs?

Patient: Oh, I know it's foolish. . . .

Therapist: Not at all. If you need someone who comes across to you in a special fatherly way, you may indeed be more comfortable and derive much more benefit from working with an older man than I, and it's very wise of you to raise this point at the very beginning. Let's look into it more closely. . . .

Comment. Some therapists may attempt to persuade this woman to remain in therapy with them in spite of, or because of, her leanings or prejudices. Issues of this nature warrant careful exploration. For some people, words spoken by a little old man with a long gray beard may have ten or twenty times the impact of identical utterances from younger men (even if they can lapse into heavy Viennese accents). If taken literally, this example may seem naive. The point being made is that it is important for therapists to assess their "reinforcement values" for individual clients and to try and remedy the situation when laboring at a disadvantage. Goldstein (1970) has provided many excellent studies on "relationship-enhancement" and indicates that therapists can structure initial sessions to augment therapeutic attractiveness.

A more precise example concerns the case of an experimental psychologist who reported that he found it incredibly simple to shape the verbal behavior of a group of female students. One of his colleagues failed to replicate these results. The disparate findings were accounted for in terms of possible differences in pretest expectancies, variations in intensity and timing of reinforcement contingencies, slight age differences between the samples, and so forth. Neither of them considered the obvious fact that the first experimenter was an extremely charming and handsome young man with high reinforcement potential for young girls whether he winked, whistled, or cackled, whereas his odd and pimply-faced counterpart required very potent techniques to compensate for his deficiencies in personality and appearance.

Example Two: The Real Thing or Nothing

Therapist: I've studied all the questionnaires you filled out and would now like to discuss my impressions and give you some idea of the way in which I think we should proceed in therapy.

Patient: Some of the questions were quite confusing. What I'm saying is that I can't vouch for all my answers.

Therapist: That's okay. All I needed were some general trends. Let me tell you what I deduced from your answers. Generally, there seemed to be three main areas of, what should we call them . . . umm . . . emotional hypersensitivity. First you seem to be really up-tight about making it with women.

Patient: That's no surprise considering what I was telling you about my dear mother and sisters.

Therapist: Right. And that brings up the second factor. You have a lot of hostility towards your mother and older sisters, yet you have never expressed your grievances directly to any of them. In fact, they probably have no idea about the way you really feel about anyone or anything. Which ties into the third factor, and that is your general secrecy and lack of trust.

Patient: Well, I'd say you've hit it on the head, but I guess there's a good reason for all this . . . umm. . . .

Therapist: Sure, but I don't think we need spend too much time on discovering *why* you act and feel the way you do as much as *what* can be done to change it.

Patient: How do you mean?

Therapist: Well, do you know anything about techniques like desensitization, assertive training, and similar methods?

Patient: It sounds like *1984*, or maybe *Brave New World*.

Therapist: Many people get the wrong idea about these procedures. It's not a matter of brainwashing or any form of coercion. Let me give you an example. Just imagine as realistically as possible that you are at a party. Close your eyes and imagine this really vividly. Try and pretend that you are not in this office but project yourself right into the scene at the party. Try to see the people and hear the hum of conversation. Look around the room. Some folks are dancing. Get the picture?

Patient: Uh huh!

Therapist: Good. There's a pretty girl sitting by herself. Look at her. Now picture yourself deciding to go up to this pretty girl and ask her to dance. (pause of about five seconds) How does that make you feel?

Patient: Up-tight!

Therapist: Okay, suppose I first trained you in relaxation so you could picture many of these scenes without feeling anxious, you would soon find yourself actually doing these things in real life without getting up-tight.

Patient: Like I said, *1984*. Or maybe Pavlov's dogs. Look here, you told me to be honest. I can see how this would be great for some people, but I want to do this thing properly; you know, like go back to my childhood and try to get some real understanding and insight into myself.

Therapist: Well, sure. To go about this properly I'm going to need your full life history. We will need to look into all your meaningful and formative relationships and explore your attitudes and values. . . .

Patient: How about my dreams?

Comment. Further discussion revealed how much this patient was conditioned by the Freudian *Zeitgeist*. For him, therapy had to consist of a couch, free association, deep introspection, and dream interpretation. Any other approach was but a poor imitation of the genuine article. It is usually bad therapeutic practice to argue and to try and sell one's own therapeutic system in place of that which the patient believes can best help him. The patient in question was accordingly referred to a psychoanalyst. In my experience, patients who specifically ask for hypnosis or dream interpretation or any other special procedure should be treated by their self-prescribed procedures. The patient often knows best. If his method of choice proves unsuccessful, it clears the way for the therapist to reevaluate the case and to apply procedures which he considers more appropriate.

Example Three: You Must Relax

Therapist: Okay, let's go on to the relaxation now. Would you like to push the chair right back so you can let your whole body have support?

Patient: I'm still not sure what you said about the incident involving my sister's husband.

Therapist: Oh, I thought we had covered that one. I think you should ignore it at this stage.

Patient: Yes, I reckon it's the only thing I can do right now. Okay, I feel better about that.

Therapist: Fine. All right, now push the chair back and get comfortable. . . .

Patient: Did I mention that Marge sends you her love?

Therapist: Yes, thank you. You can get even more comfortable by sitting farther back in the chair.

Patient: Will we have time today to talk about something that involved me and my niece's maid?

Therapist: Sure. We only need to extend the relaxation from your arms to your facial area today. It will take about ten minutes.

Patient: I also want to get into that bit about my feelings towards Janice.

Therapist: Should we forget about the relaxation today and rather talk about the matters you have raised?

Patient: Well, if you say so.

Comment. Therapists who are overenthusiastic about their own favorite techniques are apt to keep pushing them at their patients despite their obvious resistance or reluctance. A less reticent patient might not have hedged but may have expressed her need to talk about her problems rather than practice relaxation exercises during that particular session. Or she may have expressed her antipathy towards relaxation procedures in general. Even when this occurs, some therapists make the error of insisting that relaxation be applied because they consider it unwise to allow patients to control or manipulate them. Yet, sometimes a distinct therapeutic gain may be derived from allowing the patient to be controlling or somewhat manipulative, especially when he is testing out newly formed assertive skills. Passive-aggressive forms of manipulation should usually be identified and discouraged, but a patient's refusal to relax or to role play, or to carry out an assignment, is often too hastily labeled "resistance" or "contrariness" when it is nothing of the sort. In keeping with the tenor of this book, it should be noted that contrary to Jacobson (1964) relaxation is not always effective in decreasing anxiety but may, on occasion, even heighten it (Lazarus, 1965).

Example Four: Let's First Talk for a Year or Two

Therapist: Well, I would say that your anxiety seems to boil down into three main areas. First, you are over-concerned about your performance at work. Second, you really are in two minds about your love affair and need to settle it one way or the other. And third, you have a real "thing" about doctors, hospitals, and illness.

Patient: Holy cow! That's like summarizing *The Brothers Karamazov* in less than fifty words. Half a lifetime of feelings and experiences neatly cut up into three slices, filed under three categories, in three compartments. And all this after knowing me and listening to me for less than two hours. Christ! Well, how's about adding a number four while we are at it, and that is how I feel that oversimplification not only misses the boat but does the other person and yourself a grave injustice. And for a number five, you now know that I'm an angry and aggressive bitch!

Therapist: You seem to be saying that I am unaware of how extremely complicated or complex people really are and that I have insulted you by identifying three main trends which seem to account for much of your tensions and anxieties.

Patient: It's not that as much as the fact that I feel you shouldn't leap to conclusions about people that you hardly know. I mean, a hell of a lot has happened to me in thirty-five years and it's obviously going to take time for me to sort it all out with you. I mean, if you made a one-two-three statement after knowing me for a year or two, I could more easily accept that you were basing your diagnosis on some extensive facts. But to almost suck it out of the air after less than two hours. . . .

Comment. One might be tempted to explain to this patient that just as one is not required to drain every pint of her blood in order to assess its chemical content, but that a 5 cc sample can often tell us all we need to know, it is not necessary to look into every facet of her "life stream" in order to draw plausible inferences about her feelings and behavior. But this patient seemed above all else to be expressing the need for a prolonged therapeutic relationship. As I was about to move to a different part of the country in less than six months, I discussed my further impressions with her and gave her the option of continuing to see me for another few months and then, if necessary, being referred elsewhere, or of consulting someone else from the start. Not surprisingly, she considered it unwise to be "shunted from pillar to post" and chose the latter. At an earlier stage of experience, I was so technique- and problem-oriented that I would probably have missed her need for a relationship per se, or what Schofield (1964) so aptly called "the purchase of friendship." Although I am generally impressed by the advantages of short-term and time-limited therapy (Phillips & Wiener, 1966), I have seen several cases who needed more than a year's therapy to develop sufficient trust in me before they could or would reveal highly charged emotional areas which had eluded all preliminary psychometric and diagnostic evaluations.

Matching Patient to Therapist

The implicit theme throughout this chapter is that a therapist cannot adapt his therapy or himself to every patient. Sagacious referrals will continue to serve a crucial therapeutic function. The examples outlined above stress the need to fit the patient to the most well-suited therapist whose age, brand of therapy, utilization of techniques, and way of establishing rapport are all in keeping with the patient's needs and expectancies.

Considerable information about a person, apart from his chief complaints, is required before the best suited therapies and therapists can be found and properly matched to his idiosyncratic needs. We must know *when* deviant responses are elicited, by *what* they are maintained, and *how* they can best be eliminated. (Traditional psychotherapy seems to be too preoccupied with discovering *why* the person is as he is.) Effective therapy seems to require a well-balanced client- and problem-centered orientation. For instance, while most phobic sufferers can be expected to derive benefit from desensitization therapy, one needs to be on the alert for important exceptions to this rule.

Hoch (1955, p. 322) observed that "there is some relationship between the efficacy of psychotherapy and the patient's expectation of it, [his] 'ideal picture' about the therapist and also about the procedure to which ... [he] would like to respond." Similarly, Solovey and Michelin (1958, p. 1) have pointed out that "the individual who comes to consult, usually has his own mental representation of his disease, of the recovery he hopes to achieve, and often, even of the psychotherapeutic procedure he desires to have applied in his case." Conn (1968) observed that "when everything else failed, Stekel would purposely antagonize a patient. In almost every case the patient would leave in a huff and later have his glasses changed, visit a spa, or go to another doctor who would cure him. The patient would then call Stekel to report that another method of treatment had cured him."

In addition to adopting a flexible and personalistic system of psychotherapy, may I enter a plea for therapists to search continuously for new techniques in order to develop a large and effective repertoire for overcoming the anxieties, depressions, and other disruptive feelings and thoughts that mar the attainment of sustained well-being. Throughout this book, I hope to demonstrate that techniques, rather than theories, are the active means for achieving constructive therapeutic ends.

CHAPTER 3
INITIAL
INTERVIEWS

Most therapists would agree that the initial interview is often crucial. Not only do patient and therapist size each other up at this time, but first impressions often color the entire therapeutic relationship. A good first interview will tell a therapist whether or not a sound working relationship can be formed. It will also furnish the therapist with specific information concerning the patient's major presenting problems, what he hopes to derive from treatment, and the manner in which he is most likely to achieve his therapeutic goals. If handled correctly, the initial interview can set the stage for a smooth therapeutic progression. In many instances, the therapeutic interactions can be structured so that the patient knows exactly what to expect from the therapy and how to behave in therapy. Orne and Wender (1968) have shown that poorly motivated patients can profit from psychotherapy if they are taught what to expect. Ideally, the initial interview can provide hope and immediate help. In a surprising number of cases, people may require no more than an initial interview to precipitate lasting change and achieve profound behavioral readjustment.

A flexible therapist has no fixed pattern of approaching new patients. He usually perceives what his patient needs and then tries to fit the role. The shy, self-conscious, anxious newlywed may require the therapist to behave in a manner which would appear utterly absurd to a middle-aged dilettante. The structure and content of the initial interview and, indeed, the entire course of therapy, depend not only upon the problems at hand but also upon the patient's therapeutic expectations, intelligence, mental status, and socioeconomic background.

There is probably no substitute for an extensive clinical apprenticeship to learn when and how to coddle certain patients, to challenge others vigorously, to be passive or manipulative, or to be a combination of these and many other things. Nevertheless, this chapter will endeavor to do the next best thing by providing verbatim interview protocols which, despite the absence of visual and other nonverbal cues, will give the reader clinical information which should prove helpful.

Initial Interviews with Exceedingly Tense Individuals

It is common knowledge that before proceeding with clinical inquiries, diagnostic tests, or therapeutic methods, the patient should be "at ease" and a "good working relationship" should be established. In many instances, it is sufficient to listen attentively and nod sagaciously. But some highly anxious people find silence and the sound of their own voice extremely aggravating when they feel especially tense. Such cases, when met by a therapist who employs affective reflection as a standard method, often lapse into silence or run out of the therapist's consulting room. It often proves effective for the therapist to be extremely garrulous under these conditions.

Hostility

Recently, a man asked me to treat his wife whom he described as "sick in the head." The young lady was sullen and noncommunicative. I launched into a nonstop monologue to which she responded, in less than three minutes, with the comment, "Oh, shut up!" I had mistaken hostility for anxiety and responded by saying, "I thought you were up-tight when all the time you are just angry as hell." My comment unleashed a string of invectives at which point I played a clinical hunch. In her vernacular, I informed her that I regarded her husband as "sick in the head" for having brought her to me against her wishes. She immediately became contrite and confided that her husband was in fact a most hypercritical and unsympathetic person. The remainder of the interview was devoted to a productive exploration of their dyadic struggles. They are currently undergoing marital therapy with rewarding results.

The Cross Examination

A forty-two-year-old lady was referred by a physician who described her as "difficult." Since divorcing her husband two years previously, she had been seeking psychiatric assistance, had consulted five therapists, but had never returned after the first or second interview. As she entered my consulting room, the following dialogue ensued:

Patient: Are you always ten minutes late for your appointments?

Therapist: I've never been too obsessional about time.

Patient: I'm a very punctual person.

Therapist: (Smiling) Well, hopefully I can help you with that problem. Let me just get down some formal details if I may. . . .

Patient: May I ask how old you are?

Therapist: I'm thirty-eight.

Patient: Are you an M.D.?

Therapist: No, I'm a Ph.D.

Patient: Is that tape recorder switched on?

Therapist: Oh, your opening remark threw me somewhat and I forgot to ask your permission. Do you mind if I record this interview?

Patient: Don't you think it rather late to ask my permission?

Therapist: No, We've just started. I'll switch it off if you like.

Patient: Where are you from?

Therapist: South Africa.

Patient: Did you go to school over there?

Therapist: Yes. I also did some clinical work in London.

Patient: When did you get your doctorate?

Therapist: In 1960.

Patient: What did you do your dissertation on?

Therapist: New methods of group therapy.

Patient: Have you published anything on the subject of anxiety?

Therapist: Quite a bit.

Patient: Are you married?

Therapist: Yes.

Patient: Do you have any children?

Therapist: Yes. A girl of eleven and a boy of eight.

Patient: You teach at Temple University Medical School?

Therapist: That's right.

Patient: What rank do you hold?

Therapist: Full professor.

Patient: Did you get good grades at college?

Therapist: Fair.

Patient: Are you happily married?

Therapist: Yes, very much so.

Patient: Do you like living in Philadelphia?

Therapist: I'm beginning to although my family and most of my meaningful friends are all in Johannesburg.

Patient: Why don't you go back there?

Therapist: Well, for one thing, the work setup in America is much more stimulating and rewarding.

Patient:	How many cases have you treated?
Therapist:	I've lost count, but I would say well over a thousand.
Patient:	(Weeps) Excuse me. (Blows her nose and then sobs)
Therapist:	I think I know why you're crying. I'll bet I'm the first therapist you've met who was prepared to put all his cards on the table.
Patient:	(Still crying, nods her head)
Therapist:	That was quite an oral examination I just went through. Well, have I qualified to be your therapist?
Patient:	(Crying and laughing at the same time) Yes.
Therapist:	Good. Now I'd like to put a few questions to you to see whether you qualify to be my patient.

Discussion. Most therapists are taught to remain ethereal, enigmatic, and impersonal. The patient's very first comment, "Are you always ten minutes late for your appointments?" would usually be met by most therapists with some observation concerning the patient's hostility, or by some noncommittal remark such as, "Is that important to you?" Indeed, many clinicians customarily answer questions with questions. Certainly, the question, "May I ask how old you are?" would usually be met by some sort of interpretation, or a why-is-that-an-important-issue type question. None of her previous therapists had allowed her to proceed beyond three personal questions. Does this imply that I always allow every patient to interrogate me? Certainly not. This lady was obviously frightened. She was using hostility and third-degree tactics as a blatant cover-up. I decided to play along with her and to provide simple, honest, and straightforward replies to her questions and see where they led. It certainly paid off. The patient learned to trust me during those first few minutes.

A good working relationship was established soon thereafter, and during the course of subsequent sessions, the patient expressed her gratitude and amazement at the way in which her prying questions were met by straightforward facts. "I immediately felt that I could trust you and believe in you. . . . I never felt that way about the other men I consulted." Her course of treatment lasted about twenty sessions at the end of which she described herself as "a new and better person" and added, "I only wish I could have known you or someone like you twenty years ago. You were a real human being to me right from the start and I am eternally grateful for this."

The studies of Truax and Carkhuff (1967) have clearly shown that honesty, openness, genuineness, and a person-to-person relationship with the patient are important ingredients of the initial interview.

Withdrawal

Another young lady entered my consulting room, sat down, and immediately buried her head in her hands. I permitted about one full minute to elapse and then inquired, "What are you feeling?" There was no response. This type of impasse poses interesting clinical choice points. To pose the question in operant terms, should one refuse to reinforce this behavior by ignoring it and perhaps terminating the interview? Some hospitalized cases may eventually open up when placed on a "rejection schedule" of this kind. It can hardly be recommended as standard practice. Should one upbraid the patient and strongly stress one's refusal to tolerate such infantile behavior? This might be a useful last resort but seldom generates warmth and trust. Generally, verbal self-disclosure, or what Salter (1949) called "feeling talk" on the part of the therapist, will open up therapeutic channels of communication. When the young lady continued to sit in a somewhat fetal posture and made no response to my initial question, I tried a different tack.

Therapist:	You don't have to look at me or speak to me, but will you nod or shake your head to some simple yes-no questions?
Patient:	(No response)
Therapist:	Would you rather not be in here?
Patient:	(Still no response)
Therapist:	I guess you don't trust me.
Patient:	(Still no response)

Therapist: Just nod your head if you can hear me.

Patient: (No response)

Therapist: Well, I'm going to assume that you can hear what I am saying. Therapy works on the basis of mutual trust. I don't believe in forcing people to do what they don't want to do—unless it is literally a matter of life and death, of course. Now if you regard me as a policeman, or a nasty schoolteacher, or a strict parent, or as a judge, I can understand why you are withdrawing from me. But it doesn't make sense to hide from potential friends. I sort of feel rejected by you. I know it's silly, but I feel that someone else has hurt you and you are sort of blaming me, kind of taking it out on me. I'm not putting you down. I guess you are upsetting me because I want to help you and you won't give me a chance. Am I making sense?

Patient: (Nods)

Therapist: Good. Let me tell you a bit more about the way in which I like to work. I find that we live in a world where there is much ugliness and bitterness. Therapy, as I see it, should teach us how to cope with all this hate and hypocrisy and also how to rise above it. To me the most important things are genuine love and honesty. Does this sound mushy?

Patient: (Shakes her head negatively)

Therapist: Okay, then we agree, and if we get to know each other we can probably work well together. . . .

Patient: (Begins sobbing)

Therapist: I didn't mean to upset you.

Patient: (Her head still bent down) It is such an ugly world. (Sobs)

Therapist: I often feel that I should get off my ass and into

the world on some sort of crusade, a kind of big
social reform kick. But I know where that would
lead.

Patient: (Looking up for the first time and wiping her
eyes) I feel such a mess.

Therapist: Perhaps you will feel better if you go over to the
sink and splash some cold water on your face.
Would you like that?

Patient: (Walks to the sink)

Therapist: Here's a clean towel.

Discussion. It should be understood that this was no predetermined
clinical line. The computerized therapist who deliberately turns on
"warmth," or "charm," or "empathy," or who launches into other acts
such as "being understanding," "showing tolerance," or making "sympathetic clucks," usually has cracks in his streamlined veneer through
which perceptive patients can readily detect the true nature of what lies
beneath his phony facade. If a person does not possess genuine compassion for the plight of his patients and have a strong desire to diminish
their suffering, it would be a boon to psychotherapy if he could enter
some other field of endeavor.

Passive-Aggressive Reactions

There are, undoubtedly, times when the therapist must be very firm with
certain clients, but the therapist who meets aggression with his own
counteraggression will often prove antitherapeutic. At a clinical meeting,
a hostile and insecure psychiatrist who was apparently threatened by a
patient's rejecting comments responded with, "You are an unfunny
Mickey Rooney." In my opinion, sarcasm is seldom warranted in
therapy. This is different from poking good-natured fun at the patient
or enabling him to see humor in tragedy. I have witnessed too many
therapists who are inclined to indulge in cutting or contemptuous remarks. Since people experience more than enough hostility in the world
at large, let them at least regard their therapeutic encounters as one
situation in which they can express their own feelings without fear of
retaliation.

Here is an example of *understanding* as opposed to sarcastic or counteraggressive management of passive aggressive responses:

Patient: (With heavy sarcasm) Look, I know you are an excellent therapist. I mean you certainly have had a lot of experience. Besides, you are a professor. And I don't doubt that you have really been trying your best to help me, but somehow I just haven't been feeling any better.

Therapist: Don't assume that just because I have had lots of clinical experience and am a professor it necessarily means that I am a good therapist. I mean, I know some brilliant men who occupy the highest academic ranks, but who really hardly know the first thing about therapy.

Patient: (Scornfully) Oh, but I am sure that you are good at your work. I mean, doesn't everyone think so?

Therapist: I have my fair share of detractors. But you are raising an important point. It does not matter whether or not I am a good therapist in general. What matters to you is whether or not I am effective with you. And your message is that to date I have not really helped you with your problems.

Patient: Oh, you haven't been *completely* unhelpful.

Therapist: Well, maybe I've been one or two percent helpful and you are certainly entitled to question my competence.

Patient: (With sneering sarcasm) Oh, but I am not doing that. I know you are very good at your work.

Therapist: It might certainly be helpful if I could teach you to come out and state directly what you feel instead of coming on sideways.

Patient: I didn't mean to hurt your feelings.

Therapist: Believe me, it's not that my feelings are hurt. I just feel that you set things up in such a way that you have to lose out in the end, and I'm wondering how I can teach you to stop defeating yourself.

Patient: I don't follow you.

Therapist: Well, let's go over the way in which you handed me the message that you are basically dissatisfied or discouraged about your very slight progress to date. . . .

The Problem-focused Interview

Therapists with a behavioral orientation are well aware of the importance of ferreting out specific situations which arouse distress and deviant responses in their patients. Toward the end of Chapter 2, reference was made to the central importance of *when*, *what*, and *how* questions rather than *why* questions. Typically, the therapist asks, "When did you first notice that feeling?" "What was going on in your life at the time?" "How did you act right afterwards?" The following clinical excerpt should underscore the importance of tracing "stimulus antecedents," the manner in which this is carried out, and the necessity to define abstract terms and find their behavioral referents.

Identity Crisis

Patient: I don't even know how to tell you what's bugging me. My friends call it "an identity crisis."

Therapist: Well, we will have to get very much more specific.

Patient: I don't know how to be any more specific.

Therapist: Let me try to help you. In what way does your "identity crisis" interfere with your work, your sex life, or your social relationships?

Patient: Phew! Are you kidding? Just about everything is screwed up. I wouldn't know where to start. I mean, I'm just not grooving.

Therapist: No chicks? No friends?

Patient: Well, yes and no. I don't know.

Therapist: Okay. Let me review what I know about you thus far. You are twenty-three, a college senior, unmarried, only child, living in an apartment which you share with two other guys, and you feel generally unhappy.

Patient: Yeah.

Therapist: Let's get a few specific facts. Are you an acid head? Do you smoke pot? Are you hung up on speed or other drugs?

Patient: I took one LSD trip and have turned on occasionally.

Therapist: Did you have a good trip?

Patient: So-so.

Therapist: Do you booze?

Patient: Now and then.

Therapist: Are you leveling with me?

Patient: Sure, I wouldn't be here otherwise.

Therapist: Good. Now is there anything else I should know about drugs or narcotics?

Patient: No, that's not my hang-up.

Therapist: Tell me, what made you come for therapy at this specific time?

Patient: Mmmm! Uh! (Silence)

Therapist: Let's see. You called up for the appointment on Monday. Did anything significant happen over the weekend?

Patient: Well, I don't know how significant this is, but I broke up with a chick I'd been making it with.

Therapist: That sounds significant. Would you fill me in on the details?

At this point, the patient went into a rather lengthy narrative, the essence of which was that the young girl in question had hurt his feelings by criticizing his sexual performance and by calling him "unmanly."

> *Therapist:* So she really hurt your feelings?
>
> *Patient:* Uh! She wasn't much anyway.
>
> *Therapist:* That's a cop-out!
>
> *Patient:* Yeah! I guess.
>
> *Therapist:* I think we're getting somewhere. Maybe you're a lousy lay and need some technical advice on how to behave in bed. . . . Also, I think you're hung up on public opinion and bruise very easily. I think you have a "thing" about criticism, rejection, disapproval, and failure. And my hunch is that these sensitivities keep your friendships so shallow that you never really allow yourself to get into things. You sort of keep apart and feel out of things. Maybe this partly explains your "identity crisis." (Perhaps it is necessary to mention that this was said compassionately and in a very gentle tone. The tone of expression can lead the same words to have very different effects.)
>
> *Patient:* I never used to be this way.
>
> *Therapist:* Well, when did it all start?
>
> *Patient:* I would say round about the time I entered college.
>
> *Therapist:* Let's get into these details.

By the end of the initial interview, it was evident that the patient had entered college at the insistence of his demanding parents who still controlled him. He was generally timid and easily exploited and was especially unconfident around women. He was not enjoying his courses and wished to switch fields; he was exceedingly anxious to please everybody, to be liked by everybody, and never to be rejected by anybody.

At the second interview, even more specific behavioral referents concerning his identity crisis emerged, such as specific approach and avoidance responses which were clearly maladaptive.

General Guidelines for Initial Interviews

Patient types, of course, are endless. Hostile, withdrawn, passive-aggressive, and similar overdefensive individuals are likely to prove especially troublesome during the initial interview. It is hoped that the previous verbatim examples will be illuminating to novice clinicians.

Generally, the initial interview starts with the therapist assuming a nondirective role so that he can listen attentively and gauge the patient's needs. About halfway through the interview, it is usually helpful for the therapist to make leading comments and observations. Therapists will find it extremely useful to follow every comment they make with the question, "What do you think about (or how do you feel about) what I have just said?" In this way false impressions can be clarified and miscommunication can be reduced to a minimum. Here is a typical excerpt:

> *Therapist:* Well, from the sounds of it, I would say that you feel there are advantages to being a child instead of behaving like an adult. You seem to fear responsibility and you therefore want someone to take care of you and look after you. At the same time you do crave for a large degree of independence so you end up disliking yourself whenever you act like a child. I think that we will have to train you in becoming truly self-sufficient. How do you feel about what I have just said?

> *Patient:* It frightens me. I know you're right and I have to grow up sooner or later. But it still frightens me.

> *Therapist:* It need not frighten you if you realize that you will not be asked to take a giant leap into adulthood but that we will gradually have you doing more and more little things for yourself, making

small decisions alone, so that you eventually feel
more and more confident about the bigger issues.
What do you think about that?

Patient: I don't know.

Therapist: You seem puzzled.

Patient: No. It's just that I'm not sure whether I'm to
reach a stage where I never ask anybody for anything.

Therapist: I'm glad you asked that. There's a world of
difference between healthy dependency and parasitic dependency. In this complex society, we are
all mutually dependent on one another in many
respects. The hermit is not a model of good adjustment. We must look for a balance of independence or self-sufficiency and healthy cooperation and togetherness. How do you feel about
that?

Patient: Good. Yes, that makes sense.

Typically after my trainees have conducted an initial interview,
I expect them to be able to answer nearly all the following questions:

1. What maladaptive responses need to be eliminated and what adaptive responses need to be acquired?

2. Can a mutually satisfying working relationship be put into effect, or
have you (or will you) refer the patient elsewhere?

3. Can you describe the patient's appearance with respect to grooming,
physical characteristics, motor activity (e.g., rigid posture, fidgeting,
tics), manner of speaking, and attitude (e.g., friendly, obsequious, hostile, sullen)?

4. Did you notice any thought disorders (e.g., word salad, looseness
of association, flight of ideas, blocking)?

5. Was there any incongruity of affect (inappropriate laughter, anger,
or tears)?

6. Did you observe the presence or absence of self-recrimination, sui-

cidal ideas, obsessive trends, delusions, hallucinations, ideas of reference, or morbid fears?

7. Have you decided whether the patient will require you to be directive or nondirective, and do you have some idea as to the pace with which therapy should proceed?

8. Do you have a fairly good idea of what the patient wishes to derive from therapy?

9. Were you able to provide the patient with legitimate grounds for hope during this interview?

10. Do you have some reasonably clear ideas as to what or who is maintaining the patient's deviant behavior?

Unlike some therapists, I never conduct formal history taking or administer psychological tests during the initial interview (except for the procedures described in Chapter 4). I have found that case histories, questionnaires, and formal testing block spontaneity and do not permit the patient and therapist "to feel each other out" sufficiently for proper rapport to be established. It sometimes takes several interviews before patient and therapist feel that they are truly "talking the same language." With some patients it is helpful for them to take home a life history questionnaire and fill it in after the initial interview (see Appendix A).

After the initial interview, and whenever I have reason to doubt the effectiveness of any particular session, I administer the Psychotherapy Session Report (see Appendix B) as developed by Orlinsky and Howard (1966, 1967, 1968). I have found this instrument extremely valuable in gauging the personalistic needs of the patient and thereby maximizing the impact of each therapeutic encounter.

As a corollary to all that has been said thus far, the *second* interview should find the therapist immediately applying everything that he has gleaned during the initial interview. Personalistic psychotherapy has no preset structure. Thus, my second interviews have sometimes been conducted at a restaurant, at the patient's home, or in an outdoor park, rather than in the formal confines of the consulting room.

Let us now turn to verbal techniques which can facilitate the structure of the therapeutic relationship, pinpoint several important areas of adaptive and maladaptive functioning, and rapidly bring to the fore important material for therapeutic intervention.

CHAPTER 4
VERBAL
ADJUSTMENT
PROCEDURES

Clinical psychology is replete with tests which purport to measure innumerable traits, states, and functions. There is often no substitute for direct behavioral observation, but less obtrusive and more economical procedures are usually indicated. Information derived from various tests of intelligence, abstract reasoning, language and other specific abilities, checklists, questionnaires, so-called "personality tests," "semantic differentials," "repertory grids," "psychophysiological measurement," and so forth, may sometimes prove therapeutically useful. Generally, however, I have tended to veer away from many of the standardized tests on the market simply because they do not yield information that I find clinically productive. In recent years I have come to rely heavily on two verbal methods which serve a dual diagnostic and therapeutic purpose.

The Desert Island Fantasy

This may be termed a *structured projective technique* which rapidly yields important behavioral data. Generally, if applied at all, I find it most useful during early, formative sessions. As the reader will see, many inferences may be drawn, and much information may be derived from this simple procedure. When using this technique, therapists must guard against emitting "seductive cues" and tacitly reinforcing sexual fantasies. Nevertheless, some patients may misinterpret this technique, and these people should be emphatically told that the therapist is not making a covert "pass" at them.

The method is illustrated below in the verbatim transcript of the latter portion of an interview with a thirty-two-year-old housewife who had been referred for the treatment of "anxiety."

> *Patient:* So I'm like the old joke in which the psychiatrist tells the patient that she doesn't have an inferiority complex because she really is inferior.
>
> *Therapist:* Well, you certainly are a genius at putting yourself down.
>
> *Patient:* Let's put it this way. I'm a fairly good cook and I take good care of my kids. That's where my talents begin and end.
>
> *Therapist:* Look, at this stage I'd like to use a little fantasy test. Just bear with me for five or ten minutes and really try to enter into the spirit of the fantasy. I'm really going to ask you to use your imagination to the full. Try to go along with the fantasy and put yourself right into the situation I'm about to describe. I'll be asking you some impossible questions which you may be inclined to answer by saying, "How the heck should I know?" But don't answer in that way. Try to imagine how you think you might react if you really were in the situation.
>
> *Patient:* I think I follow you.
>
> *Therapist:* It's really quite simple. Just use your imagination

to the full and try to be as honest with me as is humanly possible.

Patient: I'll try.

Therapist: Okay. It is now about 9:40 A.M. on Saturday, November 2, 1968, and we are sitting and talking in this office. Suddenly the door opens and in walks a magician. Now for the purposes of this narrative, anything is possible. The magician addresses you and says, "Carol, this is a magic wand. When I wave it, you will be transported to the proverbial desert island for a period of six months." Now there's no point in saying, "No, please don't do that to me," because you have no choice in the matter. He will wave his magic wand and you will be whisked off to the island. Can you picture it so far?

Patient: Uh huh. It sounds interesting.

Therapist: Fine. Now before waving his magic wand, the magician informs you that while you are on the island, time will stand still. In other words, you will live through six long months, day and night, but when you return to this office six months later, it will still be 9:40 A.M. on Saturday, November 2, 1968. This is just so that you don't have to worry about your husband and children anxiously searching for you. Since they will be in suspended animation you don't have to worry about them.

Patient: How will I explain away my glorious suntan?

Therapist: (Laughs) I guess you will have to say that you were trying out one of those instant tanning chemicals. Of course you could hardly say, "I've been on a desert island for six months." Now, before waving his wand, the magician gives you one other choice. In effect, he allows you to choose company or solitude. Some people would welcome the opportunity to spend six months in their own company, with their own thoughts in peace and solitude. So the magician says, "Carol, before I wave my wand you may elect to take that man—pointing to me—whom you have only known for about forty minutes with you for company. Or you may choose to go on your own." Notice, he doesn't allow you to take along your husband or your favorite film star. You either choose solitude, or you can take me, a stranger who may be a real bastard for all you know. What would you choose? Company or solitude?

Patient: Company.

Therapist: Okay. In your position I would also choose company. I'd probably go out of my mind if I had to be on my own for six months. I'd always choose company, unless I had reason to detest the other person.

Patient: Few things are worse than loneliness.

Therapist: I agree. All right. The magician waves his magic wand, time stands still for the rest of humanity, and we land on the island. Now let's look around. It isn't a huge vast paradise where we can spend endless hours exploring the place and discovering all sorts of exciting things. It is a narrow strip of land with a palm tree for shade, adequate shelter, food, and provisions. Being a magic island, we needn't fear for our survival. Now here's the point. We have no books, no TV, no distractions. We are entirely dependent upon one another for entertainment and stimulation. Get the picture?

Patient: Yes, I think so.

Therapist: Imagine yourself right into the situation. Now my first question is how will we occupy our time?

Patient: Oh, gee! Well, I guess we'd first have to build a sort of hut.

Therapist: Don't worry about that. That's all been taken care of. There's an adequate shelter, lots of food. We needn't worry about our physical survival.

Patient: Umm . . . Well, I guess we'd talk.

Therapist: About what?

Patient: All sorts of things. I guess we'd want to get to really know each other.

Therapist: That's important. If, after six months, you returned to civilization knowing little more about me than you know right now, it would mean that I had remained closed, concealed, and shut off from you. I should imagine that living with such a person would be a desolate experience. I make it *me*, rather than Mr. X on that island, because I know more or less how I might respond, but I don't know what Mr. X or your favorite movie star's needs would be. I would need very much to communicate. I would want to hear all about you and I would want you to hear everything about me. And when I was telling you things about myself I would want to be sure that you were giving me your undivided attention, and that you would react at all times with your real thoughts and feelings. Now, let me ask you another question. At the end of the six months, do you think I would know *every* significant thing about you or might you hold certain things back from me?

Patient: That would depend on whether or not I found you to be an understanding person.

Therapist: If you found me nonjudgmental and tolerant would you hide anything from me?

Patient: No.

Therapist: Is it possible that I might know everything about you, good and bad, and still regard you as a worthwhile person?

Patient: I don't know.

Therapist: Why not?

Patient: Well, I get pretty moody and irritable at times. I can be a real bitch.

Therapist: What percentage of the time do you think your moods would intrude? 50 percent? 60 percent?

Patient: Oh, about 20 percent.

Therapist: That makes you 80 percent nonmoody and nonbitchy. Who could ask for more?

Patient: (Laughs) That's a good philosophy.

Therapist: I'm serious. Let's say you're selfish 30 percent of the time. Well, that makes you 70 percent unselfish. The same applies to all other adjectives such as aggressive, inconsiderate, thoughtless, stupid, etc.

Patient: You've just given me an excellent weapon to use on my sister-in-law.

Therapist: Let me ask you again whether I could know everything you have done, felt, and thought and still regard you as a worthwhile person.

Patient: That depends on what you consider worthwhile.

Therapist: You're hedging. All right, let me tell you. Remember on the island we have no distractions or external amusements. Let us assume that you are a fantastic pianist. Well, there is no piano with which to impress me. Let's say you play a remarkable game of tennis. There's no tennis court. You are left entirely to your own devices as a person. Now, I could be on the island with Miss America; beautiful, talented, brilliant, but as a *person* she may be quite worthless in my eyes. Let's assume that my companion was a female physicist who was in the running for the Nobel Prize. In addition to physics, she was a fund of information about politics, mathematics, economics, history, music, art, literature, just you name it. But as a person, she was at least 50 percent cold, aloof, uncaring. For me, it would be like living with a computer. After two days I'd probably feel like drowning her. Now, society at large might admire and revere her, but in my eyes she would not be a worthwhile human being. I would consider you worthwhile if I detected real feelings such as empathy, sympathy, and qualities such as integrity, openness, genuineness, and warmth. You don't have to be any of these things 100 percent of the time. There might be times when you are disinterested, turned off, and sort of into yourself. If this happened all the time or nearly all of the time, I certainly wouldn't regard you very positively. And as far as your own needs are concerned, let's hope that I can sense when you prefer to be left alone, perhaps just dangling your feet in the ocean, and getting lost in thought. It would be unfeeling and unperceptive of me to insist that we talk when you don't feel like talking. You have a right to your feelings and it is up to me to respect them and recognize them. But I also have feelings, and if you infringed on my rights, I would assert myself accordingly.

Patient: (Laughing) It sounds ideal. When can we leave for the island?

Therapist: Are you a worthwhile or superior person as I have defined it?

Patient: My husband and friends have always called me a good listener. They say I am sympathetic and understanding.

Therapist: Are you a good contributor? I mean is it just a one way street with you doing the listening. How much confiding do you do?

Patient: If you really came across as you have described yourself, I would confide in you completely.

Therapist: Okay. So I have the picture of the two of us keeping nothing back from each other. You soon get to know every significant thing about me and vice versa. We share ideas, exchange opinions, and find each other genuinely interested, accepting, and honest. I then say, "Carol, you are a worthwhile person. I'm delighted that if I had to be on an island with somebody, it turned out to be you." Is this likely?

Patient: Well, as you describe it, I would say yes.

Therapist: Let me emphasize that my version of life is that the things that are important on the island are the things that really count right here. Money, status, power, prestige, and so forth count for very little, if anything, on the island. What matters there is the kind of people we are. I think the same holds true in the world at large, but people are too busy chasing things that don't matter even to stop and think about the qualities that do really mean something. Do you think I am being honest or am I coming across as a phony?

Patient: But you are placing great value on things that most people take for granted.

Therapist: That's the trouble. These things shouldn't be taken for granted. How many people do you know whom you regard as genuine, authentic, open, loving, and really worthwhile?

Patient: I get the point.

Therapist: What else do you picture doing on the island?

Patient: Well, let's see. We can swim, lie in the sun, collect shells, run races, play games, and tell jokes.

Therapist: And we can concoct fancy dishes with the food, carve bits of driftwood, climb the palm tree, build sand castles, and try to catch fish. Anything else?

Patient: Well, with a man and a woman all alone on a desert island, I'm sure there would be sex. After all, if a man and a woman are relating closely and openly, it seems the most natural thing in the world for them both to want sexual relations.

Therapist: And if we did have sex would I find you warm and responsive?

Patient: I don't have any sexual hang-ups.

Therapist: Let's assume that we are on the island enjoying a complete relationship. What would happen when we returned to this society?

Patient: I'd come back a much more confident person. In fact, just the fantasy itself has somehow made me revise certain ideas. Does that make sense?

Therapist: Sure, if you have seriously thought about the humanistic values rather than the competitive hang-ups of this sick society. But how would we part?

Patient: I wouldn't want to cheat on my husband or risk breaking up either one of our families. I think as much as it would hurt, we should go our separate ways.

Therapist: You mean that we should be content with our nostalgic memories?

Patient: We won't hurt other people in that way.

Discussion. As a rule a tremendous amount of clinical material emerges from the desert island fantasy test. Some of my trainees have felt that it might be dangerous or unwise to dwell on the sexual aspects. Some patients may feel that the therapist is being sexually seductive, but their reactions can be dealt with in subsequent sessions by discussing their own sexual needs and taboos. With women who are inclined to be "hysterical" or immature, it may be wise to deemphasize the personal involvement by structuring the fantasy around a warm, empathic man instead of the therapist.

At the beginning of the fantasy, the patient who chooses "solitude" rather than "company" usually proves very difficult to treat. The patient who takes an immediate dislike to the therapist will obviously, if honest, prefer to be without him. Clearly with negative feelings toward a therapist from the outset, she would be ill-advised to continue seeing him. I make this point very clear to all my patients during the initial interview. Schizophrenic patients often choose to go alone to the desert island situation. The same is true of women who are extremely afraid of relating to men in general or who are anxious about sexual relations in particular. Those with extreme feelings of inferiority also often refuse to risk a relationship with someone they regard as learned or superior.

Some patients structure the relationship in a predominantly sexual context from the outset. As one client said, "We would have nothing else to do but make love day and night." Obviously, this will alert the therapist to the likelihood of sexual deprivation or some other sexual problem in the patient, just as a complete denial of sexual contact will necessitate more detailed inquiries into the patient's attitude toward sex. Important aspects of the patient's sexual morality and sexual preferences often come to the fore.

The presence or absence of the ordinary give-and-take qualities of personal relationships become quite evident. Some patients construe the situation as an opportunity to receive six months of free, intensive therapy. Others picture themselves in the role of a princess being served by a slave who is there merely to satisfy their whims. Self-deprecating statements often emerge. "You would be bored with me after two days." "You'd spend all the time wishing that I was somebody else."

It becomes clear whether or not the person appreciates the important factors of social relationships. It is evident from the responses of some patients that they do not know how to function interpersonally. Life with them is reminiscent of the parallel-play activities of very young children. They exist side by side but do not know how to share thoughts and feelings.

Some patients are unable to suspend their aggression, hostility, or depression, even in fantasy, and talk of committing murder or suicide on the island, or else they predict entering into six months of continuous withdrawal or melancholic preoccupations. These reactions should prompt most therapists to look into the threatening properties of close relationships per se, in addition to the more obvious aspects of their psychopathology.

Apart from the diagnostic features alluded to above, the test often proves extremely therapeutic to those patients who possess, in fantasy at least, the potential for close and meaningful relationships. They usually emerge positively reinforced, able to regard themselves as worthwhile human beings. Realizing that the qualities that are of basic importance on the island are also capable of yielding subjective comfort in a competitive culture such as ours, they are sometimes able to change their values and become indifferent to the status-power-prestige struggles that may have undermined their serenity and caused them untold grief.

Many patients have reported that the desert island situation made an indelible impression on their minds. As one woman expressed it: "Whenever I have tended to hate myself or criticize myself for falling short of society's standards, I remember the desert island, and find comfort in knowing that I possess the qualities that really matter. This has changed the way I see myself, my husband, my children, and the whole mixed up world."

Dealing with the Choice of Solitude

In the desert island fantasy, it is unusual for people to choose to go alone. When this occurs, it is necessary to try to ascertain the reasons. As already mentioned, the reasons for selecting solitude instead of company usually reflect severe interpersonal problems. Some exceptions are worth noting. One extremely adventurous girl felt that six months of solitude would be a unique experience since she had always been the center of attention. She expressed a curiosity to see how well she would withstand temporary social deprivation. More detailed inquiries showed that this was not a rationalization or a cover-up for deep interpersonal discontent. Some young women were courageous enough to choose solitude on the grounds that a cloistral existence with a man to whom they were not sexually attracted would prove burdensome.

Generally, those who have elected to go to the island alone have given the following sorts of reasons:

"I wouldn't want you to find out what a dreadful person I really am."

"I don't think I have the right to impose such a condition on you."

"I need a doctor, not a man."

"I'm a married woman and do not wish to be led into temptation."

"When you live with a man, you are bound to find out how rotten he is. I don't wish to be disillusioned about you."

"I get more bored with people than I do on my own."

"I could just sleep and eat and do whatever I please without someone else bugging me. It sounds divine."

Obviously, these reactions afford the therapist an opportunity to examine important attitudes. Evidence of autistic or overinclusive thinking or other schizophrenic patterns may emerge, and data concerning interpersonal responses are readily available. Pointed questions concerning the manner in which the person would like to be able to respond in a close personal relationship provide important clues about the way in which the therapeutic relationship should be structured. The rebellious, antiauthoritarian individual usually takes unkindly to (and resists) pedagogical assignments in therapy. The passive-dependent individual usually derives immense benefit from therapy which is strongly directive in the initial stages and thereafter centers on exercises in self-sufficiency (Salter, 1949). The highly individualistic needs with which patients enter therapy are often brought into clear focus by statements such as:

"I want someone to hear me out, but I really mean for them to hear and to listen."

"I get loads of sympathy; I want objectivity."

"I could never be open with a person who didn't reveal his own shortcomings."

"I like strong men; the strong silent type."

Of course, each of these statements may warrant further exploration in their own right, but they should also provide the therapist with important information concerning necessary dos and don'ts for establishing initial rapport.

After completing the important preliminary inquiries concerning the choice of solitude in place of company, it is usually productive to alter the conditions of the island sojourn by restructuring it so that the person is no longer afforded a choice in the matter. The therapist may say, "Now this time, I want you to meet a magician who allows no choice regarding company or solitude. He waves his magic wand and there we both are on the island for six months. We are stuck with each other and whether we like it or not, we have to try and make the best of it. Now it's up to us. We can make each other thoroughly miserable or we can have a ball. Let's take it from there. The first thing we notice is that we are on a narrow strip of land with a palm tree for shade, adequate shelter, food and provisions. . . ."

I do not know whether female therapists are generally likely to encounter difficulties with the desert island fantasy. My female trainees have indicated that male patients tend to latch onto the sexual connotations and have to be strongly coaxed into dwelling on other aspects of male-female interaction.

The Desert Island Fantasy When Patient and Therapist Are of the Same Sex

The main purpose of the desert island fantasy is to examine the patient's capacity for close, meaningful relationships. It is primarily a matter of whether the person thinks he can relate in an honest, open, basic, considerate, feeling fashion when removed from a culture that often makes deception, one-upmanship, and outright aggression necessary for survival. The main therapeutic impact is the discovery that the ingredients of basic friendship, in place of the competitive fencing that occupies so much of social parlance, often pays social and emotional dividends both on and off the island.

With male patients, I structure the desert island fantasy somewhat differently from the foregoing. It is the same "narrow stretch of land with a palm tree for shade, an adequate shelter, plus food and provisions" and equally devoid of distractions—"no books, no TV, etc., so that we are dependent upon one another as *people* for company, stimulation, and true companionship." However, to minimize homosexual complications, "there are two beautiful women awaiting us on the island. The magician has selected a woman who will be sexually attracted and responsive only to you, whereas my woman will only be turned on by me, so there is no risk of rejection or any need for competition. We, in turn, will each find our respective women most appealing." The questions then relate to how we will function as a foursome. The following excerpt, taken from the second interview of a thirty-four-year-old physician who referred himself for the treatment of "anxiety-hysteria" shows how productive this fantasy test can be, both diagnostically and therapeutically:

Patient:	Oh, God! The four of us will be there for six months?
Therapist:	Uh huh.
Patient:	Ummm, uh. Gee! Well, I will obviously be in charge of our physical well-being, you know. I'll obviously be the doctor.
Therapist:	That's taken care of. I mean it's a magic island and we are all going to be well and healthy for the entire period. We won't require your medical services, just you as a human being.
Patient:	Well, somebody has to be in charge of the place. We won't let the women take over, so obviously you and I will have to compete for leadership.
Therapist:	Why? I mean, why can't we just all be together as four human beings—sharing, experiencing, confiding, relating? Why must someone be in charge?
Patient:	I just know you'll tell me what and what not to do. And I'll kick you in the balls.
Therapist:	Would requests or suggestions be tantamount to telling you what to do?

Patient: I can be awful touchy. But let's face it. Even though you have ruled out competition between us and the women, I might still feel that your doll was closer and more loving to you than mine was to me. This would cause friction between my uh ... girl and myself, uh ... and also lead to jealousy and resentment toward you.

Therapist: It sounds as if you are just determined to look for trouble and to find deficiencies in yourself. You set yourself up so that everything becomes a competition. Couldn't you just enjoy your relationship and not even notice if I was a little closer or perhaps a little more distant from my babe? Obviously, if there was a big difference, if my woman was much more loving or attentive to me than yours was to you. . . .

Patient: How much is "much more"? Look, frankly, I'd be afraid that I wouldn't be as adequate sexually as you would be.

Therapist: In what way?

Patient: Well, in real life, my wife has only slept with me so she has no means of comparison. But maybe the girl on the island has had many lovers and I wouldn't measure up.

Therapist: What if she complimented you on your proficiency as a lover?

Patient: I wouldn't believe her. No, wait! Actually that's not true. Anyhow, I think you've picked up the need for us to examine my, umm ... sexual life more, umm ... in great detail.

Therapist: We'll do that. But just getting back to the island. I'm interested in knowing how you see the four of us functioning. Let's assume that there are no obvious discrepancies which cause you concern; can you see yourself relating openly and non-competitively?

Patient: (Shuts his eyes and appears deep in thought for about thirty seconds) It seems that I will have to kill you or you will have to kill me.

Therapist: Why?

Patient: (Sighs deeply) Well, I'd be afraid of making a homosexual advance towards you.

Therapist: Have you had any homosexual inclinations or experiences?

Patient: Not consciously. Except once when I was about nine years old. But I don't attach much importance to that. No, it's just that I get these, umm . . . perverse feelings. It's the same when I see, let's say, a place marked "Danger. Keep out!" I wonder what it would be like to ignore the sign.

Therapist: What would happen if you did make a homosexual advance to me?

Patient: Well, gee! I wonder. Look, I mean, do you realize that I would do it as a sort of compulsion? If I thought you were a homosexual or maybe bisexual and might go through with it, I'd never do it.

Therapist: Okay! I'm neither homosexual nor bisexual. So what would happen?

Patient: Well, you'd be disgusted and you'd probably half-kill me. I don't know.

Therapist: Couldn't I possibly just say, "Oh, don't be absurd! Neither one of us is a queer." Why do I have to react violently?

Patient: How can you be so certain that I'm not a queer?

Therapist: There's a world of difference between homosexual *thoughts* and homosexual *feelings*.

Patient: (Laughs) I don't know why I am laughing. (Continues to laugh) You know I just have such a strong feeling of *relief*. (Inhales and exhales deeply) Christ! What a mess! Okay! Yes! Okay! That fear has gone. Would you believe it? (Laughs) I can trust myself as a man and with a man! I know this sounds crazy. Look, I can't put it into words. I just know something has happened and the only word that comes to mind is that I am *relieved*.

The fantasy had brought the patient face to face with a hitherto unexpressed homosexual anxiety. At the time of the interview, I was puzzled as to what had lent the patient such intense relief. Subsequently, it became clear that my separation between homosexual thoughts and homosexual feelings had mitigated his homosexual anxieties. Most readers will appreciate how many other aspects of the patient's anxiety, extreme competitiveness, sexual misgivings, and insecurity were brought to the fore during the Desert Island Fantasy.

The Inner Circle Strategy

Let us now turn to a different verbal procedure which rapidly brings meaningful material to the therapist's attention and which often enables patients to dwell on crucial personal issues.

Many patients enter therapy feeling completely uncertain about the type of information which can be shared and divulged both in the therapeutic situation and in their other interpersonal relationships. Some people have to be *taught* how to confide. Unless they are gently led into "personal territory," these people can spend hour after hour discussing unimportant situational and other trivial and irrelevant aspects of their lives. At one time, I used to believe that any material which patients brought into therapy was significant. If the patient wished to spend ten sessions discussing his sexual exploits, or perhaps outlining the daily interactions among the people in his office, I used to assume that his flow of thought should not be interrupted. Indeed, there are many people who are willing to pay professional fees to have an expert pay attention to banalities. But where the patient's tendency to digress, or to focus on matters which have no obvious bearing on his major problems, interferes with the therapeutic goals, the perceptive therapist should be able to see through the verbal smoke screen and help the patient to overcome his own resistances. The *inner circle strategy* often serves a useful means to this important end.

The inner circle refers to an individual's most private and personal psychological territory. When someone says, "I'm going to tell you something that I have never told anyone before," one is usually about to be granted access to the speaker's inner circle or private zone. In therapy, this sometimes occurs only when a patient, over a period of many months, or perhaps years, has built up sufficient trust and confidence in his therapist to expose the innermost essence of his being. And when this happens, what are we most likely to be told? Almost invariably, one of three things: something sexual; something to do with the person's hostility; or something involving dishonesty in one form or another. On occasion, this highly personal information may be as trite as the individual's financial assets and liabilities, or the fact that he has had no less than five marriages. Naturally, if the patient in sharing these facts feels that he has let his therapist into a closely guarded secret, the sensitive clinician will understand that the relevation has significance for this patient and will respond appropriately. Very occasionally, the inner circle may be a beautiful, poignant, or poetic experience which one is truly privileged to share, but usually, as already mentioned, it has to do with sexual guilt, aggression, or dishonesty. The inner circle strategy will now be illustrated by means of a transcribed interview:

The Resistant Housewife

The patient was an intelligent thirty-year-old housewife who had requested marriage counseling. She had opposed the suggestion that her husband should also be seen by the therapist, separately and/or together with her. "He will just give you a snow job," she protested. "He can talk his way out of any situation. . . . I want to be seen as a person in my own right." After four sessions, very little was known about the patient other than her servant troubles, the courses she had studied before marrying, and details about each of her brothers and sisters and their marriages. Clearly, I was able to infer a fair amount about her central problems from the way in which she presented these tangential facts, but direct reference to her marital problems had been assiduously avoided. Each time I endeavored to pinpoint this area of her life, she would interject by saying, "Wait, I think this is important," or "Hang on, I think I first ought to go into something which will enable you to appreciate what makes me tick more fully." During the third session I had challenged her quite openly about the fact that she was avoiding her basic problem areas and was killing time with trivial details. Her rejoinder was, "Patience, dear doctor. You will see how the pieces all fall into place eventually." My patience was finally spent about halfway through the fifth interview when we were once again overwhelmed by trivia.

> *Therapist:* Sorry to interrupt your train of thought, but I would just like to explain something to you. Please bear with me. Now I'd like to draw a little diagram which depicts the way in which many people function. (Figure is drawn.)

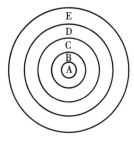

> *Therapist:* Right. Now, this diagram represents various layers of personal privacy. The little inner circle marked "A" represents the person's most private, personal territory. It can be called his "inner world." He probably keeps all the information in A all to himself. He shares these thoughts, deeds, wishes, and feelings with nobody. Sometimes he is lucky enough, or sufficiently open and courageous enough to share his inner circle with just one very special person whom he trusts com-

pletely. Usually, he only allows his very closest friends and confidants into (but not beyond) circle B. In other words, very special people are allowed all information in E, D, C, and B, but nobody, or only an extraspecial person is allowed all the way from E to A.

Patient: What are you driving at?

Therapist: Please bear with me. Do you follow what I have said so far?

Patient: You seem to be saying that we keep really private and personal information to ourselves and decide what can and cannot be shared with others. What's so unusual about that?

Therapist: Well, what do you make of these three diagrams? (Figures are drawn.)

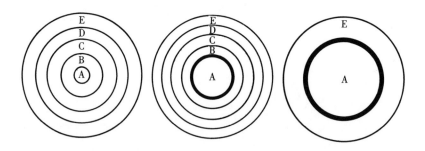

Patient: I'm still not sure what you are getting at.

Therapist: Look at no. 1. This person may or may not find someone special with whom to share E, D, C, B, and A. But he is likely to share everything up to and including B with his closest friend or friends. He will share E, D, and C with several good close friends. He will go as far as D with several acquaintances (who will not be allowed into C, B, or A). The zone around E represents the person's superficial contact with the world, the sort of information that may be gathered by minimal social contact.

Patient: I get it. The heavy line around A in no. 2 means that nobody will get past B. Am I right?

Therapist: Yes, correct. But notice another thing about no. 2. Observe how large the inner circle is. This means that person no. 2 keeps a tremendous amount of information to himself. His closest friend, who gets through E, D, C, and B, still shares very little of no. 2's inner world. I would guess that no. 1 would make closer, more meaningful, and more rewarding friendships. But now look at no. 3.

Patient: A barricade.

Therapist: That's an excellent description. We could call no. 3 "the barricaded personality." He keeps *everyone* at E and expends tremendous energy in keeping people at arm's length at all times. Now here's a question for you. How would you depict the way you function?

Patient: Hell! I don't know. What do you think?

Therapist: Well, you're probably not as closed off as no. 3. You seem to have an E, and a D, but all the rest is heavily marked "Keep out!"

Patient: You're crazy!

Therapist: Well, you certainly haven't taken me beyond D. What are you hiding from me in C, B, and A?

Patient: I've got nothing to hide. I'm not an escaped convict or a bank robber or something.

Therapist: Effective therapy usually takes place in the personal zones of A and B. What do you think is usually locked up inside of these inner circles? Something to do with sex, or something to do with the person's dishonesty or both. Everyone has probably lied, or cheated, or stolen at some

time or other. And the other thing buried inside
A often has to do with hate, anger, and aggression. Now, at our first session you mentioned that
you were having marital difficulties. Yet, I know
nothing about the way you met your husband,
why you married him, how you got along sexually, whether you have made love to other men.
I don't know whether you resent your husband
mildly or hate him bitterly. These are some of
the ingredients of the inner circle.

Patient: It sounds like professional voyeurism.

Therapist: If you can't trust me and can't confide in me, I'm
unlikely to be very useful to you as a therapist.

Patient: Okay. Sure, I've cheated on my husband. But I
don't see how this fact helps you or me.

Therapist: I can only assess the importance of a particular
piece of information when I have *all* the facts.
Let's begin by comparing your sex life in marriage with your extramarital relationships.

Patient: What do you mean "relationships"? What do
you take me for? There's been one relationship—singular. My husband never satisfied me
sexually. I never knew what sex meant until I
met Norm. . . .

With the aid of the inner circle strategy, a crucial area was
finally reached. Thereafter, therapy was no longer concerned with the
patient's peripheral defenses but came to grips with many significant
aspects of her life in general and of her marital problem in particular.
One might ask whether the inner circle strategy was really necessary, or
whether more direct questions concerning the patient's marriage might
have elicited the same basic facts without the elaborate preamble. The
reader should be reminded that this was tried several times, but before
working through the inner circle strategy, she refused to divulge any
personal information. The point of this example is to show how the
inner circle strategy orients "resistant" patients towards the revelation

of information that is central and personal, rather than trivial. The value of the inner circle strategy in counseling an aggressive adolescent girl was described elsewhere (Lazarus, 1969c) and may be of interest to some readers.

All in all, both the desert island fantasy and the inner circle strategy have been extremely useful diagnostic and therapeutic aids. They both tap crucial clinical areas and arrive at significant dimensions of aberrant behavior. They also help to develop a constructive therapeutic climate and tend to enhance the process of problem identification by fostering the development of more intimate rapport. These measures abet the process of what might be termed *clinical intimacy* by stressing the ground rules of self-disclosure, integrity, constructive criticism, and complete verbal freedom which are so necessary for the enterprise of psychotherapy (cf. Orne & Wender, 1968; Goldstein, 1970).

CHAPTER 5
DESENSITIZATION
AND HABITUATION
METHODS

It is common knowledge that repeated exposure to almost any situation is likely to change one's response to that situation. Whenever the intended change involves the lessening of fear, embarrassment, or other unpleasant feelings, graded and progressive exposure to the feared situations has been widely recommended. Overcoming fear by degrees is the keynote in most ancient ceremonial rites and rituals, old and modern child-rearing practices, and in situations as diverse as animal training, stock-car racing, combat missions, rehabilitation programs, and space travel. Sometimes, however, wisdom decrees that the total situations should be faced all at once, rather than step by step, as, for instance, when a person, after a car accident, is advised to "get behind the wheel and drive again."

To avoid fearful situations is almost to guarantee that the fears engendered by the situation will not subside. In most forms of psychotherapy, patients are encouraged to face up to their fears. Typically, they first grow accustomed to thinking about them and talking about them within the protective and reassuring context of the therapeutic relationship. Often, their fears are reevaluated so that different properties are assigned to them.

> *Therapist:* I think your fear of talking in class is tied up with your being overcompetitive.
>
> *Patient:* Do you mean I always feel that I have to appear *brilliant?*
>
> *Therapist:* Exactly. It's not that you are afraid of speaking up in class; it's that you are afraid of appearing anything less than a genius.
>
> *Patient:* So maybe I should throw in my two bits worth instead of waiting for $64,000 answers.

Many therapists combat irrational fears by advocating thought patterns which instantly neutralize unadaptive patterns of behavior.

> *Therapist:* Instead of viewing all germs and illnesses as "bad," try to regard them as immunizing agents which help your system develop essential antibodies to ward off more serious illnesses and thus serve a protective function.
>
> *Patient:* I never thought of it that way. The friendly germ. I like that!

Apart from psychoanalytic writers who have been inclined to deflect attention away from overt behavior to inner dynamics, standard antiphobic procedures have employed graded and progressive exposure to feared objects, situations, and events. Contrary to Rachman (1968) these procedures are anything but new, as the following excerpts will illustrate.

Some Early Clinical Reports

In the first German edition of a book on medical psychology published in 1922, Ernst Kretschmer outlined a typical progressive training sequence. The 1934 English translation states:

Systematic habituation-therapy has a wide scope in the treatment of the most diverse psychogenic states presenting either physical or psychic symptoms. It can serve as an important factor in treatment and after-treatment in many varieties of psychotherapy involving suggestion and persuasion; and it can be employed independently in not too difficult cases.... Unless we are dealing with barefaced malingerers, we should utter no reproaches nor use offensive expressions such as "sheer imagination," but we should tell them that their complaint arose in the same way as any troublesome physiological habit, and must accordingly be made to disappear in the same way. Habituation-therapy in cases of hysterical parakinesis, disturbances of gait, paresis, pseudo-rheumatic pains, and the like may, with patients of robust constitution, be carried out on the lines of physical exercises in the parade-ground manner; with patients of a more sensitive nature the method of application may be modified.... Habituation-therapy in cases with a purely psychic symptomatology and in the more complicated neuroses takes a rather different form. Sometimes one can successfully treat the milder phobias and compulsions with habituation-therapy supported by analysis and persuasion. We attempt a graduated, progressive hardening of the patient against his psychic symptoms; our training methods in these cases partake more of friendly persuasion than dictatorial discipline. For instance: a patient suffers from an agonizing fear of open spaces and streets, which has prevented him for months from leaving the house, and of late even from leaving his room. We proceed to make him walk short, graduated distances, at first escorted by the physician, who encourages him strenuously the whole time, later accompanied by someone else, and finally alone. We demand the minimum from the patient to start with (a few steps away from his room) and very gradually increase our demands from day to day—we encourage the patient to walk as far as the front door, then 50 yards past the front door, then we increase the distance 100 yards a day until the patient is able to reach a pre-arranged objective [Kretschmer, 1934, pp. 246–248].

Throughout a little-known book, *Dreads and Besetting Fears*, Williams (1923) stressed many modern points of view: "Dread is aroused only when a person is faced by a circumstance which experience has taught him to fear [p. xi]." "It is not the situation which causes the dread but one's more artificial notion concerning it [p. 16]." "A psychological mechanism may be sufficiently understood without the actual knowledge of the individual circumstances by which it has been produced [p. 20]." "Maladaptions are the result of faulty treatment by members of the family, and more particularly by one or both parents [p. 21]." In treating an agoraphobic patient, Williams described several objective procedures and added: "The next step in the treatment was to accompany her to a large square in the neighborhood, across which I made her go alone. Although her hands became cold and her face pale, the pulse frequency increased and her throat became dry, she declared that she had performed the feat better than she had ever done. The following day she had to do so on several occasions alone [p. 85]." Elsewhere he writes: "This process may be called reconditioning. It is the foundation of psychotherapy, all of the methods of which contain this association principle, of which there are examples in several chapters of this book [p. 143]."

Howard and Patry (1935, p. 29) also emphasized the need for "corrective habit training, necessary specific treatment for somatic disorders, and the bringing to recognition and the enucleation of 'sore-spots' or complex-determined topics, memories, associations and reactions which require desensitization and replacement by more wholesome resources and performances."

Wolberg (1948, p. 191) approached the subject from a psychoanalytic point of view and wrote that "desensitization is a process which enables the individual gradually to face and to accept painful aspects of his personality." He also stated that "much of the value that comes from confession and ventilation is based upon the fact that the patient becomes desensitized to those situations and conflicts that disturb him, but which reality demands that he endure [p. 195]." In the treatment of phobias, Wolberg urged that for purposes of desensitization, patients should expose themselves to those situations that incite painful emotions. "For instance, if the patient has a fear of closed spaces, he may be instructed to lock the door of his room for a brief instant for the first day; to increase the interval to the count of ten the next day; then to one-half minute, extending the time period each day, until he discovers through actual experience that he can tolerate the phobic situation [p. 196]."

Salter (1949) described the case of a claustrophobic surgeon who, during the course of therapy, recaptured and relived an experience that seemed to have precipitated his original claustrophobic difficulties. Recalling this incident had no obvious therapeutic effects, whereupon Salter applied hypnotic relaxation procedures and various exercises in sensory recall. Salter then adds "next I told him to practice turning his feeling of claustrophobia on and off, and conditioning relaxation to it. . . . I also told him to take care not to make his claustrophobia stronger than his feelings of well-being or the conditioning would increase his discomfort [p. 66]." The patient referred to this autodesensitization as "those anticlaustrophobic vaccinations," and by his fifth session he reported a complete absence of claustrophobia. Salter was thus one of the first clinicians to apply desensitization in the absence of the actual feared objects or situations, relying exclusively upon the patient's imagination, relaxation, and counterphobic sensations.

The period from 1954 to 1964 was extremely fertile in regard to clinical and experimental reports on the efficacy of desensitization from a behavioristic viewpoint. Wolpe (1954), as well as Lazarus and Rachman (1957), furnished the first clinical reports, while the first experimental studies were carried out by Lazovik and Lang (1960) and by Lazarus (1961). Several reports were collected by Eysenck (1960) who, in launching the journal *Behaviour Research and Therapy* in 1963, provided a ready outlet for behavioristic papers. Since then, a plethora of books, theses, articles, and several other behavioristic journals have mushroomed into existence. Desensitization and aversive training procedures, probably because of their precise and systematic properties, have received the bulk of attention throughout these publications. Excellent reviews and evaluative discussions have been compiled by Lang (1969) and Paul (1969). Franks (1969), in fact, contains a wealth of information concerning desensitization from a clinical and experimental point of view.

Experimental versus Clinical Considerations

When M. C. Jones (1924) desensitized three-year-old Peter to rabbits by gradually eliminating his fear "through the presence of the pleasant stimulus (food) whenever the rabbit was shown," the entire process was conceptualized within a counterconditioning framework. Similarly, "counterconditioning" is probably the most parsimonious explanation for the results which Wolpe (1948) obtained with cats, when he reduced their persistent avoidance responses by inducing them to eat in a piecemeal fashion. The same perhaps applies to volunteer subjects with avoidance responses to harmless snakes, or spiders, etc., who respond to desensitization techniques (e.g., Lang, Lazovik & Reynolds, 1965). It could be argued, however, that when a human subject imagines an object or situation, so many cognitive and affective processes are called into play that "conditioning" (in its proper laboratory sense) is rendered meaningless. When it comes to the treatment of phobic patients in the clinical situation (as opposed to the de-conditioning of fearful volunteers in experimental projects) the interactions are exceedingly rich and complex. Consider the following excerpt from a recent desensitization session:

Therapist: Now keep your eyes closed, relax deeper and deeper. . . . Good, now picture your mother blaming you for your father's death.

Patient: (After a pause of about fifteen seconds) The scene doesn't make me so anxious anymore but I sure had some peculiar fantasies. All at once, I remembered an incident when I was, ah, oh, about fifteen years old. My old man had been drinking and he punched the old girl right on the nose. There was blood. The same blaming look all over her face. Somehow I saw her face with blood pouring from her eyes, nose, and mouth. I was reminded of a book about "magic fluids" and wondered whether saliva, or urine, sweat, or semen would wash away her blood. Then I just saw my old man's eyes. And they had a certain look which said: "Don't let her blame you for *anything*, son." And this made me calm again. . . . Yes, I would say that scene won't disturb me again.

In the above-mentioned case, as in all clinical encounters of this kind, the simplistic notion that the affective and behavioral change was based on the neutralizing effects of relaxation upon anxiety (Wolpe 1958) is highly misleading. Even in the brief excerpt above, we see dyadic interactions between the parents and between each parent and child, coupled with implied attitudes and values which underscore the inadequacy of strict Pavlovian or Skinnerian paradigms to which radical behaviorists attempt to reduce all responses.

There is no point in dwelling on the issue as to whether the mechanism of change in clinical desensitization is a function of counterconditioning rather than cognitive restructuring, or even a product of psychodynamic processes as suggested by Weitzman (1967). Steering clear of polemics, let it simply be stated that the technique is therapeutically useful when appropriately applied. Lazarus and Serber (1968) have sharply criticized certain therapists for using desensitization inappropriately and thereby retarding clinical and therapeutic progress. Let us examine the circumstances under which it is appropriate and inappropriate to administer desensitization procedures.

Indications and Contra-indications

It should be emphasized at the very outset that, in keeping with the personalistic philosophy of this book, a statement such as "systematic desensitization is the treatment of choice in phobic conditions" is, at best, incomplete. A better rendering would be: "The skillful application of systematic desensitization will often be effective with phobic sufferers (1) who do not derive too many primary or secondary gains from their avoidance behavior; (2) whose basic anxiety dimensions are confined to the phobic area (e.g., it is futile to prepare a hierarchy of increased space constriction for a claustrophobic patient whose fear of confined spaces stems from feeling trapped in a given relationship); (3) who can experience anxiety diminution during relaxation; (4) who respond with anxiety to their hierarchical images while unrelaxed; and (5) who are not strongly averse to the method per se."

It is easy to practice the procrustean maneuver of finding almost every case a candidate for desensitization. Nearly everyone is perhaps inclined to be hypersensitive or overreactive to someone or something. This orientation or mental set can lead one to view all clinical problems, if not life itself, as a ubiquitous phobia (Wolpe, 1969a). Consider, for instance, a patient who complains that he finds life meaningless and empty. Let us assume that his problems stem mainly from the fact that he has an unrealistic level of aspiration, a negative self-image, and believes emphatically that self-worth is entirely dependent upon extrinsic achievements such as money and power, of which he possesses very little. Viewed through the lens of the arch desensitizor this case would undoubtedly add up to a cluster of hypersensitivities. He would most likely be found to suffer from at least one classical phobia (e.g., acrophobia), as well as a constellation of hypersensitivities (e.g., fears of criticism and rejection). Thus, the existential problem (life is meaningless and empty) would be presumed to rest upon, or *really* add up to, a series of phobias (a fear of heights, a fear of criticism, and a fear of rejection). According to this view, the successful desensitization of his phobias should remove his presenting complaint. Freed from his unadaptive sensitivities, he then presumably moves through life with self-respect and renewed vigor. While several cases do lend themselves to the piecemeal analysis and correction of phobialike clusters, my recent findings indicate that instances of the aforementioned kind, are unlikely to derive long-term therapeutic benefits without changing the patient's unrealistic levels of aspiration, his negative self-image, and his self-defeating values and attitudes. The point at issue is that desensitization methods often miss the interpersonal patterns of faulty communication, irrational assumptions, false ideals and expectancies, childlike demands, double binds, vague uncertainties, and confusions which most patients manifest. Those therapists with a proclivity for desensitization methods often overlook depressive and psychotic features in their patients and opt for graded exposure when chemotherapy should be the treatment of choice (Lazarus & Serber, 1968).

Basic Indications for Desensitization Therapy

Desensitization is most commonly indicated in overcoming persistent avoidance responses to innocuous events and situations. There is no *objective* reason for people to fear walking through a supermarket, riding in an elevator, eating in a restaurant, going to a beauty parlor, asking questions in class, seeing an ambulance, or for hundreds of other petty fears and foibles which seriously incapacitate certain individuals. While specific maladaptive avoidance responses typically lend themselves to desensitization methods, it cannot be overstressed that therapists should proceed along primary (not secondary) dimensions in their treatment. For instance, in discussing a fairly common phobia—men's fears of sitting in a barber's chair and having a haircut—Stevenson and Hain (1967) described many different fundamental fears which tended to underlie the secondary fear of barber shops. Some men were found to have a fear of sharp objects (e.g., scissors and cut-throat razors) usually based, in turn, upon more basic insecurities and hostilities. Other men found that the close proximity of a male barber aroused homosexual anxieties. In others, the problem was a function of social rebelliousness, or a fear of confinement, or a fear of public scrutiny. Some cases reported having had unpleasant experiences in a dentist's chair which generalized to barber chairs on the basis of their physical similarities. In the latter cases, desensitization to the presenting complaint would probably have been a necessary and sufficient form of treatment; however in the vast majority of the other cases, less obvious hypersensitivities were the proper focus of therapeutic attention. This holds true for most conditions. Interpersonal factors usually underlie most situational problems, and behavioral clinicians should guard against taking most presenting complaints at their face value.

Desensitization also has a place in reducing painful memories. While deeply relaxed, patients are asked to recollect specific events. "Think about the time your father found you in bed with your boy-friend." "Recall that incident in which your mother insulted you at the party." In addition to countering the autonomic effects of shameful, frightening, and other distressing memories via deep relaxation, it may also help to ask patients to verbalize and realize that "it really is not that important . . . so what . . . who cares . . . too bad, etc." The latter procedure (relaxation plus rational reassurance) may also be employed in overcoming the effects of a tyrannous conscience. Here, the person is asked to dwell on a series of real or imagined wrongs for which he feels personal guilt, and to erase the sting via relaxation and rational thinking. In all these instances, it is often helpful to construct a hierarchy and to proceed from the least distressing toward the most distressing items on the list.

As Cameron (1968) pointed out, successful desensitization requires "particularization." A general remark such as "My mother was such a liar" cannot be handled by desensitization procedures. The therapist, by asking for particulars, will often find scenes which lend themselves to desensitization. "Well, I remember one day when my mother distinctly told my father that I had broken his movie projector when she knew darn well that my brother had broken it." It might be emphasized that when desensitizing patients to "angry memories" of this kind, it is usually best to avoid relaxation and similar passive procedures, but instead to have patients picturing themselves attacking the offending person. As one patient said while picturing an event in her past which still angered her, "I'd like to punch my mother on the nose." Instead of relaxing to the unpleasant image, the patient was enjoined to picture the scene and to imagine herself attacking her mother. In situations where anger is present, the use of *directed muscular activity* (e.g., strenuous slamming of palms and forearms onto a sturdy and well-upholstered bed, chair, or thickly padded cushion in immediate association with a disturbing thought or image) is often extremely effective (Lazarus, 1965).

Steps in the Desensitization Process

During the course of interviews or clinical discussions, patients are apt to mention specific fears or hypersensitivities. For example: "I feel extremely ill at ease when dining in a restaurant with my husband's business associates," "My father-in-law is elderly and almost blind these days. I avoid visiting him because I have a 'thing' about blindness," "I get very nervous whenever I have to present formal reports at work," etc.

Step One. The first step, whenever specific hypersensitivities arise, is to determine whether they are basic or secondary. This is done by looking into the factors which make up the fear, as well as their consequences. The following examples should clarify this process.

> *Patient:*   I feel extremely ill at ease when dining in a restaurant with my husband's business associates.
>
> *Therapist:*   How long have you felt this way?

Patient: Oh, let me see. (Pause) I think ever since Herb went into the marketing division. That was about a year ago.

Therapist: Before that time did you suffer from a similar uneasy feeling in restaurants?

Patient: No. I still love eating out. I mean, when Herb and I go out with friends I'm fine. It's just his business dinners which get to me.

Therapist: Can you tell me what it is about these business dinners which upset you? For instance, are they formal, and are you on the spot as a sort of reluctant hostess having to entertain people who do not really mean anything to you?

Patient: I guess so.

Therapist: Don't let me put words into your mouth. Think carefully. Picture yourself in the situation right now. Imagine that you are at a restaurant with your husband and his colleagues, and tell me what associations and feelings you have.

Patient: (Closes her eyes) It makes me angry and I don't see why I have to be subjected to it.

Therapist: What does your husband say?

Patient: Oh, Herb says it brings in more business.

Therapist: How often do these business dinners arise?

Patient: About once a month.

Therapist: How do they come about?

Patient: How do you mean?

Therapist: I mean how does Herb let you know about them?

Patient: Oh, he comes home and says, "Honey, is it all right if we take the Ryans and two other couples to the Red Goblet a week from Friday?" And I usually say, "Why bother to ask?"

Therapist: So a verbal battle ensues and by the time the

dinner date is reached, you and Herb have been at each other's throats for about two weeks and a thoroughly tense atmosphere prevails.

Patient: Well I resent it.

Therapist: Why?

Patient: What do you mean?

Therapist: You know what I mean. What is really behind all this resentment?

Patient: I simply don't like dining with the Ryans and the Millers and the rest of those money grabbers.

Therapist: Wait, let's go back. You said that you have only felt this way since Herb went into the marketing field last year.

Patient: Well let me explain. He used to work for my dad, and when he died about two years ago, Herb took over the business.

Therapist: Let me guess. Was your father in charge of the marketing setup before he died?

Patient: What has that got to do with it?

Therapist: (Remains silent)

Patient: Oh for heaven's sake! You think I resent Herb because he's taken over my dad's position.

Therapist: Well?

Patient: Well it never struck me that way before.

As the interview progressed, it became obvious that we were not dealing with a specific "sensitivity to dining in a restaurant with husband and his business associates," but to a basic resentment concerning the patient's feelings that her husband was "less of a man than her father" and had profited from his father-in-law's early labors and premature demise. She was hypersensitive to all the memories surrounding her father's death, and desensitization was directed toward a death-of-father dimension. Her irrational attitudes (e.g., expecting her husband to equal her father's accomplishments) were also tackled. To have plunged ahead and desensitized the patient to the restaurant situation would most probably have proved extremely time-consuming and unproductive.

Here is another verbatim illustration of the way in which interpersonal and situational processes need to be spelled out in any comprehensive psychotherapy. The patient is a thirty-two-year-old electrical engineer.

Patient: I suffer from claustrophobia.

Therapist: Can you elaborate?

Patient: Well, I become anxious and feel I can't breathe. At times it gets so bad that I have to run outside and gulp or gasp in loads of fresh air. It's terrible.

Therapist: I would like to know two specific things at this stage. First, at what times and in what situations do you feel this way, and secondly, when did this all start? Let's begin with the second question. When did this all start bothering you?

Patient: Let's see. I'm thirty-two now. (mumbles) I first noticed it when I was about twenty-nine.

Therapist: So it has been going on for approximately three years?

Patient: Yes, I would say so.

Therapist: What were you like in this regard, say, 3½ or 4 years ago? I mean, did you have any similar problems?

Patient: Hell, no! I used to take the subway to and from work; I was quite okay.

Therapist: So what happened three years ago?

Patient: I just noticed myself getting jittery and sort of worked up, you know, sort of scared and tight. I first noticed it going up in the elevator at the office. In fact at first I just thought it was unusually hot and crowded in the elevator so I walked up the stairs. But after that even the office seemed to be too small and oppressive. I would start sweating and have to go out into the hallway. The board room has no windows and I used to try and avoid that place. But I had to attend board meetings. Boy! Do I dread these meetings. I take so many tranquilizers that I almost pass out. I can't concentrate in there and even though I always sit near the door, just in case I have to rush out, I go through hell. My first doctor said it was all repressed hostility.

Therapist: What did you make of that?

Patient: I didn't know what to make of it.

Therapist: Neither do I. Now let's get back to what happened three years ago. I don't mean only in reference to your claustrophobia. I mean what events in general can you trace back more or less to this time?

Patient: You mean just anything?

Therapist: Uh huh.

Patient: Gee! Well, let's see. (Pauses) Umm ... (Sighs) Three years. Yes, well, let's see. I've been married almost three years. But why should there be a connection?

Therapist: Could there be?

Patient: I don't see it. I mean it could be coincidence. Couldn't it?

Therapist: It could be. But you seem to be getting very defensive.

Patient: I just don't see the connection.

Therapist: Well, should we look for a possible tie-up?

Patient: Was that meant to be a pun?

Therapist: Not intentionally.

Patient: Look, I wouldn't want to get a divorce. I mean

even if there is some sort of correlation, I wouldn't want a divorce.

Therapist: Who said anything about divorce?

Patient: Well ... you know.

Therapist: Hey, listen. Even if we did establish some sort of trapped or confined feelings in your marriage, why couldn't we work on *improving* your marriage and giving you freedom of movement within the marriage instead of aiming to break it up? I mean we haven't established that the marriage has anything to do with your claustrophobia. It may or may not. But if there are problems in the marriage why not attempt to resolve them, even if they have nothing to do with your claustrophobia? They could be two separate problems, or somewhat loosely connected, or intimately related. But you immediately leap to conclusions and fear that I am going to rip apart your marriage.

Patient: Yeah. Okay. That makes sense. Well, we got married because we had to. Does that mean anything? You see we were planning on getting married but not quite so soon.

Therapist: So it seems that we can more or less time the onset of the claustrophobia to your wife's or girl friend's, as she was then, pregnancy. How did you react to her announcement?

Patient: I'll tell you. I thought if we had very vigorous intercourse it would maybe bring on her period. It didn't work, of course, but I had a hell of a peculiar reaction. I felt as though I had a kind of, quote-unquote, intent to kill. Christ! I can tie up the claustrophobia with the baby in some kind of Freudian way. For example, later on when we had intercourse and my wife was maybe four months pregnant I would think of the baby suffocating and choking to death on my semen. Maybe I wished the baby dead and developed guilt. But I don't see why this should persist even now when my little boy is two years old and I love him, you know, I mean I wouldn't want. . . . I mean I'm glad we have him. My other doctor said that I still have unconscious death wishes toward my wife and son.

Therapist: Well, in those terms that's a dead-end street. But let's see what can be maintaining your claustrophobia. How does your wife react to it?

Patient: She's very understanding.

Therapist: Maybe too understanding?

Patient: What do you mean?

Therapist: Maybe she fusses over you and encourages it?

Patient: I don't see it that way.

Therapist: Nevertheless. . . . Anyway, let me ask you another question. Do you ever have intercourse with your wife on top?

Patient: Strange you should ask that. You know it used to be my favorite position before we got married. But now I can't stand it. It really makes me feel on edge.

Therapist: What exactly do you feel?

Patient: Ha! I guess you can say like I'm trapped, weighed down, can't breathe, etc. What makes you ask that?

Therapist: It's not too farfetched to assume that the claustrophobia is tied up with guilt in the general area of marriage and sex and children. You know, you come across in a very submissive manner. I get the feeling that although you love your wife, she is, and always was, dominant. We can certainly work on your claustrophobia per se, but I think we should also train you to be more asser-

tive. I also think that there are some negative
things going on between you and your wife and
I would like to see both of you together in order
to try and improve the relationship.

Although the patient's claustrophobia seemed to be part of a
general intrapersonal and interpersonal constellation of events, it is
erroneous to assume that all therapeutic attention should be focused on
these variables. Behavioristic therapists too often err in the opposite
direction by dealing only with the target symptom while ignoring the
basic interpersonal context. Comprehensive psychotherapy calls for the
correction of all unadaptive responses, or of as many as seem feasible at
the time of treatment.

Again, it must be emphasized that before launching into desensitization programs, *it is imperative to differentiate between basic and
second-order anxiety dimensions, and also to identify the interpersonal
factors which usually underlie situational fears.* The core of the disturbance needs to be carefully identified. Even in classical phobias, the
superficial theme may be most misleading. At the very least, one should
be on the lookout for interpersonal factors and possible secondary gains
which maintain the problem by providing positive reinforcement.

Step Two. Having ascertained that the anxiety areas under scrutiny
are basic rather than peripheral, the next step is to determine whether
the specific problems can be ranked according to increasing degrees of
anxiety. Some people respond in an all-or-none fashion to their fears.
For instance, two students recently requested therapy for a public speaking phobia. Whereas the one reported feeling progressively more uncomfortable depending upon the size of the audience, the number of
strangers, the subject under discussion, the presence of faculty members,
and so forth, the other student said, "Given the presence of more than
perhaps four or five people at a time, regardless of their position or
status, regardless of whether or not I know what I am talking about,
I just go to pieces, fall apart, and become unglued." (In these cases a
flooding or implosive procedure sometimes proves helpful, although
the advisability of examining the problem more closely in order to
establish the fundamental reasons for so severe a reaction cannot be
overstated.)

The ranking of fears and the construction of hierarchies need not be the tedious and time-consuming process which Wolpe (1958, 1969) adheres to, and which Lazarus (1964) used to advocate. Having established, for instance, that a patient's dread of visiting sick friends in a hospital warrants desensitization therapy, it is obvious that most people would probably react more strongly to a crowded ward of sick people than to one which was not crowded, and still less to a private ward. Hospital hallways are apt to be more anxiety generating when ether and similar hospital odors are present, and certain other aspects of the hospital, such as walking past the operating room, seeing patients on wheelchairs and stretchers, may possess particularly high anxiety potential. But brief questioning can rapidly elicit any personal exceptions to these more usual sensitivities. Desensitization to cemeteries and funerals will usually follow a set sequence such as: driving past a cemetery in the distance (and then nearer and nearer); seeing a funeral procession in the distance (and then nearer until one is part of it); seeing a hearse in the distance etc., until one approaches the most exacting items such as the open grave and perhaps observes the coffin being lowered into the grave and covered with soil. Again, individual variations in response can be delineated during the course of a brief inquiry. Whereas I used to devote fastidious attention to compiling hierarchies in which successive items were separated by no more than five or ten "subjective units of disturbance," I have discovered that such meticulous concern with each item is needlessly time-consuming. Marquis and Morgan (1969) have compiled an excellent guidebook for systematic desensitization which lists fifteen sample anxiety hierarchies, covering such common themes as driving, heights, criticism and rejection, doctors and dentists, being the center of attention, death, shyness with women, confinement, and jealousy.

Step Three. The next step is to decide on the most appropriate anxiety reducer for each particular patient. Generally, graded real-life exposure and modeling procedures seem to achieve better results than mere imagined exposures to hierarchy items (Bandura, 1968; Sherman, 1969). Consequently, whenever feasible, I use in vivo desensitization, and try to follow and supplement imaginational procedures with graded real-life exposures to the feared events. Clinical questioning, coupled perhaps with some trial and error, will determine whether relaxation, or directed muscular activity, or emotive imagery, or implosive procedures, or the use of rational thinking is likely to prove most helpful in a given case at a given time. In a patient with an intense jealousy reaction, each of these anxiety-inhibiting responses was used in succession on each hierarchy item. A typical sequence (which I have reconstructed from memory) proceeded more or less as follows:

Therapist: Let's see how far we can get today with two additional hierarchy items. The first one is the scene where your wife is being slightly more attentive to another man than you think she ought to be.

Patient: It burns me up just thinking of it.

Therapist: Well let's cool it by starting with relaxation. Just settle back comfortably in the chair, push it right back, close your eyes. Feel the tension letting up. Concentrate on the heavy, calm feelings that grow and spread with relaxation. Breathe in and out, gently and evenly. Carry on like that for a while. Quiet and relaxed. Enjoy the good feelings that accompany muscular relaxation. Let yourself relax all over, deeper and deeper. Imagine the tranquilizing chemicals of relaxation being released into your whole body, bathing every nerve ending so that you feel serene and calm. Carry on relaxing like that for a while. (Pause of about one minute) Well, how do you feel now?

Patient: I wouldn't say that I'm *completely* relaxed, but I feel pretty calm.

Therapist: Well, let's intensify the calm and relaxed feelings with emotive imagery. Last week you told me that the picture of a log fire on a winter's evening gives you a specially good and tranquil feeling. Now as you keep on relaxing, I would like you to close your eyes again and imagine that you are sitting in front of a glowing log fire. Picture it as clearly as you can. Watch the flames dancing, notice the interesting shadows. Enjoy it to the full. (Pause of about one minute) How do you feel?

Patient: It gives me a great feeling. Really great.

Therapist: Good, keep up the relaxation and the imagery so that you become even more serene. Relax in front of the crackling log fire while it is snowing outside. (Pause of about two minutes) Now, still feeling really relaxed and calm, picture your wife at a party being slightly more attentive to another man than you think she ought to be. (Pause of about fifteen seconds) How was that?

Patient: I didn't really have enough time to think about it very clearly. Can you give me a longer time with the scene?

Therapist: Sure. First, go back to the relaxation and the imagery; see the log fire again. Relax deeper and deeper. (Pause of about thirty seconds) Now back to the party. Picture it vividly. Take your time. See your wife paying attention to this other man. (Pause of about forty seconds) How did it go?

Patient: Pretty good. It still bothers me though. It doesn't scare me as much as it makes me angry. I see one particular guy who fancies my wife and I want to smash him.

Therapist: Here, take this foam rubber cushion. Let's use some muscular activity. Think of the guy and your wife, and when the image is clear in your mind, hammer down with both fists onto the cushion. Go ahead.

Patient: (Shuts his eyes and then pounds the cushion)

Therapist: Harder! Give it all you've got. Smack it!

Patient: (Rather breathless after pounding the cushion for about one or two minutes) Wow! That feels better.

Therapist: Good. Now relax again and go back to your log fire. (Pause of about two minutes) Now back to the party and your wife paying attention to this other guy. (Pause of about one minute) What went on that time?

Patient: I thought to myself, "Maybe she's been meeting him on the sly and having intercourse with him." I know it's ridiculous. But. . . .

Therapist: Let's take that scene and blow it up, sort of implode it. Close your eyes and go along with this fantasy. They've been having intercourse regularly, and your wife tells him how much more she prefers him to you. In fact, she tells him that you are a lousy lover.

Patient: Wait. I don't think she'd ever consider me a lousy lover. She may find someone else better, perhaps even much better, but she wouldn't call me "lousy."

Therapist: Okay, she's telling this guy how much better he is than you, and how much she loves him, and she plans to leave you for him. In fact, she announces this in front of the entire gathering, and she and her lover walk out arm in arm. The other people snicker and sneer at you. You become the laughingstock of the party. The laughter echoes in your ears. They point fingers in your face and laugh right at you.

Patient: (Screaming) I want to kill them!

Therapist: Who? Your wife? Her lover? The people at the party?

Patient: (Very emotionally) Everyone!

Therapist: Go ahead. Take an ax and chop into everyone. Make the blood flow as you stab and chop and kick and kill. (These implosive methods can be accompanied by directed muscular activity in which the patient pounds a foam-rubber cushion or another thickly padded object while imagining the highly affective scenes.) How do you feel?

Patient: I would rather imagine myself using my bare hands and teeth to tear them apart and bite them to death.

Therapist: Well, imagine yourself doing that. Bite them. Feel your teeth sinking in. [One might then instruct the patient to carry out a gruesome sequence of events with various aggressive acts described by Hogan (1968) covering the range of oral, anal, and genital assaults.] Now look around at all the carnage. Blood and pieces of flesh are everywhere. You are a mess of human tissue which clings to your teeth and fingernails. Police sirens in the distance come nearer and nearer. (I find it useful to end implosive sessions which involve the destruction of people or property with "an awareness of consequences," such as being arrested and charged with mass murder, standing trial, and so forth. The effect is like waking up from a nightmare to discover, with great relief, that it was only a dream.) Now imagine yourself back at the party. You haven't murdered anyone, everything is as it was, and your wife is paying attention to another man. (Pause of about one minute) Well, how do you feel?

Patient: I'm too exhausted to feel anything.

Therapist: Well, then just relax and let's try some rational thinking. You have been telling yourself that it would be a catastrophe if your wife left you for another man, that you couldn't stand being rejected by her, and that if this awful thing ever happened to you, it would be worth your while

to commit mass murder and face the consequences. Now I ask you rationally, is anybody
worth this kind of trouble?

Commentary. The old method of having a patient, while deeply relaxed, merely picturing a graded series of anxiety-evoking scenes, is a
procedure I have abandoned for a more vigorous, multifaceted approach
which endeavors to cover a wider range of cognitive and affective processes. Methods of signaling anxiety by means of prearranged hand and
finger movements have been replaced by direct verbal communication
between patient and therapist (Lazarus, 1968b). In recent years, my
enthusiasm for desensitization procedures has diminished for two main
reasons. First, results, especially after recent comprehensive follow-ups
of *clinical* cases, have often failed to justify the effort involved. Second,
there are much more rapid and effective procedures such as behavior
rehearsal and direct instruction in rational and assertive behavior.
Carefully controlled studies of desensitization by Gelder et al. (1967)
and Marks et al. (1968) have shown that desensitization contains several
elements in common with conventional psychotherapy and hypnosis, and
is not a clearly superior technique, even for phobic states—especially in
terms of data revealing the nondurability of change.

Of course, desensitization methods are often essential when the
patient's problem precludes social action. But, as already stated, interpersonal factors usually underlie situational fears. Thus even many classical phobias call for social and personal intervention in addition to,
and sometimes in place of, symptomatic desensitization. Although I
used to employ desensitization for treating people with fears of criticism,
rejection, disapproval, censure, ridicule, devaluation, failure, authority
figures, and other situations in which social action is by no means pre-
cluded, I have rarely done so in more recent years. Again, I find that
these hypersensitivities are better treated by methods of rehearsal, role
playing, and the use of rational-emotive psychotherapy (Ellis, 1962).
The net result following, say, role playing or the correction of faulty
attitudes is *desensitization* in that the patient no longer overreacts to
innocuous events. Formal desensitization merely removes the "sting," as
it were; these other procedures provide the patient with additional skills
and coping mechanisms.

The Importance of Graded Structure

Desensitization is a highly structured and graded procedure in which new steps ordinarily follow success in all preceding steps of the process. There is reason to believe that graded structure per se has therapeutic effects (Lazarus, 1968a). In many behavioral methods, specific tasks are established and definite goals are determined. As Phillips and Wiener (1966, p. 5) point out: "Each step in structuring the elements in the client's life is a step toward the solution of his problems. The client needs to develop structure and purpose and to gain a knowledge of what leads to what." In referring to the favorable results that have been reported for desensitization therapy, Goldstein, Heller and Sechrest (1966, p. 246) suggest that these favorable outcomes "may reflect, in part, the advantages that may be obtained by providing better structure." Rotter (1954, p. 353) advocated "successive structuring" which he felt enabled the client "to attend to, react to, concern himself with the 'right' things in therapy."

The term *structure* implies that specific and well-focused therapeutic maneuvers will be prescribed and followed. This is opposite to certain nondirective practices in which sporadic and unpredictable problem-solving activities await the patient's unfocused internal motivation for their realization. *Graded structure* combines the advantages of ordinary structure (Phillips & Wiener, 1966; Goldstein, Heller, & Sechrest, 1966) with the additional sense of achievement and fulfillment that results from a feeling of success or progress per se. Graded structure provides anchor points which allows the patient to evaluate his own performance.

As the patient gains a feeling of mastery in specific tasks which he perceives as relevant to other areas of his life, his incentives for further change presumably increase. This ties in well with established principles of programmed learning which indicate that graded steps, active participation, immediate reinforcement, and knowledge of results promote more rapid and efficient learning.

Graded structure in psychotherapeutic situations implies that treatment programs should be divided into introductory, preliminary, intermediate, and advanced stages and that therapist and patient should be in agreement concerning the particular stages which have been successfully covered or completed. In a recent clinical trial, Lazarus

(1968a) employed graded structure as a placebo control. Contrary to the experimenter's bias and expectancies, the patients who received graded structure responded almost as favorably as those who were treated by behavior therapy.

In searching for some of the active therapeutic ingredients in desensitization in particular, or in psychotherapy in general, the importance of structure (e.g., fixed time and place of meeting, prearranged frequency of visits, fees) and the particular importance of graded structure (i.e., the subdivision of therapeutic interviews into stages and phases arranged in ascending order) should not be overlooked.

CHAPTER 6
ACQUIRING
HABITS OF
EMOTIONAL
FREEDOM

People who derive benefit from therapy, regardless of the type of treatment they undergo, often state that they have become more outspoken, less inhibited, and able to stand up for their rights. For example, Storrow and Spanner (1962) reported that after short-term insight therapy, patients who described themselves as more dominant after therapy than before, (i.e., "able to give orders," "manage others") also tended to describe themselves as improved.

When stressing the need for dominance, it is necessary to emphasize that the goal is not to become domineering. Similarly, the difference between assertion and aggression should also be noted, since outbursts of hostility, rage, or resentment usually denote pent-up or accumulated anger rather than the spontaneous expression of healthy emotion. Habits of emotional freedom imply the ability to give honest feedback (i.e., to show one's true feelings, and to do so in a frank and open manner). Emotional freedom opposes hypocrisy, phoniness, and deception. Contrary to popular belief, the result of emotional freedom is not alienation or increased vulnerability, but decreased anxiety, close and meaningful relationships, self-respect, and social adaptivity.

The virtues of emotional freedom were eloquently documented by Salter (1949) under the term *excitation* (as distinct from *inhibition*). Since Salter's Pavlovian underpinnings seem tenuous, and since many people confuse excitation with excitability (which it is not intended to connote) I prefer to avoid this term. Wolpe (1958) proposed the term *assertiveness* in place of *excitation,* but many people associate "assertive training" with one-upmanship and other deceptive games and ploys which Wolpe includes under this heading and which have no place in the forthright and honest expression of one's basic feelings. Besides, the word *assertive* cannot (unless stretched beyond its lexical boundaries) convey all the nuances of "emotional freedom" which would include the subtleties of love and affection, empathy and compassion, admiration and appreciation, curiosity and interest, as well as anger, pain, remorse, skepticism, fear, and sadness. Training in *emotional freedom* implies the recognition and appropriate expression of each and every affective state. Throughout this book, the term *assertive behavior* will denote only that aspect of emotional freedom that concerns standing up for one's rights.

Many conventional psychotherapists are extremely skilled at bringing people in touch with their affective states. This is often insufficient, for patients, in addition to recognizing their emotions, also need to learn how to express their feelings in a mature and honest fashion. Specific techniques are often necessary to teach people to express feelings appropriately. One of the best ways of achieving this end is by means of role playing or behavioral rehearsal (Lazarus, 1966; Friedman, 1969; Piaget & Lazarus, 1969). Instead of describing the process in generalities, a slightly edited interview protocol will be presented.

Case Background

Sam, a bright twenty-eight-year-old tax lawyer, complained that he felt "nervous, confused, and unfulfilled." He was divorced, had no children, and viewed himself as "a failure and a loser." His father, a surgeon, and his mother, a teacher, were deeply religious and raised Sam and his sister to "mind our P's and Q's." Sam had always excelled in school, although he had no close friends and usually felt uncomfortable around people. His ostensible reason for seeking therapy was to overcome his claustrophobia.

Toward the middle of the second interview, the following dialogue ensued:

> *Therapist:* I sense a lot of anger in you.
>
> *Sam:* Anger? I don't see how you arrived at that. I'm not aware of any special anger as such. I'll admit I was pretty peeved at my ex-wife, but even then, I showed no violence or undue harshness toward her.
>
> *Therapist:* Yes, but how did you *feel*?
>
> *Sam:* Well, I thought she was extremely immature.
>
> *Therapist:* Never mind what you thought. How did you feel?
>
> *Sam:* I was going to say that I resented her, but I think that would be considered normal under the circumstances.
>
> *Therapist:* Anger is a normal and basic emotion. You don't have to apologize for it.
>
> *Sam:* But you seem to be implying that I have more than my normal share of anger. You said that I struck you as being extremely angry, or words to that effect. Obviously I get irritable at times and perhaps minor things annoy me more than they should, but I don't walk around with a chip on my shoulder as far as I can see. Or are you saying that I do?
>
> *Therapist:* Well let me ask you how much resentment you feel toward your parents. You mentioned that they were very strict, and I gathered that they often withheld privileges to which you were entitled. . . .

Sam: If you are asking whether I felt mad at them when I was a kid, obviously I did. But in retrospect I realize that they meant well and did the best they could. But when I was a kid, I did get awful mad.

Therapist: And when you were a kid and felt mad at them, how did you show your anger?

Sam: What do you mean? I guess kids wail or gripe. I don't know.

Therapist: Whenever I zero in on your anger, past or present, you start intellectualizing. Never mind what kids in general do when angry. For instance, did you ever have a temper tantrum and really blow your stack?

Sam: I guess I must have. Which kid hasn't? I really don't remember.

Therapist: When you were a child and threw a real tantrum, such as screaming, cursing, kicking, biting, maybe smashing things, and so on, what did your parents do? How did they handle it?

Sam: I don't know. I mean I can't remember anything of that sort. I know I sometimes cried and my dad would tell me to be a man or something to that effect. I don't know.

Therapist: In other words, be a man and don't show your emotions, hide your feelings, keep a stiff upper lip, etc., etc.

Sam: Yeah, that about sizes it up.

Therapist: So with that background let's just suppose that little Sam had a temper tantrum. How would mom and dad react?

Sam: Well, they certainly wouldn't like it.

Therapist: Would they beat little Sam, lock him up, verbally reprimand him, or what?

Sam: Oh, I would say they'd do all of it. My dad used to hit first and my mother was called "crab" because she would pinch my sister and me when she was riled.

Therapist: And all of this gives you no cause for anger or resentment?

Sam: Are you deliberately trying to create a feeling of antagonism in me? Do you want to hear that I hate my parents?

Therapist: Only if it's true. I feel that you deny your own emotions and that you find anger especially threatening. I'm trying to put you in touch with your anger so that you can learn to express it in a socially acceptable way. With your background, I would find myself hating and resenting certain things about my parents while, at the same time, loving other qualities and attributes. But I wouldn't deny the negatives, and while focusing on them, I would feel aggressive if not rather murderous.

Sam: Maybe you should have some treatment yourself. (Laughs) I'm only kidding.

Therapist: That, in the profession, is what we call a passive-aggressive reaction.

Sam: Oh come now. I was only kidding.

Therapist: But let's look at it seriously. I am advocating responses that are quite foreign to you. I am saying the very opposite of the things you were raised to believe in, such as don't hide your feelings, do express your true emotions, let people into your real thoughts and attitudes, say what's on your mind.

Sam: I'm all confused. When we spoke on the phone last Monday and I asked what you thought of the rational approach used by Ellis you said that you were all for it. Now you are telling me to blow my top which seems to go against what Ellis advocates. A rational person wouldn't be bugged by things. As I understand it, he would reason them away.

Therapist: Let me try and clarify my position. Your point is an excellent one. When a person recognizes his self-worth and acquires a fitting indifference to the stupid or inconsiderate reactions of certain people, he will indeed be governed by rational and logical perceptions. But, hopefully, he will always be capable of emoting and feeling. When something annoys him, he won't catastrophize. He will be annoyed and express his proportionate anger, and do so toward the source of his irritation. He won't rationalize and kid himself that he is not angry. Being rational is not the same as rationalizing. The irrational person compounds the situation and works himself up into a disproportionate rage, or he may deny that he is angry. The rational person says, "I found Tom's behavior very annoying, and I will tell him so the very next time I see him. I didn't get a chance to do so when it was happening, because I didn't want to embarrass him in front of his employer." Observe that he is showing consideration despite his anger.

Sam: But why give someone the satisfaction of letting him know that he can bug you or hurt you?

Therapist: Meaning that you should pretend that Tom isn't capable of bugging you?

Sam: Exactly. Why play right into his hands? If he knows what hurts you or bothers you, he has a weapon to use against you whenever he feels like it.

Therapist: Many people make the same error that you are

making. Rationally speaking, you can only be hurt by someone in a physical or economic sense. If our hypothetical friend Tom beats you up or causes the loss of your job, you have indeed been injured by him. But we are not talking about that. If you tell Tom that it bothers you when he keeps on making wisecracks, or if you tell him that it hurts you when he makes nasty remarks about your brother, you are being truthful and not placing yourself at his mercy. If Tom is even slightly reasonable, he can apologize and change his behavior, or he can discuss it more fully and inquire why you feel so strongly about the matter and ask you to examine whether you are needlessly supersensitive.

Sam: But what if he decides to needle me still further?

Therapist: Then you inform him that you find him a real pain in the ass and that you intend severing all connections.

Sam: But what if Tom happens to be your boss or if you need him for other reasons?

Therapist: In that case, you have to decide whether the price is right. I once worked for an outfit where I could have made a mint if I was prepared to pander to a vicious millionaire who headed up the board of directors. All it needed was some double talk and duplicity. But I hated this sort of thing, and so I cut out leaving others to do the brown-nosing which they didn't mind doing.

Sam: I can see how you can cut relations with friends, acquaintances, or even employers, but how can you escape from parents? Look, you know I think you're right. I do resent a hell of a lot of things about my parents. My dad has the typical surgeon's sense of humor. As a kid he used to threaten to cut off my toes and fingers unless I behaved. The Freudians would enjoy that one, hey? And my mom has always been a goddamn teacher. All she does is lecture. "Sam, I told you not to marry so young. I knew you weren't ready for it." And so on ad infinitum. So tell me, how the hell do I get them off my back?

Therapist: So how do you handle matters that arise with your parents?

Sam: I've tried everything. If I talk back my mother gets hurt and says, "Don't talk to your parents like that!" My dad chips in and says, "Have you no respect?" They have an incredible knack for putting me on the defensive and for making me feel guilty.

Therapist: Do you think the four of us could meet together? If I could have you and your folks interacting with me being present. . . .

Sam: We went through that act once when we saw a family therapist. He also had my sister in on it. My folks succeeded in twisting everything to their own advantage. It was a disaster.

Therapist: When was all this?

Sam: Just before I got married. I was very unsure and went to a psychiatrist. He said he practiced family therapy and he had us all in together for three or four visits. Then I quit because it was leading nowhere. So what I'm saying is that I don't want to go through all that again.

Therapist: Can you be specific about the sorts of binds you get into with your parents?

Sam: Oh man, these can vary from my mother telling me to have a haircut, or to keep my apartment more tidy, or to visit them more frequently, or to shave off my mustache. And my dad keeps on about the fact that I don't visit my grandmother, and that I am too much of a pleasure seeker. Here's his favorite line: "I'll never understand how any son of mine can have fast cars, fast women, and wear those garments you pass off as clothes." And another favorite line whenever I try to get my point of view across is: "Sam, I'm not *asking* you to show us some respect. I'm *telling* you to."

Therapist: So how do you handle these situations?

Sam: Pretty poorly, I guess. Look, I know they mean well.

Therapist: The intention may be good but the effect of it all seems to keep you a boy instead of a man. It's the usual conflict of wanting to be a part of mommy and daddy versus the desire to become an autonomous adult. This seems to be a good opportunity to do some role playing or what I call "behavior rehearsal." Let me play the role of your father and let's see how well you can handle his onslaughts in a rehearsal situation.

Sam: You mean you want me to pretend that you are my father?

Therapist: Right. I'll say the sorts of things he says to you and let's see how well you can handle them in this situation.

Sam: But I know it's phony and we're just acting. What good will that do?

Therapist: I'll explain the theory behind role playing another time. Let's just see how you make out. Okay, now I'm your father. (role playing) Sam, I agree with your mother. You shouldn't have married so young, and you should have more respect for us. Shave off your mustache and start wearing some decent clothes.

Sam: Go to hell!

Therapist: (role playing) How dare you speak to me like that! You little, ungrateful upstart. You apologize this instant or I'll disown you completely.

Sam: (role playing) Drop dead!

Therapist: Is that the way you'd really like to handle it?

Sam: Well, that's what I say under my breath. No, I realize that's no way to set things right but I feel kind of foolish doing this sort of thing.

Therapist: Just try to pretend that you really are talking to your father and try to be as realistic as possible. (role playing) Sam, when are you going to grow up, listen to your mother, have a haircut, wear some decent clothes, and be a man?

Sam: (role playing) I am a man.

Therapist: (role playing) Men don't go in for fast cars, flashy clothes, and cheap women.

Sam: (role playing) That's your opinion.

Therapist: (role playing) Are you questioning my judgment?

Sam: (role playing) No, I'm not questioning your judgment but I'm also entitled to an opinion.

Therapist: Hold it! You are in fact questioning his judgment. Why deny it?

Sam: Yes, yes I know what you mean. But if I said, "Listen, you old goat, your judgment's way behind the times" nothing except maybe hysteria and a real ugly scene is likely to follow.

Therapist: Now that's the aggression or the anger to which I was referring earlier. There's a vast difference between an *assertive* and an *aggressive* response. I think that your anger is legitimate. In fantasy, you can picture yourself going even further than merely hurling verbal insults. You can fantasize punching him and really letting rip. In fantasy, you can even imagine yourself committing murder, but in your real confrontations you don't have to be either submissive or aggressive. Here we should aim for a balanced and rational response.

Sam: Okay, so even if I just told him, "Yes, I am questioning your judgment" there'd be a big row.

Therapist: Right. So what I want you to learn is how to express your feelings. For instance, instead of saying, "Yes, I am questioning your judgment," what would happen if you said, "Dad, you're making me feel like a little kid"?

Sam: He'd snap right back with, "Well, you are nothing but a kid."

Therapist: Let's reverse roles. Let me be you and you act as your father. Why don't we take it from the part where your father comes on all critically?

Sam: You want me to act as my dad? Okay (hesitates) here goes. (role playing) Mother and I deserve better treatment, more respect, and a bit of consideration. Are we any worse than Aunt Hilda and Uncle Mike? And you know how nicely your cousin Herb treats them.

Therapist: (role playing) Dad, I wish you wouldn't make comparisons; it makes me feel like a kid. Besides, since Herb is someone I do not particularly admire. . . .

Sam: (role playing) Well you are a kid. You think that being divorced adds up to being a man. And you're always criticizing other people. Believe me, you can learn a lot from Herb.

Therapist: (role playing) Dad, I don't wish to get into an argument. I get the message that I am a disappointment to you, that you wish Herb was your son, and that you look upon me as a child who should make no independent decisions but....

Sam: (role playing) Don't get smart with me, young man!

Therapist: (role playing) Dad, will you please stop talking to me like a ten-year-old child.

Sam: (role playing) Well, you don't act much different.

Therapist: (role playing) Look, Dad. By the time a person reaches my age he has gone beyond the stage where he is open to parental guidance. You and Mother have done the best for me, and if I am a failure and a disgrace in your eyes try to look upon it as my bad luck instead of worrying about the way it reflects on you.

Sam: Actually, I'd like to go further than that and point out to him that ever since I can remember he's never had anything positive to say about me. Whenever he opens his mouth to speak to me he invariably puts me down or finds fault with me.

Therapist: Excellent. You should certainly make that point. But why is it, in fact, so important to you to win your father's approval? Let's say you heeded all his advice and lived your entire life according to his specifications, would he approve of you then?

Sam: I see what you're getting at. I think I've been avoiding an inevitable showdown. It's like you said. There is a certain amount of security in knowing that you can turn to your parents if necessary. Actually, I don't have to put up with their carping criticisms. I'm financially independent for one thing. But before I can become, what's the word . . . fully emancipated, we'll have to work on my feeling of guilt. Also, back of it all I guess, there's a sneaky feeling that daddy really knows best and I really am some kind of louse.

Therapist: Yes, we can try to change all that. Let me make one important suggestion. Instead of waiting for your father to attack you or to criticize you, why don't you approach him at a time when he is not on the attack? For instance, when all's quiet and all's going well, why not go up to him and say, "Dad I'd like to talk to you," and then tell him how you feel about the fact that he seems to think so negatively about you.

Sam: Um . . . yes. I suppose there may be an advantage in tackling it cold like that.

Therapist: Before going ahead with Plan A, I'd like to rehearse it with you to be sure that your overall tone is assertive but conciliatory.

Sam: I think I can handle it.

Sam was an apt pupil, verbally facile, intelligent, personable, and ready to implement the various therapeutic suggestions. He seemed to need explicit approval from an objective outsider to accept his own anger and to give vent to his feelings. At the next interview he reported that the actual confrontation with his father had proceeded extremely well. He reported that his father was eminently more reasonable than he had anticipated ". . . and for the first time that I can ever remember, he said some really positive things about me . . . like he thinks I'm a good lawyer, and that I'm honest, and some other things of that sort." After four sessions, Sam was no longer troubled by nervousness or claustrophobia.

In more disturbed patients, assertive training and role-playing techniques may augment their anxiety and render them evasive or overdefensive. It is often necessary to apply behavior rehearsal within a desensitization framework so that the patient receives the simultaneous advantages of both processes. This method, termed *rehearsal desensitization* (Piaget & Lazarus, 1969) follows a fairly typical sequence:

1. Nonthreatening role-playing situations are employed until the patient enjoys the procedure per se.
2. Very mildly threatening encounters, arranged on a hierarchy, are enacted. The items on the hierarchy must consist of specific anxiety-producing situations which can be enacted in the consulting room.
3. The therapist models the way in which he thinks the patient should respond to each item (i.e., the initial presentation of each item calls for role reversal).
4. The patient attempts to enact the role only when the therapist's modeling leads him to feel that he can do so quite adequately.
5. New items are attempted only when patient and therapist are satisfied with each performance.

The therapist makes sure that his patient understands that he has graduated to a more difficult item because he has succeeded at a task which earlier would have been difficult for him to perform. Results are often rapid and quite dramatic. The expressive behavior seems to intensify counteranxiety responses. At the same time, if the new expressive behavior is followed by positive consequences of various kinds (e.g., the achievement of respect or control in situations that were previously out of hand) they become an integral part of the person's repertoire.

The following case history taken from Piaget and Lazarus (1969) should illustrate specific applications of the steps described above:

Case History

Mrs. T. was a plump, soft-spoken housewife of thirty-seven years who, during her initial interview, never once established eye contact with the therapist. Her presenting complaint involved a fear of crowds, particularly in situations where attention might be focused on her. It soon became apparent, however, that Mrs. T.'s functioning was severely impaired in nearly all interpersonal situations. She complained of chronic depression and severe anxiety which three years of "existential therapy" had been unable to overcome. When the therapist suggested assertive training as a possible starting point, Mrs. T. smiled sadly and said that such a method had been attempted by a previous behavior therapist. She explained that she was simply unable to carry out her previous therapist's instructions.

The therapist then described rehearsal desensitization to Mrs. T. He suggested that in this way she might acquire assertive skills, at her own pace, within the safety of the consulting room. Mrs. T. expressed initial doubt as to the outcome of the procedure, but finally agreed to give it a try.

The next four sessions were used to complete the behavior analysis and to build an appropriate hierarchy. During this time, the therapist was extremely supportive and gentle with Mrs. T. in order to gain her trust and confidence and to establish a relationship between them conducive to optimal rehearsal desensitization. A twenty-four-item hierarchy was constructed along a continuum of progressively more assertive behavior in the presence of one other person. The lower end of the hierarchy consisted of such items as: maintaining eye contact with herself in a mirror while speaking, and maintaining eye contact with the therapist while silent. Middle-hierarchy items were: complaining to a waiter about food, and asking a stranger on the street for directions. High-hierarchy items involved: expressing and defending an opinion, discussing a controversial topic, and expressing, in a loud, clear voice, a novel ideal regarding teaching methodology to a supervisor.

Mrs. T. had considerable difficulty with several of the items, but the hierarchy was completed to the mutual satisfaction of patient and therapist after fourteen sessions. Concurrently she reported substantial improvements in her reactions to similar real-life situations.

Phase 2 of therapy involved the completion of a similar hierarchy consisting of graded behavioral interactions with two or more persons. Secretaries, research assistants, and other departmental personnel were employed in the behavior rehearsal. Mrs. T. needed only seven sessions to complete a fifteen-item hierarchy, and subsequently reported marked improvements outside the consulting room. Her depression vanished and she referred to herself as a "new woman with a renewed interest in living."

To check the validity of this report the therapist accompanied Mrs. T. on a shopping trip one afternoon. During this time he encouraged such in vivo behaviors as initiating a conversation with a stranger, criticizing the manners of a salesgirl, and returning an item she had just bought. Mrs. T. needed little encouragement. Although reporting a certain amount of anticipatory anxiety, she was more than willing to test her new skills. In addition, she initiated several "assertive performances" on her own.

Mrs. T. was accompanied by her husband to the final consultation. He stated that the change in Mrs. T. was amazing, that she seemed happier than he had ever known her to be, and that she was now a "much more interesting person to live with." He also expressed a desire to undergo similar treatment for "a much more moderate kind of problem."

Mrs. T. terminated therapy after a total of twenty-eight sessions. A six-month follow-up indicated that her assertive behavior and general positive attitude had become even more pronounced.

"Encapsulated Personalities"

The virtues of tact, diplomacy, and discretion, if carried too far, become a barrier to communication and result in "constipation of the emotions . . . . and psychological toxicity [Salter, 1949, p. 47]." There is a general tendency to imply, infer, hint about, suggest, or allude to matters instead of stating them directly. The fawning sycophant and the obsequious hypocrite are all too common in our society. This is largely attributable to the fact that most people seek to remain enigmatic on the false assumption that it is always safer or wiser not to reveal themselves freely and openly (cf. Jourard, 1964). The end result is a network of folkways, mores, customs, and taboos, coupled with ambiguous moral, ethical, and religious prohibitions that renders every act of omission or commission capable of arousing guilt, suspicion, and fear. The person who takes his cultural heritage too seriously is bound to face so many contradictory "dos" and "don'ts" that almost every interaction will be fraught with tension and uncertainty. Borrowing from Kurt Lewin, it may be said that such people have an extremely constricted range of free psychological movement or territory.

Distressfully concerned with an arbitrary range of "rights" and "wrongs," they permit themselves so little freedom of movement as to exist in an emotional prison or in a confined capsule. To a psychoanalyst (Hammer, 1968, p. 5) the patient is seen as "imprisoned to varying degrees, in a mental cage whose walls are made of the forces of his inner desires and his defenses against them." Emotional freedom versus emotional restriction or "encapsulation" may be depicted by a simple figure which most patients find illuminating.

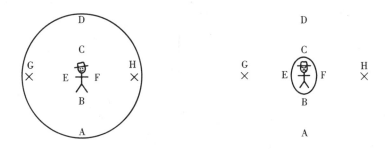

Emotional freedom   Encapsulation

The timid, inhibited, or "encapsulated" individual has been robbed of his legitimate territory of free movement. Therapy should aim to show him the freedom to which he is entitled and to teach him how to set about regaining his lost space.

In the figures above, the emotionally free individual considers the territory bounded by the poles AD and GH his own psychological terrain, or his own life space. He can move readily anywhere within these boundaries without feeling that he has overstepped his limits or encroached on someone else's emotional property. If somebody enters his territory uninvited he will unceremoniously stand up for his rights and tell the trespasser to leave.

The encapsulated person is uncomfortable or afraid, and very insecure when venturing beyond points B, C, E, or F. He usually feels that he is not entitled to any territory beyond his narrow range inside the capsule. Nevertheless, cramped for space and hungry for freedom, he may sometimes turn vicious and attempt to steal territory from those around him. He is often confused about what constitutes his own legitimate rights and the rights of others. "Have I the right to ask my mother to baby-sit occasionally?" "Am I really entitled to a raise?" "Do you think that my father is entitled to open my mail and to censor the books I read?" "Every day my sister borrows money from me but she never pays her debts." "My husband won't allow me to see my mom and dad." "Do I have to forfeit every weekend to visit my grandmother?"

There are many situations in which it is difficult to decide whether one's own legitimate rights are being usurped. At certain times one's demands might seem to deprive others of their legitimate rights. There are some especially delicate interactions (e.g., marriage and child-parent relationships) in which it is exceedingly difficult to define the rights of each individual. Group therapy seems to be most helpful in bridging these difficult discriminations. Within the context of open group discussions, sufficient shades of opinion are often expressed to cover most nuances of interpersonal functioning (see Chapter 9). But many situations in which people fail to stand up for their rights pose no special problems of interpretation. Some people almost apologize for taking up space, breathing in oxygen—indeed, for being alive. I tell my patients that for each one of the following questions to which the obvious yes-or-no answer is not forthcoming, therapeutic intervention or behavior change is distinctly necessary.

Assertive Questionnaire

When a person is blatantly unfair, do you usually fail to say something about it to him?

Are you always very careful to avoid all trouble with other people?

Do you often avoid social contacts for fear of doing or saying the wrong thing?

If a friend betrays your confidence, do you tell him how you really feel?

If you had a roomate, would you insist that he or she do their fair share of cleaning?

When a clerk in a store waits on someone who has come in after you, do you call his attention to the matter?

Do you find that there are very few people with whom you can be relaxed and have a good time?

Would you be hesitant about asking a good friend to lend you a few dollars?

If someone who has borrowed $5 from you seems to have forgotten about it, would you remind this person?

If a person keeps on teasing you, do you have difficulty expressing your annoyance or displeasure?

Would you remain standing at the rear of a crowded auditorium rather than look for a seat up front?

If someone keeps kicking the back of your chair in a movie, would you ask him to stop?

If a friend keeps calling you very late each evening, would you ask him or her not to call after a certain time?

If someone starts talking to someone else right in the middle of your conversation, do you express your irritation?

In a plush restaurant, if you order a medium steak and find it too raw, would you ask the waiter to have it recooked?

If the landlord of your apartment fails to make certain necessary repairs after promising to do so, would you insist upon it?

Would you return a faulty garment you purchased a few days ago?

If someone you respect expresses opinions with which you strongly disagree, would you venture to state your own point of view?

Are you usually able to say "no" if people make unreasonable requests?

Do you think that people should stand up for their rights?

Dozens of similar questions can be asked about all sorts of specific encounters. The twenty questions above will suffice to indicate general deficiencies in assertive behavior. Of primary importance, however, is a full knowledge of each patient's *specific* interpersonal deficiencies. For instance, someone could answer each of the questions above with exemplary assertiveness but, nevertheless, prove to be completely intimidated by their parents, or a spouse, or by other situations not tapped by the questionnaire.

A caveat about the evils of "compulsive assertiveness" might be timely at this point. Some therapists induce guilt in their patients for all nonassertive acts. Thus, they encourage them to take pride in pedantries that spell inconsiderateness rather than social-assertiveness. A patient who received assertive training elsewhere narrated with pride that he had "chewed out" an elderly lady for walking too slowly in line ahead of him. When treating timid but hostile individuals, one must take care that they do not use the philosophy of emotional freedom as a license for vulgarity and disrespect. All human beings are entitled to dignity, respect, and courtesy. One of the troubles with our society is that all too often we have to demand these rights instead of receiving them as a matter of course.

Friendship and Marriage

The other, and by far the more important, aspect of emotional freedom concerns the expression of affection, endearment, and togetherness. Basic relationships, such as genuine friendship, presuppose a climate in which all emotions are given ample freedom of expression. There is consistent and appropriate ventilation of feelings. It is *easy* to know what each person really feels and thinks about the other. The full expression of each other's genuine thoughts and feelings is totally welcomed. Even anger is never stifled but is expressed in a spontaneous, warm, and constructive fashion (Bach & Wyden, 1969; Rubin, 1969). In this setting, people do not *feel* one way and *act* another. They play no false roles and do not attempt to fool themselves or other people. And the fundamental attraction between true friends is predicated upon the mutual desire for cooperation rather than competition. When good things happen to one, sincere pleasure, not even a tinge of envy, is experienced by the other.

Cynics will maintain that such relationships are impossible. Skeptics might hasten to point out that true friendships are exceedingly rare. But the person who does not enjoy one or two of these precious interactions is emotionally impoverished and underprivileged regardless of other gratifications such as wealth, status, power, prestige, or intellectual achievement. It is my contention that the Marilyn Monroes of this world could avert their tragic endings and buffer the whiplash of overwhelming fame and fortune by acquiring the capacity to form and place value on enduring A-to-Z friendships. "A-to-Z friendship" implies complete openness and intimate sharing. There are no "keep off the grass" signs, no emotional taboos, no unmentionable subjects, no secrets whatsoever. Self-disclosure and personal transparency are the keynotes. According to the concepts referred to in Chapter 4, no barriers are erected around the person's "inner circle."

Many people contend that marriage is a relationship which carries the principles of friendship to its ultimate and most intimate degree. I think they are mistaken. Many an excellent premarital and extramarital friendship has come to grief soon after the parties married. The structure of marriage overlaps with friendship but is not synonymous with it. A colleague of mine who has had a remarkably happy marriage for the past fifteen years, openly stated that although he loves his wife dearly and adores her as a wife, as a companion, and as the mother of his children, he very much doubted whether he would seek out her company *as a friend*. Those who conclude that his attitude betrays a grave defect in his marriage are probably themselves victims of false romantic ideals. What are the differences between a good marriage and a good friendship?

Basically, marriage is intimate sharing whereas friendship is shared intimacy. Friends typically are not expected to live under the same roof year in and year out. As such, their shared intimacies are intensive rather than extensive. Marriage involves the sharing of many daily events in which the feeling tone of one partner has a direct effect upon the other. Consequently, it is easy to overload the system. Besides, the focus of marriage usually ends up being family-centered whereas in friendship the investment is mainly between the two people. Hence, factors such as intellectual compatability and common interests and ideals, are probably more necessary for successful friendship than for successful marriage.

In marriage, the continuously close physical proximity and all the shared burdens and responsibilities dictate the need for some degree of emotional privacy. Whereas the ideal friendship is an A-to-Z relationship, the ideal marriage should proceed no further than A-to-W. Marriage is not ownership. Each partner is entitled to his or her individuality, emotional privacy, and, as mentioned earlier in this chapter, considerable freedom of psychological movement. The only proviso is that when exercising freedom of movement and individuality, one must take care not to encroach on the partner's rightful territory. When discussing these issues with patients, the following simple diagrams have proved useful:

This depicts a poor marriage relationship. There is very little togetherness or common ground.

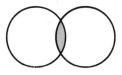

This depicts an excellent marriage. There is about 80 percent togetherness but also sufficient separateness to permit individual growth and essential privacy.

This represents the romantic ideal where two people merge so completely that they become as one. In practice, were this possible, it would probably result in emotional suffocation.

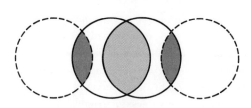

Here is a reasonably good marriage in which each partner has an independent interest or relationship which in no way interferes with or threatens the marriage as it occupies only each one's own individual territory.

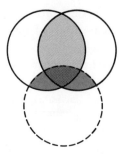

In this figure, one of the partners has an interest or relationship which not only occupies some of his or her own territory but which also intrudes into their (the marriage) territory as well as encroaching upon the other partner's individual zone.

In the treatment of married couples it is often necessary to examine how they can best pursue their independent interests without creating distance between them. It is easy for a hobby, a sport, or a friendship to come between husband and wife. Yet these same factors can help to cement marriage relationships and accentuate their togetherness if managed correctly. The principal process is for couples to learn to express their feelings and desires and for each partner to respond in turn to these freely stated opinions with equal candor. Even small gains in emotional freedom often return big rewards, so one's therapeutic efforts in this regard seldom go unreinforced.

Constructive and Destructive Criticism

In marriage, the ridiculous ease with which intimacy can turn to enmity is all too obvious. Bach and Wyden (1969) have written an interesting commentary on marital interaction with special emphasis on the need for couples to learn clean and constructive marital fighting in place of dirty and destructive feuds which often cause rifts too damaging to mend. There are several distinctly helpful ways of expressing inevitable disagreement and criticism which tend to draw people closer together. This refers simply to profound differences between constructive and destructive criticism. Destructive criticism carries messages which are totally condemnatory as opposed to constructive criticism which places the specific negative overtone within a general positive undertone. Here are a few typical examples:

Destructive Criticism	Constructive Criticism
"You are stupid."	"That was a stupid thing you did."
"You are ugly."	"I think you look ugly with a beard and mustache."
"I hate your guts."	"Right now I am really mad at you for what you did."
"He's a nasty specimen."	"He has some nasty ways about him."
"He is a thief."	"He once stole some money."
"You are a pig."	"You have bad table manners."

If the recipient of constructive criticism is even vaguely interested, he will be given specific dos and don'ts which will enable him to mend his ways. This ties in with many of the points more fully discussed in Chapter 8. At this stage the reader should observe that destructive criticism attacks the entire person and leaves him no escape, whereas constructive criticism is not directed at the person but toward specific offensive actions which can be remedied.

Training in Positive Expressiveness

The behavior therapy literature devotes disproportionate space to assertive training, to the expression of anger, and to the need to be able to contradict and verbally attack other people. This is all very important when appropriate, but a large proportion of people are all too good at asserting their rights, often to the detriment of/ others. I should now like to try and achieve some equilibrium by emphasizing the other side of the coin—the expression of compassion, tenderness, warmth, and other positive feelings. Balanced emotional freedom implies not only the ability to demand one's own rights, but also the willingness to protect the rights of others. Many of our patients are able to contradict and attack, or to criticize and defend, but are completely incapable of volunteering praise and approval, or of expressing love and affection. Even in behavior rehearsal or role-playing situations, some of these individuals experience inordinate difficulty in uttering the following sorts of statements:

"That was an excellent piece of work you did."

"I like that outfit you're wearing."

"Your soup is delicious."

"You are an excellent athlete."

"I truly appreciate your concern."

"Our friendship means very much to me."

"I love you."

The most common objection to verbalizing positive feelings is that it should not be necessary to express in words what actions themselves can convey. My rejoinder is that actions and words (when in the same direction) speak loudest of all. As an example, I often tell my patients, "If I allow my friends to *infer* that I enjoy and value their friendship because I obviously like to go out with them and actively seek out their company, it is still not as satisfying to all concerned as being told in so many words that I am genuinely happy to be with them."

In the same way as it is relatively easy to overstep one's assertive prerogatives and behave aggressively, so it is easy to overdo positive expressiveness and end up oozing and gushing sickly sentimentality. Sincere expressions of appreciation and positive regard should not be confused with saccharine-coated compliments or perfunctory flattery. The goal is to aim for a balanced outpouring of anger (when appropriate) and love (when appropriate).

Case Illustration: From Anger to Love

I recently treated a very unhappy girl of nineteen who made a serious suicidal attempt before being referred to me. The initial phase of therapy consisted mainly of an endeavor to teach her to stop denying her hostility. "How much anger have you been expressing?" was the stock question at the beginning of each session. We would review and examine many specific personal encounters and the manner in which she had dealt with each of them. I would constantly coax her to assert her rights, to stop being pushed around, to give vent to her anger, and not to permit her family to make a scapegoat of her. (I had suggested seeing the patient together with her parents and her younger sister, but they refused to embark on family therapy and preferred to cling to the fiction that the patient was the only "sick" member of the family.) Within a few months the patient was notably less anxious and depressed but she was far from happy. She remarked, "Your treatment has brought me from negative to neutral. Now can you teach me to be happy?" I replied, "In addition to expressing anger, it is also necessary for you to express love and warmth." The stock question at the start of each session then became, "How much love have you been expressing?"

Detailed inquiries revealed a wide discrepancy between her newfound assertiveness and her chronic inability to display either spontaneous or contrived affection. Here again it was necessary to discuss specific situations and to encourage her to express positive feeling whenever the opportunity arose. "Well, you could have said to your cousin, 'I was very touched that you remembered my birthday,' and when your mother said nothing about the dented fender, you could have hugged her and said, 'Thanks for being so understanding'." From time to time it also became necessary to provide a "refresher course" in the appropriate expression of anger, but most of the therapy was centered on role playing frank and forthright statements of love, adoration, affection, and appreciation.

After we had embarked on the "love phase" of therapy for about six weeks, the girl's mother called me to report that she and her husband were having marital difficulties. (This is consonant with theories of "family dynamics" which hold that many problems are family-centered, so that improvement in one family member may result in disruption elsewhere in the system. See, for example, Jackson, 1965; Nagy & Framo, 1965; Watzlawick, Beavin & Jackson, 1967.) Again I extended an invitation to the entire family to work together as a unit in therapy. This time my advice was heeded and we embarked on a course of family therapy. Here it was necessary to point out the double binds which arose, the needless rivalry between the sisters, the mother's tendency to use guilt as a controlling device, and the damaging effects of the father's bad temper. But the mainstay of therapeutic attention soon shifted to the necessity for each family member to learn the true meaning and application of emotional freedom. Significant change was noted when the father stopped "pulling rank" and gradually became a friend and confidant to his daughters. The mother felt that the change in father-daughter relationships enabled her to become more of a wife and less of "an evil guardian." The outcome was most gratifying for all concerned.

CHAPTER 7
OVERCOMING
SEXUAL
INADEQUACY

Effective psychotherapy frequently necessitates an appreciation of the subtle interplay between biological, psychological, and sociological factors. Nowhere is this more fundamental than in the treatment of sexual problems. To consider sexual intercourse merely the expression of a "drive" or "need" is to ignore the network of social values, cultural taboos, and personal attitudes that permeate every aspect of this frenetic embrace. Very few sexual problems stem entirely from structural, hormonal, or neuronic deficiencies. The overwhelming majority of sexual problems stem from psychological (attitudinal) determinants.

Sexual information, despite the efforts of many enlightened educators, remains confusingly fragmentary and contradictory. Many forces favoring sexual obscurantism still retain an unhealthy measure of support in our society. Puritanism, although waning, is still responsible for disseminating sexual myths and superstitions. It is hardly necessary to labor the point that many people are uninformed and uncertain about sexual matters. But as Fromme (1966, p. 7) points out, the situation is not easily remedied. "Although sex is here to stay there are many people and many forces attempting to drive it underground. In addition to legal censorship, we have religious bans and, probably most pervasive of all, just plain common prudishness."

The strongly inhibitory sex training that predominates in North American society is described by Bandura and Walters (1963, p. 149) as being "accomplished mainly by the transmission to children of parental anxiety reactions to the exploratory, manipulative and curiosity behavior that inevitably occur during childhood." Consequently, it is not surprising that even in this supposedly enlightened era, clinicians' caseloads are replete with sexually disturbed individuals. In this chapter we are concerned with the understanding and correction of sexual insufficiency or inadequacy (commonly referred to as "frigidity" in the case of females and "impotence" and "premature ejaculation" in the case of males).

Forms of Sexual Inadequacy

In general, the terms *frigidity* and *impotence* refer to the inability to initiate, enjoy, or complete sexual intercourse. Successful coitus presupposes that this most intimate act be taken to the point of mutual fulfillment. Obviously, there are degrees of impotence and frigidity. Some men display almost complete absence of sexual arousal. Others, although easily aroused, nevertheless lose their erections before reaching orgasm. Similarly, sexual problems in women range from those who find coitus completely revolting to those who experience difficulty in reaching a climax.

While the term *impotence* usually implies various degrees of difficulty in obtaining and/or maintaining erections, it also refers to those males who are capable of prolonged coitus but who have difficulty in achieving orgasm or ejaculation (known as retarded ejaculation or ejaculatory impotence). The term also describes those men who report minimal or limited pleasure in sex, especially ejaculation without sensation. Some authorities view premature ejaculation as a form of impotence, whereas others regard it as a separate condition. Kinsey et al. (1948, p. 580) consider rapid ejaculation a superior biological trait! But the man who ejaculates too soon is obviously unable to maintain an erection to the satisfaction of the female and is certainly considered "impotent" in her eyes.

It is uncommon to find women who find all sexual contacts anathema. Most "frigid" women occasionally experience mild but essentially fleeting pleasure during sex. Frigidity parallels the features of impotence in several respects. Some women fail to become sexually aroused; others tend to lose their response before reaching orgasm (corresponding to loss of erection in the male); and some, although adequately aroused, experience great difficulty in achieving orgasm. However, whereas "orgasmic impotence" is common in women, it is rare in men, and whereas premature orgasms are common in men, this condition is probably nonexistent in women. Absence of pleasure in sex is the most common feature of frigidity. Some writers (e.g., Kant, 1969) define frigidity as the absence of orgasmic response. But surely, those women who enjoy coitus by obtaining sensual pleasure, emotional closeness and physical excitement, and who feel satisfied despite the lack of a true orgasm, should not be called "frigid." Unfortunately the term *frigid* is often used in a pejorative manner.

In broad outline, impotent men usually desire or even crave sexual intercourse but are unable to perform the act; frigid women usually have no desire for sex and derive little or no pleasure from the act, but are generally able to go through with it. A condition known as *vaginismus* (conditioned involuntary spasm of the perivaginal and circumvaginal muscles) makes intercourse painful or impossible for certain frigid women. But whereas the impotent male is usually traumatized by his condition, the frigid female may sometimes be proud of herself.

Causal Factors in Impotence and Frigidity

The causes of sexual inadequacy are varied. Numerous drugs, chemicals, or toxins may impair sexual functioning. Most physical illnesses that produce general malaise tend to decrease sexual capacities. Certain systemic diseases can produce chronic sexual problems, and local diseases of the genito-urinary tracts may also interfere with sexual drive and performance. Sexual apathy is often seen in psychotic syndromes, especially in certain depressive conditions. Ellis (1961, p. 450) contends that certain cases of frigidity may be due to "innate or constitutional lack of sexual responsiveness."

The vast majority of impotent males and frigid females, however, do not suffer from any of the aforementioned conditions or any other organic lesions. In most cases of impotence and frigidity psychological factors play the major role. This implies that past experience or learning is usually responsible for the origin and maintenance of sexual inadequacy.

In broad neurophysiological terms, sexual arousal depends upon discharges of the autonomic nervous system. Erection in the male and clitoral enlargement and vaginal distension in the female are predominantly parasympathetic functions. Discharges of the sympathetic division exert an inhibitory effect on sexual arousal and performance. Thus, doubt, fear, guilt, shame, conflict, embarrassment, tension, disgust, irritation, resentment, grief, hostility, and most other "negative emotional reactions" will tend to undermine diminish, or extinguish sexual capacities in men and women. In certain instances, however, negative emotions may heighten the sexual drive, akin to some compulsive eaters who use food to inhibit their anxieties. The sexual response is in fact a very delicate and vulnerable mechanism, perhaps more quickly and readily disturbed than any other aspect of behavior.

The "sexual drive" and its expression are often likened to the "hunger drive" and its ramifications. Despite obvious differences between so-called "hunger pangs" and a "sexual appetite," both are stimulated by complex central and peripheral physiological processes, and both show wide individual differences in taste and appeal which, in turn, are a function of past experience and cultural conditioning. The crude and hurried ingestion of an ill-prepared meal and the gourmet's epicurean delights serve the same physiological processes but occupy vastly different psychological planes. And so it is with sex where the flimsy division between ardor and obscenity can transform passion into an assault. The sexual anorexia of many a frigid female may be traced to formative encounters with insensitive men who provided crudeness and vulgarity in place of tenderness and consideration.

Simplex and Complex Factors

In reviewing the life histories of impotent men and frigid women, diverse causative factors are evident. "I believe that I have damaged myself through excessive masturbation," said the twenty-year-old son of Calvinistic parents. A twenty-two-year-old frigid social worker stated, "The way my clients behave sexually doesn't offend me, but I personally have been raised to regard sex as an evil and degrading pastime." Frequent antecedents include fear of unwanted pregnancy (despite the advent of oral contraceptives), hostility toward the sexual partner, and various patterns of guilt and anxiety. Since the male's image of his own masculinity is so often dependent upon his sexual performance, he can readily develop a "fear of fear." The man, for instance, who enters sex with the thought, "Wouldn't it be awful if I became so tense or anxious during sex that I lost my erection!" may thereby engender sufficient anxiety to suppress all sexual feeling. Certain women these days also place such a premium on sexual adequacy that they inadvertently sabotage their sexual pleasures by becoming too concerned about their own level of performance. In some cases, sexual difficulties stem directly from doubts which people have about the appearance and adequacy of their bodies in general and their sex organs in particular. Indeed, causal factors may range all the way from simple squeamishness, to the complex personal philosophies concerned with the concept of pleasure.

I have observed a tendency among some psychologists and psychiatrists to view sexual difficulties with unnecessary pessimism. This stems from the habit of compounding sexual problems by insisting that nearly all cases of sexual inadequacy are deep-seated in origin and require extensive reconstructive therapy.

A case worth citing is that of a nineteen-year-old lad, seen at a psychiatric ward round, who mentioned his overriding fear of sexual intercourse, and described how friends had informed him that in certain women the vagina was capable of such violent spasms and contractions as to endanger the male organ. The chief psychiatrist accordingly referred to "deep-seated castration anxieties" and predicted that even long-term analysis might not yield improvement. Yet, when one of the doctors simply corrected the lad's misconceptions and offered him factual information bolstered by the force of his own prestige, the problem was instantly resolved. In this age of psychological oversophistication, the search for complex answers to simple questions has become an international malady.

Pseudoinadequacies

A number of people who consult therapists for the treatment of frigidity or impotence suffer only from misinformation. It is extremely common, for instance, to find women who consider themselves frigid (or are regarded as such by their husbands) on the basis of being capable of achieving only manually induced clitoral orgasms. Freud (1938) is probably responsible for popularizing the myth that the woman who achieves a clitoral as opposed to a vaginal orgasm is immature and emotionally disturbed. Bergler and Kroger (1953, p. 711) exemplify this erroneous point of view: "Frigidity is the incapacity of a woman to achieve a vaginal orgasm during intercourse. It is of no matter whether the woman is aroused during coitus or remains cold, whether excitment is weak or strong, whether it breaks off at the beginning or ends slowly or suddenly, whether it is dissipated in preliminary acts, or has been lacking from the beginning. The only criterion of frigidity is absence of vaginal orgasm." Yet when reviewing the role of clitoral versus vaginal orgasms on the basis of experimental data, Masters and Johnson (1966, p. 66) arrive at very different conclusions: "Are clitoral and vaginal orgasms truly separate anatomic entities? From a biologic point of view, the answer to this question is an unequivocal No." Ellis (1962a, p. 97) is equally explicit: "Penile-vaginal intercourse may abet orgasm through providing indirect stimulation for the clitoral situated genital corpuscles; or in some copulative positions, it may result in direct stimulation for the clitoris itself. No matter: the female orgasm is still mainly clitoral and not vaginal. So-called vaginal orgasm, therefore, is a myth." In *The Sexually Responsive Woman* (Kronhausen & Kronhausen, 1964, p. 26) the authors emphasize the following: "We now know, on the basis of such solid scientific research as is available, that there is no need for a shift or transfer of sensitivity from the clitoris to the vagina. On the contrary, it is not the vagina but the clitoris which remains throughout the woman's life the organ with the greatest potential for erotic stimulation." It is rather tragic to contemplate how many "man-years of analytic hours have been spent with presumably frigid women in exploring the causative psychological factors which prevented the clitoral-vaginal transfer (Hastings, 1963, p. 35)."

Another pseudoproblem involves the male who considers himself impotent because he is either sexually unresponsive to some women or incapable of immediate sexual arousal. Men's erotic boastings have led to a stereotype of the male as a most undiscriminating animal who desires to cohabit with almost every female, and in whom physical proximity with any woman will lead to immediate and sustained sexual arousal. Some men view any personal deviation from this putative norm with concern if not distress. Thus, a thirty-five-year-old man sought therapy after an unsuccessful encounter with a paid companion at a motel. He considered irrelevant the fact that he was somewhat fatigued after a long journey, had imbibed a fairly large quantity of alcohol, found the girl relatively unattractive, and was preoccupied with various business negotiations. "The way I see it is that if you're in bed with a woman, bombs could be bustin' up the joint and you shouldn't even notice it." This attitude typifies a widely prevalent contention that men, worthy of the name, should be capable of instant erections almost regardless of the prevailing circumstances. It is interesting that as one proceeds up the scale of refinement and sophistication, men, no less than women, pride themselves on their discernment, their discriminative selectivity, and upon their insistence that sexual intercourse is so much more enjoyable when it involves more than mutual friction of erogenous zones.

Marked individual differences in the need for sexual expression often occasion discord in marriage. If consistent discrepancies exist between the husband's and wife's respective potential for arousal and sexual gratification, attendant resentments may lead to specific impotence or frigidity (i.e., only with the marriage partner). This type of impasse is exceedingly difficult to remedy, especially in the case of highly sexed women married to sexually cold (but not necessarily impotent) men. Drugs, hormones, and other medical treatment are at best of limited value. The undersexed (but not necessarily frigid) female is usually capable of having intercourse even though she has no sexual desire or interest at the time. The male, of course, cannot have coitus unless he is sexually aroused. However, the sexually passive husband might be well-advised to learn that many women prefer frequent digital stimulation combined with overt affection to infrequent coitus. Indeed, as will be discussed in the section on treatment, it is important to realize that sex need not be an all-or-none activity dependent upon adequate penile-vaginal stimulation.

A very common malady is the "frigid" woman who complains that her husband displays affection only in bed. Men who regard the expression of love and tenderness as vaguely, if not strongly, unmasculine, not only abound but may even, regrettably, be in the majority. Yet many women find consideration and affection an essential precursor to sexual arousal. Verbal communication of an intimate and personal nature is almost nonexistent in many marriages in which time is absorbed by business and domestic chores, separate hobbies, sports, and other recreational pursuits. These and many additional dehumanizing forces can give rise to resentment where sexual withholding is ultimately used as a retaliatory weapon. However, it would be a misnomer to label this a form of impotence or frigidity.

Assessment Procedures

That therapy should always be based upon a comprehensive regime of problem identification and a thorough behavior analysis is an obvious but frequently neglected fact. Clearly, an individual whose sexual avoidance stems from irrational fears of contamination must proceed along a different therapeutic route from a patient who equates "carnal desire" with guilt and sin. The many and varied antecedent factors that can produce frigidity and impotence dictate the need for thorough and systematic assessment procedures. Apart from possible organic factors which have to be excluded whenever there is reason to suspect physiologic dysfunctioning, the therapist must acquire precise insights into the basic dimensions of each patient's problem.

The Presenting Complaint

The starting point is to focus upon the presenting complaint, using the following questions as a guide:

Is the patient engaging in some sort of marital "game" as described by Berne (1964)?

Does the difficulty stem from a distinct absence of feeling or attraction between the partners?

Does the problem stem, perhaps, from simple naïveté and inexperience?

Is the problem the result of simple or complex misconceptions?

Have there been specific traumata which have occasioned or reinforced a pattern of sexual withdrawal and avoidance?

Is there perhaps a latent homosexual preference?

Is the problem a manifestation of overgeneralized hostility toward the opposite sex?

Are the difficulties associated with human relationships in general rather than sexual contacts in particular?

To what extent is the problem compounded by superstitions and various inhibitions?

The Sexual History

When the ramifications of these nine questions have been explored, the history of the patient's sex life should be traced in detail:

When and how was knowledge of sex first acquired?

Was there any sex instruction in the home? (It is important to obtain precise information about parental attitudes, whether negative or positive, to sex.)

At what age and under what circumstances did the patient first become aware of his or her sexual impulses?

Were there any developmental problems relating to menstruation, breast development, growth of pubic hair, voice change, etc?

Did masturbation arouse fear or guilt?

When did dating commence and what forms of petting occurred? (Information should be obtained about preadolescent sex play as well as subsequent sexual patterns.)

What were the details, circumstances, and repercussions of the first coital experience?

Is there relevant information about any other significant heterosexual (and/or homosexual) encounters?

What are the patient's prevailing attitudes and knowledge about sex? (Particular attention should be paid to the person's views on sexual morality.)

What are the patient's feelings about his or her own physical appearance?

What circumstances are inclined to result in sexual arousal and/or the achievement of orgasms (e.g., erotic literature, daydreams, masturbation)?

What is the patient's reaction to partial versus total nudity?

What information can be obtained regarding the patient's feelings about various coital techniques and positions?

Is there any preference for lovemaking in full light, subdued light, or in the dark?

Are there any specific reactions to the absence or presence of sexual arousal in his/her partner?

It may also be necessary to explore various additional topics such as venereal disease, prostitution, contraception, abortion, perversions, and so forth.

It is important to remember that sexual disturbances may also emanate from nonsexual emotional sources. For instance, I treated a young man who achieved sexual potency after being desensitized to fears of blood. As a child he had felt acutely upset when seeing the slaughter of poultry, and had thereafter remained squeamish toward blood. His impotence clearly dated from a sexual experience with a woman who, unknown to him, had not quite completed menstruating.

Treatment

The preceding sections have stressed the fact that the terms *frigidity* and *impotence* refer to a wide range of sexual insufficiencies and inadequacies which stem from diverse causes. Therapeutic strategies differ both according to the type of problem and the antecedent conditions. The man, for instance, who cannot obtain an erection usually requires different therapeutic management from the patient who suffers from premature ejaculation. In women, techniques for overcoming orgasmic impotence differ markedly from those required in the treatment of vaginismus. Furthermore, two cases of sexual apathy will each require very different forms of treatment if the one is a manifestation of moralistic guilt and the other stems from homosexual inclinations. A number of specific therapeutic techniques will now be described.

The Correction of Misconceptions

Direct advice, guidance, information, reassurance, or instruction may suffice to overcome the milder, simpler, and more transient cases of impotence and frigidity. The correction of faulty attitudes and irrational beliefs is often an essential forerunner to specific techniques of lovemaking. One should endeavor to impart nonmoralistic insights into all matters pertaining to sex. It is often helpful to prescribe nontechnical but authoritative literature (e.g., Ellis, 1958, 1962a, 1965; Kronhausen & Kronhausen, 1965; and McCary, 1967). Patient and therapist may then exchange views on a variety of topics and examine sex in a rational, objective, and enlightened manner.

Graded Sexual Assignments

Wolpe (1958) evolved a simple but effective procedure for promoting sexual adequacy and responsiveness in those cases where anxiety partially inhibits sexual performance. Although intended primarily for the treatment of impotence, I have used this method in overcoming frigidity (Wolpe & Lazarus, 1966 pp. 110–111). A cooperative sexual partner is indispensable to the success of the technique. The patient is instructed not to make any sexual responses which engender feelings of tension or anxiety, but to proceed only to the point where pleasurable reactions predominate. The partner is informed that she must never press him to go beyond this point, and that she must be prepared for several amorous and intimate encounters that will not culminate in coitus. The theory is that by maintaining sexual arousal in the ascendant over anxiety, the latter will decrease from one amorous session to the next. Thus, positive sexual feelings and responses will be facilitated and will, in turn, further inhibit residual anxieties. In this manner, conditioned inhibition of anxiety is presumed to increase until the anxiety reactions are completely eliminated.

An excerpt from a patient's letter should clarify the procedure:

"You will recall that both Julie and I were skeptical of the sexual program you advised. All the same we went through the paces. I think I went slower than anybody. The first few times we just sort of cuddled in the living room. In less than five minutes I became tense so we quit. A few nights after that we were, as the teenagers would put it, 'making out,' and I had my hand inside Julie's bra. I didn't feel tense but nor was I aroused. I don't remember exactly how soon afterwards—about a week I'd guess—we'd go through the motions of intercourse with our clothes on in the living room and I'd become semierect. It got to the point where we would masturbate each other in the living room to climax, but in the bedroom nothing would happen. I'm sure this was because the bedroom reminded me of all my past failures. In fact I think it had something to do with beds. It had gotten to the point where I could perform just fine on the living room rug when Julie surprised me by buying one of those sofa-bed arrangements. At first I was impotent until we moved back onto the floor. In fact one night we were in bed and kind of stroking each other. As usual nothing happened, so I suggested that we move onto the rug. There I was fine and we had intercourse. We used to kid each other about this floor angle, but it sort of bothered me. We overcame this problem in two ways. First, we would stimulate each other in bed, knowing full well that if nothing happened we could always move onto the floor. This was most reassuring. Secondly, we would make love in bed in the early morning when I tended to have an erection anyway."

When a man fails to obtain or maintain an erection, he often feels greatly embarrassed and somehow needs to "save face." It may be helpful for him to explain to his partner that ambivalance, or tension, or similar stressful factors can readily produce a state in which it becomes *physiologically* impossible for him to feel sexually aroused. He may wish to explain that the erotic needs of a sensitive, aesthetic, and cultured man can fairly easily be undermined even by subtle innuendos, whereas an uncouth male is probably incapable of having his sexual ardor dampened by anything less than a well-armed and irate husband. The refined and cultivated man could probably never perform rape!

Many impotent men require no formal treatment once they accept that penile-vaginal intercourse is but one way (not the only way, or the "proper" or "normal" way) of satisfying a woman. It is emphasized that a truly proficient lover should be so adept at manual, digital, and oral manipulations that he can induce multiple orgasms in most women without involving his penis at any stage of the proceedings. It is also stressed that when the onus of an expected level of performance is removed from the sufferer (i.e., by the knowledge that his partner need never emerge sexually frustrated whether or not he obtains or maintains an erection), adequate sexual adjustment usually ensues. When a man engages in oral and manual caresses, he will usually find that these actions not only arouse and satisfy the female but also arouse him, especially when he focuses on pleasures being bestowed on his partner instead of dwelling on his own genital problem. Some men may achieve "reflex erections" simply by relaxing while their partner manipulates, massages, or lubricates their genitals. If successful coitus then ensues, a generalization of sexual potency is often achieved without further treatment. Another helpful method is for the man to rub his flaccid penis on his partner's vulva and to use his fingers on her clitoris. If the woman achieves orgasms or very much enjoys this technique (and many women do), the man will often himself achieve a sufficient erection to enter her and thereby complete the sex act. The confidence which accrues from these maneuvers usually renders them redundant after a short while.

More serious sexual disorders usually necessitate the application of several procedures as exemplified by the case of Roy published in Ullmann and Krasner (1965, pp. 243–245). This patient required many discussions aimed at the correction of his misconceptions, as well as assertive training, specific advice, and desensitization all within the context of a nonjudgmental therapeutic relationship.

The Role of Desensitization Procedures in Overcoming Frigidity

Treatment of chronic frigidity by systematic desensitization was first reported by Lazarus (1963). Therapeutic success was achieved with nine of sixteen recalcitrant cases after a mean of 28.7 sessions. Brady (1966) achieved marked improvement in four out of five chronic, severe cases of frigidity treated over an average of eleven sessions by desensitizing the patients after administering subanesthetic doses of methohexital sodium (Brevital) as a means of producing muscular relaxation. Desensitization has also been successfully applied to groups of impotent men and frigid women (Lazarus, 1961, 1968d, 1969b). The preferred size of desensitization groups is between four and eight members. The sessions are conducted at the pace of the slowest (most anxious) individual. If one group member obviously delays the progress of the other patients, he is given a few individual sessions to expedite matters. The typical hierarchy applied to the frigid women consisted of the following progression: Embracing, kissing, being fondled, mild petting, undressing, foreplay in the nude, awareness of husband's erection, moving into position for insertion, intromission, changing positions during coitus. Madsen and Ullmann (1967) have noted the advantages of enlisting the husband's assistance in the therapy room during the construction of hierarchies and in the presentation of hierarchy items.

Reference has already been made to the desensitization of nonsexual fears which may nevertheless impair sexual functioning (e.g., fear of blood, general squeamishness, fear of injury). Improvement in sexual functioning and responsiveness has been a fairly frequent byproduct of desensitization programs directed at themes of criticism, rejection, disapproval, and ridicule. A frigid woman was unresponsive to many forms of treatment until she received desensitization along a dimension of "bodily criticism." A tactless, if not sadistic, husband from whom she was divorced had made numerous adverse comments about her body which had undermined her self-confidence over the years. Consequently, she avoided all sexual contacts. An eight-item hierarchy was constructed: You have gained weight; your thighs are flabby; your stomach sticks out; your breasts are drooping; your stretch marks will turn off any man; you have a masculine shape; your vagina has an odor; you have absolutely no sex appeal.

Only three desensitization sessions were required to lend her the courage finally to accept a boyfriend's sexual advances. Not only was the sexual experience per se successful, but she reported a newfound readiness and ability to believe that her lover genuinely considered her feminine and attractive.

In the treatment of vaginismus (as well as in those cases

suffering from generalized fears of penetration), desensitization, first in imagination, followed at home by gradual dilatation of the vaginal orifice, has proved highly successful. The patient, under conditions of deep relaxation, is asked to imagine herself inserting a graded series of objects into the vagina. When she is no longer anxious about the imagined situation, she is asked to use real objects. One might commence with the tip of a cotton bud, or the tip of the patient's little finger, followed by the gradual insertion of two or more fingers, internal sanitary pads, various lubricated cylinders, and eventually by the gradual introduction of the penis, culminating with vigorous coital movement. A detailed case study along these lines was presented several years ago by Rachman (1959). Masters and Johnson (1970) consider it necessary for husband and wife to cooperate in all phases of dilatation therapy.

Assertive Training for Impotent Men

Many impotent men appear to have servile attitudes toward women and respond to them with undue deference and humility. Their sexual passivity and timidity are often part of a generally nonassertive outlook, and their attendant inhibitions are usually not limited to their sex life. These men feel threatened when required to assume dominance in a male-female relationship.

Therapy is aimed at augmenting a wide range of expressive impulses, so that formerly inhibited sexual inclinations may find overt expression. This is achieved first by explaining to the patient how ineffectual forms of behavior produce many negative emotional repercussions (see Chapter 6). The unattractive and exceedingly distasteful features of obsequious behavior are also emphasized. The patient is then told how to apply principles of assertiveness to various interpersonal situations. For instance, he is requested to "express his true feelings; stand up for his rights," and to keep detailed notes of all his significant attempts (whether successful or unsuccessful) at assertive behavior. His feelings and responses are then fully discussed with the therapist, who endeavors to shape the patient's behavior by means of positive reinforcement and constructive criticism. Behavior rehearsal (Lazarus, 1966), a special form of role playing, is often an integral part of assertive training. This procedure enables the therapist to model desirable patterns of behavior and affords the patient a means of learning by imitation.

Case Illustration: The Use of a Prepared Script. A twenty-four-year-old lawyer after 6½ months of marriage, was perplexed and distressed by his partial impotence. He was sexually adequate some of the time, but was generally inclined to obtain only a semierection. His case history indicated that his domineering mother had taught him to fear and revere women, and that he was therefore unwilling, if not unable, to challenge or upbraid his wife on any terms whatsoever. Further inquiry revealed that he had accumulated considerable resentment towards his wife but felt, paradoxically, that giving vent to his feelings would be unmanly. Therapeutic attention was accordingly directed at his absurd and irrational attitudes which led him to regard women as objects rather than as people. These topics were covered during the course of three interviews.

The patient was then required to memorize a carefully worded speech which he and the therapist composed together:

"Grace, I have something very important and very serious to discuss with you. It concerns you, me, our marriage, and life in general. I want you please to hear me out without interrupting me. I've spent a hell of a lot of time mulling over these points, and finally I think I've straightened out my ideas, and I want very much to share them with you.

"Let me put it as clearly as possible. I was raised by my mother to bottle up my feelings, especially in relation to women. In thinking over this attitude, I now realize that this is crazy and even dishonest. I feel, for instance, that if I resent the fact that you turn to your father for advice in matters about which I have more knowledge than he, I ought to express my resentment instead of hiding it from you. I feel that when you order me about and treat me like a child, I ought to tell you how I really feel about it instead of acting like an obedient puppy dog. And most important of all, when you go ahead and make plans for me without consulting me, and especially when you yell at me in front of your parents, maybe I should quit acting as if I didn't mind and let you know how strongly I really react inside.

"What I am getting at is simply that in spite of my love and affection for you, I would really rather be unmarried than be a henpecked husband like my father."

This little monologue was rehearsed several times during a one-hour session until playbacks on a tape recorder convinced the therapist that the client was ready to confront his wife and that he could do so in a forthright and sincere manner. His wife's most probable reactions to the various accusations and insinuations also received careful consideration. Rehearsal techniques were used in preparing the patient to cope with tears, interruptions, denials, counterallegations, etc. His assignment was then put into effect. The patient reported that his wife "heard me out without interruption . . . seemed a little upset, but agreed that I should not withhold or conceal my feelings. I felt incredibly close to her and that night we had very good sex."

The patient was seen once every two or three weeks to reinforce his newfound assertiveness. He also had a successful confrontation with his mother and reported therapeutic gains which extended beyond his original marital and sexual impasse.

Not all cases are so readily resolved. The passive man who marries a domineering woman may require more than mere assertive directives. Frequently both partners require conjoint therapy involving the exploration of attitudes and communication patterns, as well as complex desensitization regimes (Lazarus, 1968c).

Aversion-relief Therapy in the Treatment of a Sexually Unresponsive Woman

It is well-known that an unpleasant electric shock in the presence of a given object tends to produce an *avoidance* reaction to that object. Conversely, *approach* responses may be conditioned to a stimulus repeatedly presented at the moment of termination of an electric shock. Thorpe et al. (1964) and Feldman and MacCulloch (1965) have successfully applied therapeutic procedures based upon these principles mainly to homosexuals and transvestites. The treatment of a sexually unresponsive woman by an aversion-relief method is outlined below:

Case Illustration. The patient, a twenty-six-year-old unmarried school teacher, complained that she was so repelled by male genitalia that sexual relations were impossible for her. A defloration experience some four years earlier had induced violent nausea, despite the fact that her lover had shown much skill and tenderness. Since that time she had abstained from sexual contacts except for several "platonic affairs" which involved activities "above the waist." She denied having any homosexual inclinations. Therapy was requested as she had become involved with a man whom she very much wished to marry "if I can get over my sexual hang-up."

Attempts to desensitize her failed because she experienced difficulty in visualizing the scenes. Accordingly, the following aversion-relief method was applied:

The leads of a faradic shock unit, powered by a 9-volt dry battery, were strapped to her left palm. The therapist said, "Shock!" and switched on the current. The patient was instructed to endure the pain and discomfort for as long as possible, while the current was gradually increased. When the electrical impulses became intolerable, she was required to turn her attention toward several photographs of nude men on the desk in front of her. Upon looking at the pictures, the shock was immediately terminated (producing definite signs of relief). She received intermittent shocks when averting her gaze from the pictures. After three separate twenty-minute sessions during the course of a week, she declared that "at least I now quite enjoy the penis in picture form." Various so-called "pornographic" photographs and drawings were used as relief stimuli during the next three sessions. Finally, a slightly modified method was employed during six additional interviews. The therapist said, "Shock!" and administered a very strong burst of electricity to the patient's palm if she did not proceed to look at the pictures within eight seconds. She was told that she could avoid the shock by looking at the pictures in good time.

After the tenth treatment she went home and had intercourse with her boyfriend. She described the encounter as "slightly successful." After the twelfth session she telephoned to report that during coitus she had achieved two orgasms in quick succession, stating rather coyly, "and that's the best form of anxiety relief on the market." Several months later she reported that she fully enjoyed most aspects of foreplay and coitus but that she was inclined to draw the line at oral-genital contact.

It should be noted that only the very naïve clinician would attribute change in the preceding instance to conditioning. The active variables at the very least involved a therapeutic relationship and an abundance of persuasion and suggestion. None of the foregoing may have sufficed, however, if not for the primary incentive derived from the patient's love for her boyfriend.

The Treatment of Premature Ejaculation

Premature ejaculation is sometimes a symptom of anxiety. The amelioration of anxiety by such techniques as relaxation, desensitization, and assertive training has therefore proved helpful in certain instances. In general, however, it should be noted that psychotherapeutic efforts have not proved especially effective in altering the premature response pattern. Nevertheless, some essentially simple tricks may occasionally meet with gratifying success. For instance, some individuals have managed to delay orgasm and ejaculation merely by dwelling on nonerotic thoughts and images while engaged in sexual intercourse. Others have found it more effective to indulge in self-inflicted pain during coitus (e.g., pinching one's leg, biting one's tongue). Masters and Johnson (1970), however, are not in favor of distraction techniques. The use of depressant drugs (e.g., alcohol or barbiturates) may also impede premature ejaculation in some individuals. The reduction of tactile stimulation (e.g., by wearing one or more condoms, or by applying anesthetic ointments to the glans penis) is also often recommended. All of the foregoing procedures are of limited value.

A fairly useful method of delaying orgasm is by means of a training program designed to increase the threshold of excitability. Extravaginal stimulation of the penis during erection is continued until a sensation premonitory to ejaculation is experienced by the patient. Semans (1956) states:

Stimulation is then interrupted until the sensation has disappeared. Penile stimulation is repeated until the premonitory sensation returns and then is again discontinued. . . . By repeating the procedure the response of ejaculation becomes no longer premature; that is, it can finally be delayed indefinitely until female response has begun or is complete [p. 356].

A case illustration clarifying this procedure will now be outlined:

Case Illustration. A twenty-two-year-old college student complained that he always ejaculated a few moments after insertion. He was able to delay orgasm by masturbating with a dry hand, but use of a lubricant, even during masturbation, resulted in rapid ejaculation. By means of the procedure described by Semans (1956), he was soon able to delay ejaculation during masturbation with or without the use of a bland cream. Next, his girl friend was instructed to stimulate him manually. Upon reaching a preorgasmic sensation, he was to remove her hand until the sensation disappeared. Stimulation was then to be resumed and interrupted again when the preorgasmic sensation returned. Within three weeks the patient reported that when he and his girl friend engaged in mutual masturbation (even with a lubricant) she would invariably achieve an orgasm before him. Next, the patient was told to insert only the glans of his penis into his girl friend's vagina and to avoid any movement. If ejaculation became imminent, he was to withdraw immediately. In a gradual manner, he was to increase the depth and duration of insertion and also the amount of movement. He was always to try and remain well within his capacity to avoid ejaculation.

Approximately a month later, "after one or two mishaps," he reported a distinct breakthrough. A few moments after intromission he nearly always felt like ejaculating, whereupon he would immediately withdraw and wait for the impulse to subside. Upon resuming coitus, some thirty seconds afterwards, he invariably found himself able to delay and control orgasm and ejaculation. A follow-up some ten months later revealed that apart from a tendency to ejaculate prematurely when embarking on a sexual relationship for the very first time, he generally maintained excellent control and regarded his own level of sexual performance as "far better than average."

The Squeeze Technique. Masters and Johnson (1970) have found the "squeeze technique" the most effective procedure for overcoming premature ejaculation. When the man is about to ejaculate, instead of stopping stimulation as in Semans's technique, the woman is instructed to squeeze her partner's penis for about three seconds. Rather strong pressure is applied under and behind the glans around the coronal ridge. During the first training session, four or five repetitions of the pressure are applied each time the man feels an incipient ejaculatory urge. After several manual sessions with the technique, the progression includes nondemanding and nonvigorous intromission, gradually introducing increasingly powerful pelvic thrusts. Whenever the man feels a pending loss of ejaculatory control, he withdraws and the woman applies the squeeze technique before reinserting the penis. It is of interest that in emphasizing dyadic factors in the genesis and resolution of sexual problems, Masters and Johnson stress the fact that the squeeze technique employed by the man in solitary masturbation does not produce gains which transfer to the heterosexual situation. The main drawback to the squeeze technique is that it sometimes produces temporary impotence. A urologist has expressed the opinion that the procedure may produce prostatitis, but Masters and Johnson make no reference to this possible side effect.

Walter Knopp, M.D., has drawn my attention to the following procedure for the management of premature ejaculation which appeared in the *International Drug Rx Newsletter*, September, 1966, Vol. 1, No. 7:

> Depending on the dose administered, a unique pharmacological action of the phenothiazine, thioridazine (Mellaril-Sandoz) is retardation or inhibition of ejaculation. To relieve premature ejaculation prescribe 25 mg., two to four times daily (occasionally a higher dose may be required). Some men respond immediately; others only after taking the drug up to two months. After two months of symptomatic relief, reduce dosage by one-half for another month. If relief is maintained, for this month, thioridazine should be discontinued. If premature ejaculation recurs, a second course of thioridazine therapy, with the same or slightly higher dosage, for two or three months, often produces lasting relief.

Addendum

The case histories and the various maneuvers described above may lend a deceptive aura of oversimplicity to the actual procedures involved. Some of the mechanistic procedures and precise clinical strategies may even suggest a computerized form of sex without love. Two points should therefore be emphasized:

1. It is hoped that persons who administer the techniques outlined in this chapter will be endowed with sufficient warmth, wit, and wisdom to operate within a context of empathy, sincerity, and flexibility.

2. It is erroneous to assume that spontaneity, affection, tenderness, and

love are undermined by recognizing the existence and importance of various mechanisms. Scientific psychology is, in fact, only possible if lawful mechanisms of behavior can be identified.

In summary, the purpose of this chapter is to call attention to a variety of methods which have proved highly effective in overcoming many sexual inadequacies. The practitioner well-versed in these procedures can, with confidence, offer a positive prognosis in most instances of frigidity and impotence.

CHAPTER 8
COGNITIVE
RESTRUCTURING

Nearly all therapeutic methods applied to human beings probably result in cognitive changes. It is the complexity of his cerebral cortex which sets man apart from the rest of the animal kingdom. In terms of cortical structures his closest rival is said to be the dolphin. Dolphins evidently communicate with one another by sounds and signals which are perhaps the nearest counterpart to the miracle of speech in man, but while numerous parallels can be drawn between the behavior of humans and animals, the hazards of extrapolating from one level to the other should constantly be remembered. Ethologists, for instance, cannot be expected to shed light on those aspects of behavior which are "exclusively human." Wolpe (1967), in emphasizing the parallels between the neurotic behavior of animals and men, stresses that the differences between them are purely a matter of "complexity." But the greatest danger lies in leaping from the simple to the complex, "for it is precisely what is not in the simple system that may constitute the essential character of the complex [Boulding, 1968, p. 85]." Harlow (1953) has commented that "the results from the investigation of simple behavior may be very informative about even simpler behavior but very seldom are they informative about behavior of greater complexity."

Speech and symbolic processes add an entirely different dimension to man's otherwise animal behavior. When does a quantitative difference become qualitative? As Boulding (1968) has pointed out, many parallels may be drawn between automobiles and jet planes. They both have the same primary function—rapid transportation. The different dimension, *flight* is purely a product of structural complexity. Even a wheelbarrow may have elements in common with a rocket (e.g., plastics and metals) but wheelbarrows and cars cannot teach us anything about flight. As long as we remain grounded, there is much to be learned from wheels and wheelbarrows, just as there is much to be learned from animals as long as we stay speechless.

Is it not obvious that B. F. Skinner's ingenious operant conditioning principles have had the greatest clinical effects on people who have lost, or never had, the capacity to speak and reason abstractly? Amaurotic idiots, drooling saliva, smearing and eating excreta, and formerly confined to back wards, can be shaped and conditioned to follow habits of cleanliness and to perform simple but useful tasks. Echolalic children can be taught to communicate. The bizarre behaviors of certain chronic schizophrenics can be modified or eliminated, all through the direct application of reinforcement contingencies formulated in animal laboratories (e.g., Ayllon & Azrin, 1965; Lindsley, 1956). But to argue, as one of my colleagues recently did, that people who withstand torture for the sake of an ideal are in all essential respects the same as animals who endure electric shocks to receive a reward, seems to me an incredible instance of fallacious reductionism. Ellis (1962, p. 16) has stressed that a human being, unlike an animal "can be rewarded or punished by his *own* thinking, even when this thinking is largely divorced from outside reinforcements and penalties." Stated boldly, the point at issue is that "thinking behavior" transcends data derived from reflexology. Many disorders of language and thought must be dealt with in their own right and at their own level. "We might summarize the situation by stating that while animal experiments cannot themselves confirm hypotheses about human behavior, their usefulness in clarifying problems makes them valuable as a research tactic (Maher, 1966, p. 107)."

The bulk of therapeutic endeavors may be said to center around the correction of misconceptions. The people who consult us tend to view innocuous events as extremely noxious, and may disregard objectively noxious situations. Therapy often strives to show people how to separate subjective from objective dangers. Thereafter, the emphasis is on avoiding or coping with objectively hazardous events while ignoring the innocuous situations. There are many means toward these single ends.

It is fatuous to ask whether a change in cognition leads to a change in behavior or vice versa. "Insight" may often *precede* an observable behavior change; at other times, insight clearly *follows* an individual's changed behavior. A good case in point concerning the importance of insight is born out by a thirty-two-year-old man who had unsuccessfully been treated for impotence by a well-known behavior therapist. He was extremely despondent by the time he consulted me as he had entered his previous course of behavior therapy with great optimism, only to have his hopes dashed by the complete failure of desensitization and graded sexual practices. After the initial interview it was evident that the patient had numerous gaps in his self-knowledge, and I was able to offer hope that "cognitive restructuring" might overcome his sexual difficulties. It required several months of therapy for the patient to assimilate certain facts about himself. He began to recognize his hostility toward his mother—a feeling he had emphatically denied at the commencement of therapy. He began to perceive many connections between his feelings toward his mother and his attitude toward his wife. After recognizing his hostility he was able to oppose numerous irrational generalizations by employing prescribed sentences. "It is crazy to think that all women are like my mother." "Why should I punish my wife for my mother's misdeeds?" He came to appreciate the manner in which his sexual needs were linked to his dependency needs. He reported a fantasy of being "enslaved and owned" by a woman through craving for her sexual favors. He expressed the belief that, "a sex addict is worse than a heroin addict" which, in turn, unlocked a chain of feelings and ideas to the effect that sexual indulgence would indubitably weaken his constitution. The strange link between postorgasmic lassitude and the decrepitude he associated with prolonged drug addiction became the focus of considerable therapeutic attention. Can a man be potent if sexual indulgence brings to the fore his hatred toward his mother, fears of enslavement, negative associations with drug addiction, and the aftermath of venereal disease? It was necessary to change the patient's perceptions in each of these areas before his sexual performance was considered normal by his wife and himself.

Conversely, it has been well-documented that a change in behavior can lead to insight and produce an entire sequence of different perceptions (e.g., Taylor, 1964). "Since following your advice and standing up for my rights I see the whole world differently." "It was only when I stopped crying out for help that I came to terms with myself as an adult and saw what my family was doing to me." "I first had to *do* those things before I realized their true significance." After laboriously, but successfully, desensitizing a fearful concert pianist to public performances, he said, "I now *realize* that before your treatment I failed to separate my music from my own being. The desensitization made me *aware* of the fact that a poor performance would not end my life or my career."

All forms of psychotherapy, including behavior therapy, try to teach people to think, feel, and act differently. Cognitive, affective, and overt response patterns are not separate units but interactive processes which constitute *behavior* in its broadest sense. The notion that emotional states are a function of the autonomic nervous system and originate solely in subcortical or hypothalamic brain centers (Wolpe, 1958) is open to dispute. This notion was questioned many years ago by Bousfield and Orbison (1952) and more recently in the two-volume study of emotions by Magda Arnold (1960). The so-called "schism" between thoughts and feelings has been questioned. Rokeach (1960) has claimed that "every emotion has its cognitive counterpart, and every cognition its emotional counterpart." Over the past fifteen years, Albert Ellis has evolved and practiced a system of therapy called "rational-emotive psychotherapy," which bases most of its methods upon the overlapping of reason and emotion and which views behavior as a "sensing-moving-thinking-emotion complex [Ellis, 1962]." Much of this chapter is based upon rational-emotive psychotherapy and some additional notions and observations of my own.

In reviewing my case notes over the past decade, I find that several themes emerge repeatedly and that many hours each week have been spent emphasizing identical points to dissimilar people. Of course, in keeping with the personalistic notions already covered in preceding chapters, the different ways in which identical points are impressed upon a variety of people constitute the essence of clinical skill. Let us dwell on some of these recurrent themes.

Dichotomous Reasoning

There is a widespread proclivity to divide everything into two opposite forces—good versus evil, black versus white, right versus wrong—and to avoid the gray areas or middle ground. Politicians most often fall into this trap with their tacit, and sometimes blatant, insistence that "Those who are not for us are against us!" Kelly (1955) has ascribed a dichotomous quality to all human thinking and has devised tests based upon perceived opposites to see how people structure their world and the roles they need to play. But what Hayakawa (1964) terms the "two-valued orientation" seems to be a factor in many areas of miscommunication and emotional suffering. As an antidote, Hayakawa advises one to attach a *truth value* to every statement. Instead of considering any statement as "true" or "false" one should assume that its "tentative truth value" stands somewhere between 0 and 100 percent. Consider a fairly typical domestic battle which can only exist between people who think in all-or-none terms.

> *Wife:* You're always criticizing me, always putting me down, and always finding fault with everything I do. I never do anything right as far as you're concerned.
>
> *Husband:* That's not true. (Instead of entirely disagreeing with her, even a facetious response such as, "Would you say I do this to you more or less than 67 percent of the time?" may expose the basic fallacies in her argument and open more constructive channels of communication.)
>
> *Wife:* Yes it is.

> *Husband:*   No it's not.
>
> *Wife:*   See, there you go again, always disagreeing with me.
>
> *Husband:*   I'm not disagreeing with you.
>
> *Wife:*   Oh yes you are.
>
> *Husband:*   No, I'm not.
>
> *Wife:*   So then you admit that you always find fault with me.

These marital games often go further than they were intended to and may herald more serious problems. Most marital clashes seem to hinge on some area of dichotomous reasoning. Couples often adopt opposite positions on money, sex, birth control, relatives, alcohol, table manners, dress, the "right" way to discipline children, and so on ad infinitum.

Rokeach (1960) in *The Open and Closed Mind* refers to the things a person believes in as that person's "belief system" and to the things that person does not believe in as his "disbelief system." (For example, to a practicing Jew, Judaism is his belief system and Catholicism, Protestantism, Hinduism, and so on is his disbelief system. Anxious, frightened, and insecure people cling tenaciously to their belief systems and close their minds to all favorable information about their disbelief systems. Thus, we may meet people who find absolutely no virtues in socialism, or capitalism, or television, or legalized abortion, or in psychoanalysis. I have found it extremely helpful to assign to some of my patients the task of discovering some facts and accurate information about their very strong disbelief systems. When they become more open minded, it is often impressive to observe the ensuing reduction in their overall tension and anxiety.

Overgeneralization

Closely allied to problems of dichotomous reasoning are those which stem from overgeneralization. The dichotomous reasoner sees individual doctors, policemen, priests, lawyers, teachers, etc., as either good or

bad. The person who overgeneralizes sees *all* women drivers as dangerous, *all* salesmen as crooks, *all* politicians as corrupt, and *all* insurance
companies as unreliable. "Julie let me down so badly that I'll never trust
another woman as long as I live!" "All men are the same!" "Never trust
anyone who wears striped shirts; Arthur always wore striped shirts and
you know what he did to me!"

The other side of the coin consists of false positive overgeneral-
izations which can produce dismay or disillusionment when events run
counter to these ideals. "All psychiatrists are warm, empathic, and
open." "All policemen are honest." "All clergymen are kind and trustworthy." "All mothers love their children." "Black people can always
trust their soul brothers." "Doctors really do the best for their patients."

There is a wealth of literature on the subject of prejudice which
pertains to problems of overgeneralization. It may be sufficient for present
purposes to point out that in therapy, one of the best ways of overcoming prejudice, overgeneralization, and dichotomous reasoning is to constantly emphasize that *hardly anything is quite certain but is only probable to a greater or lesser degree.* Bertrand Russell (1962, p. 83) has
stated, "Not to be absolutely certain is, I think, one of the essential
things in rationality."

Excessive Reliance on Other People's Judgement

Overconcern about public opinion is one of the most widespread
maladies. Unfortunately, in raising their children, too many mothers
employ public shame as a controlling device. "What will other people
think of you?" "What will the neighbors say?" "Wait until your friends
find out what you are really like." In this way, criticism becomes something to be dreaded and avoided at all costs. At the same time, other
people's opinions and judgments are invested with tremendous value.
I point out to my insecure patients who are anxious to please everybody
all of the time that this is simply impossible. "There are some people
who are bound to dislike you no matter how hard you try to please
them." It sometimes helps to emphasize that many personal likes and
dislikes are based upon irrational factors. "Some people may dislike you
simply because you remind them of someone whom they have good reason to dislike. You may just happen to resemble someone who was really

nasty to them." Nevertheless, many of my patients constantly indulge in the following illogical sequence of ideas: "Jones dislikes me. This proves there is something wrong with me." When my patients believe that "this probably means there is something wrong with Jones because I have never done him any harm," they seldom require further treatment.

There is a crucial difference between a person who says, "I am stupid," and someone who says, "I have done many stupid things." A smart or basically nonstupid individual is capable of doing some stupid things. A basically honest person may be dishonest on occasion. A successful person may nevertheless meet with certain failures. These self-evident truths sometimes have to be emphatically impressed upon people in therapy. "Yes I agree that you did a foolish thing, but that does not make you a fool." "Okay, if you want a value judgment, I would say that you did a shocking thing fourteen years ago. That is *in the past*. What does it prove about you *today*?"

It is helpful to make one's patients fully aware of the differences between reports and judgments. "I am a housewife." This is a report. "I am *only* a housewife." This is a judgment. On closer examination, the judgment may proceed as follows: "I should have gone to college and taken up a profession. It is a disgrace that I failed to do so. It is shameful that I am what I am. Most people look down on housewives." Thus, people apologize for their jobs, their cars, their homes, their wives and children; they are ashamed of their parents, their religion, their appearance, and their personal tastes. Insecure people uncritically accept other people's standards and judgments. Every effort should be made to train one's patients to be nonjudgmental toward themselves and toward others as far as this is humanly possible. I recall a dialogue with a patient that went something like this:

> *Patient:* I just feel so deeply ashamed. It's such a disgrace.
>
> *Therapist:* What are you referring to?
>
> *Patient:* To the fact that I lost my business and let those crooks cheat me out of my money.
>
> *Therapist:* I can see that anyone would have regrets but why do you feel so ashamed about it?
>
> *Patient:* Well, my whole family thinks I'm an idiot.
>
> *Therapist:* So do you have to agree with them?

    Patient: I shouldn't have been taken in like that.

    Therapist: Why shouldn't you have been taken in? You trusted them.

    Patient: That proves how stupid I am.

    Therapist: Maybe that proves that you were too trusting. What have you learned from that experience?

    Patient: To be more careful in the future.

    Therapist: Excellent. That experience should tell you to be more careful, but it should not end up in the dead-end idea that you are a shame and a disgrace to your family.

Enculturation and Oversocialization

Emotional suffering is often a consequence of cultural enslavement. Many people regard cultural values as absolutes and have never paused to consider their relativity. They are entirely molded by the culture and assimilate all its contradictions. Conventionality is seen as extremely important rather than superficial, and folkways and mores are considered anything but perfunctory. Thus, millions of people are capable of justifying bloody warfare but not masturbation or birth control. If therapy is to have any enduring value, it should communicate the full meaning of social change and heighten one's concern with culture improvement. When unhappiness is clearly the outcome of passivity and an uncritical yielding to cultural shaping, the therapist's task is to train the person to gain sufficient detachment necessary to make more or less independent decisions. In this regard, Shakespeare's quotation from Hamlet has often been cited: *"There is nothing either good or bad but thinking makes it so."*

    A number of therapeutic methods may prove effective in freeing people from unnecessary taboos and redundant guilt feelings. A brief survey of some anthropological and sociological facts often highlights the relativity and arbitrariness of ancient and modern customs and beliefs. An astonishing number of people are unaware that few, if any, taboos cut across all cultures. Other people are ignorant of the fact that social change, despite its generally slow and tedious evolutionary process, nevertheless exists, and that in time many "don'ts" will become "dos" and vice versa. It is useful to compare the dos and dont's between different cultures. One may then ask, "Is any one set of values necessarily more correct or better than another?" This didactic emphasis often permits people to recognize the fatuity of most of their own beliefs.

Another method which often liberates people from orthodox enculturation may be termed "The Two-peach Parable." This method is perhaps best illustrated within the context of an actual clinical example.

Case Illustration. A thirty-two-year-old man was extremely guilt-ridden over an extramarital affair which had lasted approximately three months and which had terminated a year before consulting me. Although we had examined the circumstances surrounding his need for another woman at the time, and although he came to appreciate the fact that his extramarital liaison had strengthened his marriage, he nevertheless remained guilt-ridden because he had "sinned in the eyes of God." At this stage "The Two-peach Parable" appeared to be the method of choice:

"Let me tell you a little story and see whether you can apply the moral of this story to your own situation. Once upon a time there was a primitive island community. This little community was very poor and very simple. In good years there was just sufficient food to go around. Most of the time it was not unusual for many people to go hungry. The wise old men of this community got together and made many rules. These regulations were necessary for the survival of the community. One of these rules went as follows: *When thou goest into the orchard, thou shalt have one peach and one peach only.* The reason for this was simply that the limited food supply made it imperative to impose restrictions on the amount of food consumed by any one individual. If you went into the orchard and ate two peaches, you would be depriving someone else of his right to a peach, and through your gluttony and inconsideration his belly would be empty and he would go hungry. So it was incumbent upon you to honor the one-peach rule in any twenty-four-hour period. 'Thou shalt have one peach and one peach only.'

"Many years later, this little community learns about modern methods of cultivation and farming, and these new agricultural methods produce surplus food and especially an overabundance of peaches. Peaches now fall off the trees and rot on the ground. Despite the plethora of peaches, the ancient rule remains, 'Thou shalt have one peach and one peach only.' This rule, passed down from one generation to the next, like many other rules, fails to keep pace with the times. Some people, especially children, may ask. 'But why can't we have more than one peach?' They may be told not to question the law. They may be told, 'What was right for our great-grandfathers is right for us.' 'If you eat more than one peach you will go blind.' They may even be told, 'If you pick more than one peach at a time your arm will fall off.' 'It is the will of God.' Thus, in this community, as in most other communities, what was once a sensible and pragmatic rule has become part of the community's mysticism and superstition.

"Now if we examine the behavior of the people in this community, we will find several distinct patterns. There will be those who adhere religiously to the one-peach rule and would never deviate from it. Some of them would dearly love to have more than one peach at a time, but they wouldn't dare. Others among them are not at all fond of peaches to begin with, and so they easily uphold the law. Those who are not so fond of peaches, or are perhaps too old to eat them with relish, are likely to be in favor of meting out the most severe punishment to all violators of the one peach rule.

"Other people may have two or more peaches and feel guilty. If they continue feeling guilty each time they take their second peach, or each time they think back to past episodes of indulgence, they are probably best advised to return to and observe the one-peach custom or law.

"Then there are those who have deduced that there is no valid reason whatsoever for upholding the one-peach dictum. They consume two or more peaches at a time with neither guilt nor remorse. The more enterprising and courageous members of this group may even endeavor to introduce social reform. In this community, the people may eventually become so enlightened that they will obtain blessings from their elders to bottle and can peaches for daily use through all seasons."

In applying this parable to issues involving monogamy and marital fidelity, it is hoped that the allegorical content will not be taken literally! In the case of the guilt-ridden thirty-two-year-old ex-adulterer, as in many other cases, the parable enabled him to gain a somewhat more objective perspective concerning his own misdemeanor. As usual, the conversation turned to the general area of morality, with special reference to many of the antiquated taboos of our society. The inevitable conclusion was that the only moral precept worth upholding is that:

You are entitled to do, think, and feel whatsoever you please provided no one gets harmed in the process. It should be clearly noted that immediately upon hearing the patient's story of guilt and remorse over his extramarital affair, I had endeavored to impart the "no harm done— no need for guilt" philosophy. As often happens, the patient remained unreceptive to this notion until the "parable technique" was applied. He then concluded, "Basically, I guess I'm a one-peach man. . . . But I agree that I don't have to keep on giving myself a hard time about those few months when I sometimes ate two peaches a day."

It is my impression that the most effective therapists have a rich fund of parables, metaphors, and analogies and tend to cite examples and stories from past cases, from learned men, and from their own experiences in living.

A procedure termed *After the Holocaust* also has the effect of reducing guilt and often awakens some awareness of areas in which culture change may be necessary and desirable. This method is also recommended for people who seem to suffer as a result of too literal and rigid an adherence to narrow religious values and beliefs.

> *Therapist:* I want you to imagine that everyone has been wiped off the face of the earth except for a few dozen people. You and I are among those who have been spared and we are placed in charge of drawing up a new code of morals and ethics for ourselves and for future generations. Get the picture?
>
> *Patient:* Like "Noah's Ark Revisited"?
>
> *Therapist:* Right! Or like "After the Holocaust." Anyhow, we have an enormous responsibility. As such, we both have equal say, and for any rule to become effective we both have to agree 100 percent.
>
> *Patient:* What happens if we can't agree?
>
> *Therapist:* In that case, you and I would have to debate the point and keep at it until some compromise was reached which pretty much pleased us both.
>
> *Patient:* I wouldn't know where to start.

Therapist: Well, let's pretend we're in the situation. Why not start with God? Now remember that we want to build a better world. Or perhaps you disagree and feel that before the bomb, or whatever it was that destroyed the world, our society and civilization was not "sick"?

Patient: Oh, it was "sick" for sure.

Therapist: Okay, so we want to build a completely new and better world from scratch. Now, what do we tell the people about God? Should we depict God as a picayune being who is likely to seek revenge on people and their children and their children's children? Of course, if I alone was in charge of the situation, I would opt for atheism, but since you have an equal vote, I imagine that we would have to reach a compromise.

Patient: How about a God of Love?

Therapist: Sounds great. But would your God demand that we erect temples or churches, that we pray regularly, that we observe commandments and that we don't sin?

Patient: Well, if we didn't set down certain rules people would just murder each other and become like wild animals.

Therapist: Maybe and maybe not. But could we not train our people to respect human dignity and property, to act out of love and compassion, without creating a deity to watch over them?

Patient: I think there is a God. Call it Nature if you like. But there is some Divine force.

Therapist: Just tell me if your "Divine Force" will lay down rules about birth control, sexual intercourse, and dozens of petty "dos" and "don'ts" in all other areas of behavior?

Patient: Oh, gosh! I don't know. I've never thought about

it this way. I mean, suddenly you're asking me
to examine and maybe revise my whole thinking.

Therapist: That's exactly what I'm asking you to do.

After entering the postholocaust fantasy, the ensuing discussion
usually enables patient and therapist to examine the range of rules which
are necessary for governing human conduct. Spurious values which
are a burden and serve no useful purpose become identified and can be
debated. It is often doubly helpful to narrate "The Two-peach Parable"
and then to fantasize "After the Holocaust." The end result again is
to achieve a fitting detachment from arbitrary regulations which only
limit human happiness and mar the pursuit of pleasure.

Thoughts and Feelings

People often remark, "I understand and accept certain things intellect-
ually but not emotionally." Upon closer examination it may be discovered that they are in fact merely verbalizing certain thoughts that
they do not fully accept or believe. An intelligent social worker who had
been raised in an extremely narrow-minded home claimed that, "Intel-
lectually I am fully aware that there's nothing wrong with kissing and
necking, but every time I do anything like that I, nevertheless, get consumed by guilt." Is it possible for someone to be *fully aware* that something is irrational and still react irrationally? Or do people just say that
they are in complete accord with an idea when they are merely mouthing
the correct words with basic disbelief? "I realize that I shouldn't get
upset when my mother yells at me. After all, she's a sick woman. But
every time it happens I get up-tight, right here in the stomach." Is this
an example of a conditioned autonomic response devoid of any significant intellectual or cognitive referents? Or is it more likely that, upon
closer examination, the person is telling himself something along the
following lines: "I've never had proper and sufficient maternal love and
it's awful to be yelled at by someone who should know better!" One may
ask which comes first: the cognition or the affect? Beck (1967) indicated on the basis of clinical and experimental findings that depressed
and anxious feelings often *follow* cognitive processes. He cited several

instances bearing out the intimate relationship between patients' conceptualizations and consequent feelings of depression.

Albert Ellis has emphasized that several Greek and Roman philosophers as well as ancient Buddhist thinkers had perceived the close connections between reason and emotion or between thoughts-perceptions/feelings-emotions several thousand years ago. The essence of the process may be captured by simple aphorisms. "As you think so shall you feel." "If you are not feeling well you are probably not thinking right." "'Tis but saying so makes it so." This is in keeping with the collapse of behavioristic S-R theories which tried to bypass anything "mental" but finally had to be modified to account for those events which occur between the input of a stimulus and the emission of an overt response. Thus, S-O-R theories gained prominence (a *stimulus* impinges on a unique *organism* which then emits a *response*). The conception of stimulus-response bonds has given way to a mediation model. The rational-emotive approach, like Tolman's and Lewin's models may be conceptualized as a S-CM-R Model (stimulus→ cognitive map→ response). Ellis (1962) refers to it as "the ABC theory of personality and of emotional disturbance," and stresses that it is not the events at point A that cause the reaction at point C, but rather the thoughts at point B about what occurs at A. He noted that almost two thousand years ago, the Stoic philosopher Epictetus wrote: "Men are disturbed not by things, but by the views which they take of them."

Any number of clinical examples may be cited to clarify the ABC philosophy, but let us take one very typical case in point. A young man looks downcast and unhappy. We may ask, "Why are you so miserable?" (Let us call this point C. We are asking, "What caused C?") He replies, "Because I was rejected by my girl friend." (He says in effect, "I am C because of A." He maintains that the rejection caused the depression.) The majority of people make the same error of leaping from A to C, completely forgetting that it is *B* which leads to C. And what is B? It is the person's perception of A, his subjective interpretation of A, the things he tells himself about A. Rejection (A) cannot cause depression (C). Someone else may be rejected (A) and become *elated* (C). To say, "I am elated because I was rejected" sounds irrational and one may inquire by what process rejection can lead to elation—in other words, what is happening at point B? But people often fail to see that it is just as irrational to conclude that depression is caused by rejection, without asking, "What is the person telling himself at B?" In the case of the elated young man, point B might unfold along the following lines: "At last I am free of a relationship that was a drag and an inconvenience. I didn't want to reject her because she is basically a very decent person and she was dependent on me, but now that she is the rejector, I can withdraw gracefully and develop a new and better relationship with someone else." The depressed young man would be telling himself something quite different at point B, "It is awful to be rejected. I can't stand it and it shouldn't happen to me. It proves that I am not a man, that I am unattractive, and that I am a failure." Of course, it proves nothing of the sort, and this might be the first illogical conclusion to bring to his attention in an endeavor to change B and thereby constructively alter C.

But it can be argued that if any young man is rejected by someone whom he loves very deeply, it is "normal" for him to be upset. Indeed, a sensitive and feeling person who is nevertheless a rational human being, may reason at point B as follows: "I am sad that Betty Lou rejected me, because I enjoyed being with her and I will miss her stimulating company. I had hoped that we would be able to develop a mutual love bond, but it seems as though the relationship was one-sided. This is unfortunate, but it certainly is not the end of the world." Thus, rejection leads this young man to tell himself certain things about the situation that results in feelings of "normal sadness" rather than "abnormal depression," which as Beck (1967) has shown, usually contains the non sequitur "therefore, I am worthless."

Rational Imagery

The foregoing lends itself to the use of a procedure which may be termed *rational imagery*. Whenever a person feels extremely upset (angry, anxious, or depressed) he should imagine himself confronting a group of his peers (objective onlookers) with a question: "What would you consider a reasonable response under the circumstances?" Let us say that a man is fired from his job. His immediate reaction, based on years of irrational propaganda, is to feel defeated and humiliated. In the past he would usually reach for a bottle and drink himself into a stupor. He had to find relief from his biting and destructive thoughts at point B, acquired no doubt from his parents and associates who taught him to accept the warped and irrational values. "I'll never amount to anything. I'm just no good. I'm a worthless slob. I can't do anything right. I'm just a total failure. I can't stand it. I wish I were dead. How can I face people now? What will everyone think of me?" Instead of reaching for the bourbon, he carries out his therapist's advice and conjures up an image of "rational observers" (or one "rational observer") with whom he has the following sort of dialogue:

Patient: Is it irrational to feel upset about losing my job?

Observer: No, there are a number of inherent frustrations about which you probably can't help telling yourself some realistically negative things. So to feel "rather frustrated" under the circumstances is a logical reaction. But you feel more than "rather frustrated." Look at yourself. To feel so dreadful about it surely means that you are compounding the facts with irrational assumptions.

Patient: Losing one's job is more than "rather frustrating."

Observer: Why? Is it a catastrophe? Would you say that losing one's job is worse than losing an eye?

Patient: Losing an eye is far worse.

Observer: But your grief and anguish seemed to fit the situation of someone who had just lost both eyes, 50 percent of his hearing, plus an arm and a leg, and who was in acute physical agony from his festering wounds.

Patient: Well, at least he'd have everyone's sympathy, whereas everyone will know that I am a failure.

Observer: It sounds as though you want to be pitied? However, are you a total failure or have you merely failed in a few specific situations?

Patient: Well, it is very upsetting.

> *Observer:*   *It* is not so upsetting. *You* are upsetting yourself.
>
> *Patient:*   So then what would be a rational course of action?
>
> *Observer:*   First, start looking for another job. Second, try to determine what acts of omission or commission caused you to lose your last job. Third, try to correct these errors in future. And above all, stop telling yourself that because you are a fallible human being this means that you are worthless, useless, and a complete failure.

When the basic assumptions of rational-emotive therapy have been explained to my patients, and after they have read and understood the contents of Ellis and Harpers' (1961) *Guide to Rational Living*, I often ask my patients to enact these dialogues so that I can help them parse any residual irrational assumptions. We usually record their dialogues on tape, listen to the playbacks, and try to improve upon the quality of the various rational self-corrections. Most of the patients with whom I have employed this method report that it is most helpful. A patient who had made no progress with desensitization methods responded very rapidly to rational imagery. He stated, "Now, whenever I become upset over something, I first ask myself if I am responding rationally. I picture myself talking to you and I can almost hear you pointing out the distortions in my reasoning. I soon see how *I* may still tend to exaggerate and magnify things. As soon as I spot the magnification I say 'Stop magnifying!' and within minutes I feel quite calm and relaxed.... Of course, these days it takes a lot more than it used to before I even start feeling anxious."

Rational Points of Emphasis

Our irrational society indoctrinates all of us with numerous superstitions, prejudices, and senseless notions. Following Ellis (1962) there are eleven specific rational judgments that need to be strongly emphasized.

1. *It is not a dire necessity for an adult to receive love or approval from* *all significant others.* The emphasis here is on teaching people to separate that which would be *desirable* from that which is *necessary.*

2. *It would be better not to determine self-worth by external competence, adequacy, and achievement.* The difference must be emphasized between striving for various accomplishments which bring pleasures and rewards, and compulsively driving oneself to excell for the sake of excelling.

3. *Wrongdoers ought not to be blamed or punished and labeled "bad," "wicked," or "villainous."* Criminal and antisocial acts are committed out of ignorance, stupidity, or emotional disturbance. While protective measures must be adopted (e.g., incarceration), the stress should be upon trying to correct *past* errors so that future responses will be more prosocial. The same applies to *self-blame* which should be replaced by a full acceptance of the fact that one is fallible, followed by a sincere endeavor to become less fallible.

4. *It would be better not to catastrophize when things are not the way one would very much like them to be.* Frustrating circumstances obviously lead to feelings of frustration, but too many people become angry or depressed over the fact that they feel frustrated, and end up thoroughly miserable.

5. *Nearly all instances of unhappiness are due to internal thoughts rather than external events.* It is seldom other people or external events that cause unhappiness. People define various annoyances or dangers as "very upsetting" and then proceed to make themselves "very upset."

6. *Worrying about dangers and dwelling on the possibility of dreaded events will not ward off the feared situations.* It is well known that the anticipation of a dreaded event is often worse than the actual event itself. One's patients often need to learn this truism, as well as the fact that worrying serves no prophylactic purpose.

7. *Constantly taking the "easy" way out by avoiding difficulties and responsibilities usually leads to indolence, fear, and boredom.* The emphasis is upon setting a middle course between those individuals who are overdisciplined and are too hard on themselves (usually a sign of guilt and self-punishment), and those who avoid making decisions and run away from challenges. "Drop-outs" usually suffer from needless anxiety or rebellion.

8. *Everyone should strive to achieve a healthy independence instead* *of leaning upon and relying on someone stronger than oneself.* To aim for complete independence is both unrealistic and undesirable, as we are all somewhat interdependent in this complex society. But there is a vast difference between parasitic dependency and rational patterns of togetherness, friendship, and cooperation.

9. *Everyone's past history has inevitably influenced his present behavior but need not keep on directing and affecting it.* It may be *difficult* to break away from one's past experiences and set a new and different course through life, but to state that this task is *impossible* merely results in a chronic give-up reaction.

10. *There is no value in becoming upset over other people's problems and disturbances.* To provide constructive advice and loving help to others is very different from becoming terribly upset for them or over them, and thereby hoping that this will magically improve matters.

11. *Any quest for perfection or absolute control over the exigencies of life is likely to produce panic and inefficiency.* To err is human because people are fallible. The world is one of probability and chance. It is important to encourage people to learn from their wrong or mediocre decisions instead of waiting for "perfect" solutions which probably do not exist. Many unfortunate people drift from psychiatrist to psychiatrist, from one church to another, and from movement to movement looking for "the answer."

The application of rational-emotive psychotherapy is not a mere intellectual exercise. Reading, understanding, and agreeing with the tenets of rational living is but the initial or preparatory phase of incorporation and change. Thereafter, the therapist helps the patient to discover and ferret out his own self-defeating sentences and shows him how to substitute constructive and sensible conclusions. The intention is for the patient to learn to do so on his own. As Ullmann and Krasner (1969, p. 314) point out, "the therapist may punish the emission of irrational labels by arguing against them, by showing that they are foolish, and in other ways making the verbalization of these ideas itself a characteristic of being 'bad.' At the same time, the therapist reinforces the emission of different evaluations of situations." The closing phases of cognitive restructuring are illustrated in the following therapeutic excerpt:

Patient: So I became upset when my father disagreed with me and I found myself doubting.

Therapist: What were you really telling yourself?

Patient: I'm not sure.

Therapist: Let me guess. I would say that your internal sentence went something like this: "Authority is always right and should never be challenged."

Patient: That could be it. My dad always said that he knows best and that we should not question his opinions or judgments.

Therapist: Okay, fine. Now think over the argument again, only this time remember that we never bow to authority but we always examine the evidence, no matter how dependable and knowledgeable the source of the evidence may be. What conclusions do you arrive at?

Patient: That I was right and he was wrong. But he has a way of throwing his weight around that undermines my confidence. There's another irrational sentence in there somewhere, and I haven't been able to find it. I wish I could identify it. What do you think?

Therapist: Well, tell me what else went on during the discussion?

Patient: I began to buckle, you know. I mean, I just felt like a kid again. Is that what you mean?

Therapist: What else did he do or say?

Patient: I don't remember. I mean he got nasty all right and that's maybe when I kind of gave in.

Therapist: What do you mean when you say "he got nasty"?

Patient: He started cursing at me. Like, I mean, you know, putting me down.

Therapist: Maybe that's the missing sentence.

Patient: What?

> *Therapist:*   *Words can hurt me.*
>
> *Patient:*   "Words can hurt me." Yeah! I think that's it. Of course, I said to myself that being cursed was like being whipped. I let them hurt.... No I *made* them hurt me. Yeah! I'll watch out for that from now on. He sure as hell didn't use sticks and stones to break my bones.

The Importance of Anticipatory Processes

The fundamental postulate underlying Kelly's (1955) elaborate theory of personal constructs is that: "A person's processes are psychologically channelized by the ways in which he anticipates events." In other words, an individual's behavior is governed by his own predictions. The rejected lover who predicts that he will never be able to find anyone to replace his beloved, presents an entirely different clinical picture from the distraught lover who predicts that, in good time, an adequate replacement will be found. In short, therapy should endeavor to imbue our patients with realistically positive anticipations.

This ties in with the evidence presented by Frank (1961) that procedures which arouse hope may have curative power in themselves. Providing encouragement and mobilizing the patient's expectation of help is crucial. A useful ancillary technique in this regard is to have the patient regularly practicing imagery in which he clearly sees himself responding in a nonneurotic manner.

The anticipation of threat and the confrontation with harm are key variables in the sophisticated theory of psychological stress presented by Richard Lazarus (1966). As Lazarus clearly demonstrates, threat involves some *anticipation* of future harm and is dependent on various perceptions, memories, judgments, and similar cognitions. Comprehensive therapy implies that patients will learn to overcome or cope with ongoing harmful events while, at the same time, learning to deal with threatening circumstances (i.e., potentially harmful events). As Richard Lazarus points out, therapy should aim to increase an individual's *counterharm resources*. Indeed, all the methods described in this book are assumed to reduce vulnerability to threat and facilitate healthy or adaptive forms of coping.

CHAPTER 9
GROUP
METHODS

The age of the group is upon us. Throughout the nation people are meeting and encountering themselves and each other in various group settings. From "growth centers" to "laboratories in communication," minithons, marathons, T-groups, and sensitivity training programs abound. In a potpourri of philosophy, psychology, and mysticism, the participants go through a gamut of experiences limited only by the constraints of the group leader's imagination. The quest is to place people in touch with their feelings, and to achieve "self-realization." The most enterprising leaders now favor nude encounters with much sensual rather than sexual massaging, hugging, stroking, and kissing, offset by exercises in meditation and imagery. Mixed bathing in body-temperature water is also popular and is said to generate a mystical, regressive, or religious experience which unfetters deep-seated inhibitions.

Group processes have become big business for some, a religion or subcultural way of life for others. The so-called "growth movement" or "human potential movement" is supposed to provide personal fulfillment in place of dejection, with creativity and social togetherness filling the voids of apathy, alienation, loneliness, boredom, and disillusionment. Nearly all the methods employed—fatigue, heightened anxiety, the presence of a guru, monotonous stimuli, observation of others, mass attacks, and persuasion—are familiar to students of religious conversion and brainwashing (Sargant, 1957; Frank, 1961). And, not unlike reports from Lourdes, miraclelike changes are sometimes witnessed. As might also be expected, it is not uncommon for some people to emerge badly sensitized. Encounter-group victims suffering from "fallout" as the result of violent emotional explosions have almost become a new clinical entity. In California, I was once consulted by eight persons in one week. This could be avoided by a more careful selection of participants. Within the personalistic philosophy discussed in the earlier chapters of this book, I have referred selected patients for marathon encounters, feeling fairly certain that open confrontations and subtle (or not so subtle) coercive procedures would be beneficial for them. Most of these people seemed to derive distinct therapeutic gains. On the other hand, I have patients for whom an encounter group would be as helpful as surgery without suturing. Jaffe and Scherl (1969) have reported on psychotic reactions precipitated by T-group experiences.

It is my impression that for most people, group encounters produce a short-lived *high* or state of euphoria. At first, a single prolonged encounter or sensitivity training session was considered sufficient to promote long-term change. Thereafter, repeat sessions were deemed necessary. Although an attempt to provide follow-up data on the (hopefully) lasting effects of group encounters is underway, long-term outcome information is at best fragmentary. We need evidence that the changes observed during group encounters transfer to the individuals' daily encounters outside of the group, that the participants become generally freer, more authentic, more expressive, less defensive, and less vulnerable human beings. One of the most serious concerns in this regard is how to differentiate between expert imitations of authenticity, or simulated sincerity, and the genuine article.

One of the prime examples of phony unphoniness is a current patient of mine, a veteran of more than 1,200 hours of sensitivity training and marathon encounters. He has learned how to appear honest, sincere, genuine, empathic, and turned-on. He knows how to "unmask," "express gut feelings," and "display love," but our therapeutic task is to eliminate the myriad anxieties which force him only to *appear* real rather than to *be* real. The same, I fear, is true for most group hoppers who get a druglike "fix" from playing games of authenticity instead of really living and relating meaningfully to real people.

If the foregoing is critical, it is aimed at certain charlatan group members and group leaders who undermine the very genuine and careful efforts of those who are truly concerned with humanity, social reform, and meaningful relationships. As a participant, participant-observer, and leader of numerous groups since 1955, I am completely confident that certain types of groups have definite value for some individuals. I have previously described specific group procedures such as group desensitization (Lazarus, 1961), assertive-training groups (Larazus, 1968d), and a time-limited group for overcoming impotence and frigidity (Lazarus, 1969b). I now wish to outline a series of group-training procedures which combine specific and comprehensive techniques in keeping with all that has been said up to this point in the book.

Personalistic Group Meetings

The group usually consists of between fifteen to twenty members. The first meeting lasts for about six hours. Thereafter, the group meets for three to four hours once a week and usually extends over twenty-four weeks. People may leave the group whenever they please, but no new members are accepted after the sixth session, at which stage the group is "closed." The participants are told all these facts beforehand.

Selection of Group Members

Most of my groups are composed of people who have been or still are in individual therapy with me and whom I think will derive benefit from a group experience. Occasionally, I have accepted patients referred by colleagues who knew them well and felt that they could profit by being in a group. Now and then people specifically requesting admission to a group have been accepted after one or two initial interviews.

Unsuitable Candidates

People who are extremely depressed, or hostile, or paranoid, or deluded usually have a disruptive effect on the rest of the group and seldom seem to derive much benefit themselves. Similarly, highly obsessional individuals locked into their own thoughts and rituals often require individual training in becoming less self-preoccupied before being capable of benefiting from a group.

Excessively timid and hypersensitive people would be well-advised to undergo a regime of desensitization and assertive training before having a group confrontation.

People with limited therapeutic objectives (e.g., "I merely want to overcome my fear of traveling in airplanes") usually make poor group members—unless they are placed in a specific or homogeneous group (Lazarus, 1968d).

Some people appear to require an intensive and personal 1-to-1 relationship in therapy. A group may provide supplementary assistance for them but can seldom take the place of individual therapy.

Most Suitable Candidates

People with obvious interpersonal difficulties usually do well in a group. The presence of several people with similar problems provides a medium through which they can resolve conflicts in a realistic manner. Open confrontations and the opportunity to observe people with dissimilar problems handling relationship factors in very different ways, provide active and vicarious learning of numerous interpersonal skills.

All problems which lend themselves to role playing seem to acquire additional leverage in a group. Role playing a mother-son situation, for instance, with someone whom the "son" regards as maternal, has advantages over mouthing appropriate words with an essentially nonmaternal male therapist. In addition, the opportunity to observe other people role playing singnificant events in each other's lives has the effect of introducing a wider range of possible response patterns.

Those individuals who are afraid of people or of groups per se, often find that several group meetings can provide a direct way of overcoming their social and interpersonal fears.

People who appear to do best in groups are those relatively stable individuals who can profit from several shades of opinion concerning their values, attitudes, and other aspects of their behavior. Instead of receiving one opiinion (the therapist's), no matter how learned and authoritative, it often helps to receive confirmation or refutation of one's ideas and actions from several interested people. Constructive criticism often carries more weight in a group than it does individually.

Matching in Heterogeneous Groups

The easiest groups to conduct are those which are relatively homogeneous—married couples, frigid women, obese or overweight people, alcoholics, or, say, a group of unassertive and inhibited men. Heterogeneous groups consisting of men and women with a variety of problems, a considerable age range, different socioeconomic backgrounds, etc., are more challenging and tend to provide the members with wider opportunities for acquiring social and personal awareness. In these mixed groups one often sees a narrowing of generation gaps and the weakening of other sociological barriers. When group members are too dissimilar, however, it is difficult or impossible for them to identify with one another or to communicate meaningfully. I have found that group members should, at the very least, be reasonably well-matched in terms of intelligence and social outlook. An unintelligent person among a group of bright and reasonably talented individuals often feels a heightened sense of insecurity and inferiority, and can retard the group's progress at every level. A staunch racist among a group of liberals will tend to engender nontherapeutic aggression and cause the sessions to deteriorate into unproductive intellectual debates.

Perhaps one of the greatest benefits of a constructive group is that while placing people in touch with their feelings, it also provides a *frame of reference* for them to reevaluate their own behaviors according to rational standards. This should become clearer as some of the group processes are described below.

All in all, group members are carefully chosen to form a reasonably intelligent and relatively well-functioning group in search of general rather than highly specific goals (e.g., "I want to learn how to relate less fearfully and more openly to people," versus "I need some relaxation exercises so that I can sleep better"). The methods employed often overlap with those used in individual therapy, but distinctive features and special group techniques will also be quite evident.

The Group Leader's Orienting Address

It is impressed upon the members that the group procedures are all predicated on the assumption that it is possible to learn to relate openly, nondefensively, and yet assertively, with mutual trust and genuine concern. The use of first names is obviously required since all group processes take place under the rubric of friendship. Thereafter the group is given the following structure and orientation by the leader:

"Picture what it would mean to belong to a club or to have some similar place where you could go and have people level with you completely. Imagine an ideal community where everyone is helpful, honest, cooperative, and sincere. In this club or community, people are valued and rewarded for their human qualities rather than for their extrinsic achievements. Such a setting makes it safe to reveal oneself entirely because ridicule, scorn, and derision are outlawed. Helpful or constructive criticism is always welcomed. But whenever anyone criticizes someone, the critic may be asked, 'In what way do you think that remark was helpful to so-and-so?' If the critic fails to convince the majority that his comments or actions were indeed helpful, he will be shown how he could have responded more constructively. In this setting, people will not be afraid to make mistakes. They will simply be shown how to profit from their errors.

"What I have just outlined, of course, is the climate of interaction for this group. In here you may set aside your games, your phony facades, your pretentions, and your false social graces. We want none of them. Instead, we want you to take the risk of being yourselves, of saying what you really mean and what you really feel. If you show an ugly side to your makeup, we will try to teach you how to change this negative aspect while still accepting and valuing you as a human being.

"Another way to understand and get a feeling for the group situation is to realize that we are a small community with the common objective of helping one another grow emotionally. As the weeks go by, we should all feel very safe with each other. We should learn to trust and confide in each other. The group should become a model of honest and satisfying social interactions. It should become the first place where you can feel confident that honest feedback will be forthcoming, and where kindness and compassion are the rule rather than the exception. In here, your fellow man should take pride and pleasure in your new adaptive behavior as in his own. This is because everyone will be responsible to a greater or lesser extent for the good things that happen to everyone else in the room.

"This group should become one place where you can air your grievances to a sympathetic audience, where if problems crop up in your daily life you can be sure that at the next group meeting you will receive emotional support and helpful advice. And if good things happen you can look forward to sharing your happiness with the group, and perhaps of serving as a model for those less fortunate than yourself.

"Right now, think what it would be like to reveal yourself as you really are, rather than to let the members of this group see you only as you appear to be. If this seems dangerous or frightening, I trust that it will become less so as we proceed. Please understand that nobody will be forced to say or do anything they do not consider within their capabilities. Everyone will proceed at his or her own pace. But obviously, the more risks you take and the more emotional investments you make, the more you will derive from the group.

"One final point. People are bound to reveal emotionally charged and personal information. I want you to treat everything that transpires as strictly confidential. You are on your honor not to divulge any information outside of the group that may hurt someone in the group.

"Would anyone care to respond to my soliloquy?"

After these opening remarks I usually allow about fifteen minutes of general discussion. People tend to question or challenge my utopian ideas and often voice their personal misgivings. Three distinct camps usually emerge rather quickly: (1) "I don't think group therapy is for me," (2) "I am very optimistic about this group," and (3) "Let's give it a few meetings and see what happens." I then say something like, "Okay, let's start shaping up your powers of perception. Would someone care to comment on their observations and impressions about anyone present?" This promotes a fair amount of personal interaction in the group. Since the group leader is well-acquainted with most of the people present, he is in a position to confirm valid observations and to dispel false impressions. It is especially useful to inquire why certain people emit or perceive false cues or signals.

Group Leader: Greg, you called Pamela a "militant feminist." I know her pretty well and I haven't picked that up in her and I'm wondering why you feel as you do? Would you mind telling us exactly what you meant?

Greg: You want me to tell you why she seems to come on that way? Well, I have an aunt who is a real man-hater. Boy, the way she treats my uncle makes me want to puke. Anyhow, Aunt Jean's view of men is that they have been put on this earth to serve women. I've heard her say it, in so many words, ever since I was a kid.

Pamela: Do I look like your aunt or something?

Greg: No, you *sound* like her. Remember when you told Virginia not to be bugged by Bert's comment? Well, the way you told her to ignore what you called his "boyishness" is a typical put-down that my Aunt Jean uses all the time.

Another Group Member: I think Greg's got a thing about women.

Pamela: Or at least he's got a thing about women who remind him of his Aunt Jean.

Greg: Well, maybe Bert can tell us whether he found that remark about "boyishness" a kind of put-down.

Pamela: The word *boyish* isn't necessarily a put-down.

Greg: Well, anyhow, let's hear from Bert. Bert, how

about it? When she made that remark tell us how you really felt.

Bert: Gee! I don't know. I did notice that Pamela did seem to take it upon herself to protect the other women at times. Especially Virginia, who comes on kind of helpless. Greg, I don't know why you jumped on her for calling me boyish because, I mean, it didn't bother me. Do you know what I think? It seems to me that Greg has hit on something about Pamela but he hasn't labeled it correctly. I think Pamela has a thing about men, sort of that she's afraid of them and that she projects her own fears onto other women and ends up overprotecting them.

Group Leader: Hey, that's pretty close to the truth. I'm impressed. What do you say, Pam?

Pamela: Well, I think it's mostly tied up with this need I have to be liked by everyone. . . .

The Inner-circle Exercise

Depending on the quality of the discussion, it can continue for more than an hour, after which the inner-circle exercise is introduced to the group with the following type of comments:

"When I talk about the 'inner circle' most of you know to what I am referring. (Diagrams with explanations similar to those outlined in Chapter 3 are presented mainly for the benefit of those members who are unfamiliar with the concept.) For the last hour or so we have been making educated guesses and inferences about the territory bordering each other's inner circles. Now it might be useful for everyone to allow us to come reasonably close to their inner circles by telling us why they are in this group and exactly what they hope to get out of it. Who would care to start?"

The discussion of goals and objectives is openly evaluated by the group leader in terms of their overall feasibility. Vague or very general objectives are broken down into specific areas of functioning:

"I hope that I can learn to be a happier person."

"What would make you a happier person?"

"Well, for one thing, I would like to find a better paying job."

"That's clear enough. What else would make you happier?"

"Oh, to love and be loved."

"That makes sense. What else?"

"To overcome my lack of self-confidence."

"So if you find a better job, enter into a meaningful love relationship and feel generally more confident, you will be a happier person and feel that the group experience was worthwhile."

"I sure would."

The next phase of the inner-circle exercise is to have the group ask questions (but not to feel constrained to answer them) which would get to the core of everyone's inner circle. It is interesting to note how questions nearly always commence with external or situational issues and proceed toward internal or personal areas. "How do you feel about your physical appearance?" "How much money do you earn?" "How old are you?" "How often do you have sexual intercourse?" "Do you ever masturbate?" "How do you really feel about your spouse?" "What are the things about yourself that you dislike?" "What is the worst thing you ever did?"

The upshot of these core questions is usually a pertinent conversation concerning real and imagined dangers involved in divulging personal information. Most of these discussions usually dwell on the fact that occupational situations generally call for the careful concealment of all information and behavior that could be considered "questionable." Positions involving security clearance and jobs on which one's performance is constantly evaluated by supervisors tend to heighten one's feelings of insecurity and promote anything but openness, authenticity, and meaningful relationships. But even in these situations one endeavors to show the group that the areas of actual danger are much fewer than might be supposed. Even if most work situations call for discretion and careful judgment, this circumspect behavior can be overgeneralized. While in many work situations it is wise to think carefully before expressing one's views on politics, religion, morality, company policy, or the behavior of a fellow employee, it is a grave mistake to carry over this guarded behavior into one's marriage, one's friendships, and one's social contacts.

Blackmail almost invariably becomes a central topic of conversation. It is usually helpful to divide group members' responses into "paranoid reactions versus healthy suspiciousness," and to discuss these implications. This, in turn, usually prompts group members to disclose their own personal misgivings and suspicions. The discussion often turns to ideas about *trust*—the importance of trust and the varieties of trust (e.g., "I would trust him with money but not with information." "You can trust her to be by your side when needed, but don't believe anything she tells you about her marriage or her business." "I don't trust his judgment on financial matters." "I wouldn't trust her with my husband.") General I-don't-trust-people reactions are fairly closely examined ending with each person's frank statements concerning how trustworthy they consider themselves to be.

Throughout all these discussions, the group leader constantly strives to elicit *feelings* from the participants rather than intellectual opinions. Phony or defensive statements are constructively challenged. In most of the groups I have conducted, these proceedings have usually been extremely animated and have evoked a good deal of emotion, soul searching, and productive insights.

Life History Phase

It is pointed out that people cannot respond closely and meaningfully without a "three-dimensional" view of each other. Inferences that may be drawn from actions and reactions in the group would have more "meat" if placed within the context of each member's own background and experiences. The participants take turns in telling the story of their lives. In my earlier groups, each member was given a maximum of thirty minutes in which to sketch the most salient features of his life history. Other members were free to ask questions or to make observations during each person's narrative. The main disadvantage of this procedure was that some members grew impatient and felt somewhat alienated from the group when waiting over three weeks for his or her turn. Consequently, my present method is to have people divide their life histories into consecutive ten-year periods, and to take turns describing their most relevant experiences during each period. In this way, the group qua group atmosphere is maintained because each member always has the opportunity of sharing at least one segment of his life at each group meeting and thus does not feel left out of the proceedings.

In order to maintain interest and promote continuity, the group is asked to provide a brief resume of each person's life history to date before proceeding with the next phase:

Example.

Group Leader: At this stage we have all completed two life history phases. We should have a pretty thorough idea of the first twenty years of each others' lives. We are ready to hear about the third period, your most relevant experiences between the ages twenty to thirty years. Why don't we start with Judy today? But before Judy goes on, who would care to recap her first twenty years?

Group Member: I'll try. Umm . . . as I recall it, she described her first ten years as "uneventful" except for the death of her grandfather. Also, she spoke a lot about her schoolteachers. Her second ten years. . . .

Another Group Member: Wait, during her first ten years she was bullied by her brother, which she told us was kind of important.

Group Member: Oh yes. But the years ten to twenty were especially important. Her family moved from New Jersey, and she met her friend Dora and also got to know those very rich folks next door.

Judy: Can I interrupt? Don't forget I met Norman round about that time too. I also told you how I felt about my dad's carrying on with other women.

Group Member: I hadn't forgotten that. Shall I go on? Well the first part of Judy's second phase was the "board-ing school era," as she called it. She told us about the lesbian happening and also how she tried to kill herself when Norman and Dora started going together. I think those were the main points. Did I leave anything out?

Judy: I think you touched on the main points except for the way I felt about my mother when I came home for vacations. Anyhow, the third period, especially the years twenty to twenty-five were much more important. . . .

If for any reason the first session becomes sluggish or heavy-going, the *life history phase* can be introduced and will tend to add zest to the proceedings. Generally, I introduce the life history phase approximately one hour after the beginning of the second session.

Ensuring Therapeutic Transfer

Patients whom I have treated individually have commented that they have felt free enough to disclose themselves to me completely. They were nondefensively authentic and spontaneous in all our person-to-person interactions. Their trust and confidence in me, however, did not neces-sarily diminish their mistrust and oversuspiciousness of others. Before they were able to develop greater tolerance and understanding toward others, it was usually necessary to dwell on the various ways and means of achieving emotional freedom (see Chapter 6) and engage in consid-erable cognitive restructuring (see Chapter 8). In other words, the likelihood of therapeutic transfer is often remote unless one deliberately works at it.

In the group situations that have been outlined above, the sup-portive and accepting atmosphere soon makes it relatively easy for group members to engage in self-exploration, to exude confidence, to display wholesome and nonjudgmental reactions, and to show appropriate emo-tions under many circumstances. To assume that these gains will auto-matically transfer beyond the confines of the consulting room or outside the handful of supportive group members is a serious error. Too many group members become good group members but still remain ineffective outside of the group.

My major means of endeavoring to ensure therapeutic transfer is to ask each group member the following question, "What negative, destructive, or antisocial responses have you managed to curb or curtail this week, and what positive, constructive, or prosocial responses have you succeeded in performing?" The question is repeated more succinctly, "What maladaptive habits have you stopped and what adaptive responses have you started?" Group members usually report having quit smoking, drinking, or overeating; stopped nagging their wives, putting themselves down, engaging in self-pity, and so forth. On the question of new adaptive behaviors, they tell of forming new friendships, not avoiding phobic areas, expressing more overt love and affection, going out on dates, pursuing new interests, etc. It is constantly impressed upon the members that the 4 hours of group training are but a springboard for the remaining 164 hours each week which constitute their lives in the full sense of the word (Lazarus, 1968d).

Not infrequently, the group meetings end by asking each member to make a pledge either to stop some old unadaptive behavior or to implement some new adaptive behavior. "What will you try to stop doing that is destructive and/or what will you try to start doing that is constructive?" Often two or more members make pacts with each other to stop smoking, or to start jogging, or to lose weight, and so on.

In essence, by focusing considerable attention on matters which take place in each person's life *outside* of the group, and by encouraging each member to make specific changes in his or her conduct during the "other 164 hours," the likelihood of constructive transfer and generalization of gains is greatly augmented.

The Personalistic Behavioral Emphasis

In the same way that individual patients follow no predetermined structure or preset regime of therapy but receive the methods that appear to suit their particular needs, personalistic groups, apart from the introductory launching procedures described above, are extremely flexible and versatile. As the meetings proceed, the discerning observer will usually note how the members graduate from self-disclosure, to self-discovery, to self-understanding, and eventually progress to experimentation in vivo with new and significant behavior change becoming evident in many important areas.

If a casual observer were to sample random segments from various group sessions, much as one would sample several radio programs by tuning rapidly from one station to another, he would find a bewildering contrast of methods and procedures. Perhaps the greatest contrast would be between the violent gut-rendering cacophony of shouting and stamping as group members give vent to their pent-up aggressions by screaming louder and louder, over and over, "I am angry! I hate! I could kill!" to the silent meditative qualities of group relaxation, as each member quietly lets go of his tensions, and concentrates on soft tingling sensations flowing through his body. The entire group descending en masse upon a department store to witness a member's newfound assertiveness with salesclerks, or a group visit to a cemetery in order to help one or two members overcome "death phobias," literally takes personalistic group therapy beyond the confines of the consulting room.

The behavioral emphasis finds expression in the fact that group members are trained to specify what they and other people *do*, instead of using vague descriptive labels. For instance, if a group member described his wife as "lazy," he would immediately be asked to list the precise behaviors his wife fails to perform in order to justify this label. In this way unrealistic demands are easily discerned and can be challenged by the group. Furthermore, the axiom that *behavior is often a function of its consequences* is strongly impressed upon the group. They are shown how the events which follow most acts of behavior will tend either to encourage (reinforce) or discourage (extinguish) the ongoing responses. Thus, many undesirable behaviors which take place in the group are deliberately ignored so as to discourage their performance. New and adaptive behaviors meet with praise and approval. In addition, what Schaefer and Martin (1969) simply, but appropriately, term *odd behavior* is clearly enumerated in the group with a view to determining (1) who or what is maintaining each person's odd behavior, and (2) how this odd behavior can best be eliminated. Apart from the life history phase described above, all the proceedings are present and future oriented.

It is beyond the scope of a single chapter to enumerate all the techniques employed in the group setting, but nearly every procedure described in this book (and many others not contained herein) can be incorporated with benefit into a group. Generally the members enjoy the emotional support, the opportunity to release pent-up feelings, the personal reassurance and acceptance, as well as the direct reeducative, explanatory, and insightful experiences. All constructive group encounters provide members with the chance to see themselves in relation to others, thereby obtaining a realistic appraisal of their adaptive and maladaptive habits, plus specific suggestions and encouragement for remedying the latter. Loss of isolation by discovering that one is not alone in many unusual or disturbing thoughts and feelings, is often exceedingly helpful. When members learn to give to others and help them through trying times, additional gratification and feelings of self-worth often result.

The only negative group meetings have been those in which I experimented by having cotherapists whose methods and techniques differed from my own. Instead of augmenting my own repertoire as I had originally assumed, the impact upon the group was one of rivalry and confusion.

In the majority of instances, however, gains which accrued to the people who participated in personalistic groups have been impressive.

CHAPTER 10
LEARNING
PRINCIPLES
IN THE
TREATMENT
OF DISTURBED
CHILDREN

In many instances, problem children cannot be helped substantially without the active cooperation of their (problem) parents and other significant family members. This does not imply that the treatment of deviant children must always take place in a family-centered environment. A *personalistic* emphasis attaches due credence to the necessity of treating unique individuals within their social contexts. A behavioral orientation (Lazarus, 1958) seems to permit or encourage one to "swing the focus of attention back and forth from the individual and his or her parts to the individual in his or her social setting." In the treatment of disturbed children, the implications of this individual-social emphasis becomes central when deciding (1) who or what is maintaining the deviant behavior, and (2) what is the most effective way of changing the untoward responses. These points should become obvious as specific modes of intervention are outlined below.

A Note on Matters of Upbringing

My most difficult and problem-ridden adult patients usually give a history of overdiscipline in the absence of overt love, coupled with harsh criticism, rejection, and inconsistent parental behavior. Also prevalent are those with a history of neglect, semiabandonment, or unstructured permissiveness. Coopersmith (1967, p. 236) has concluded that: "the most general statement about the antecedents of self-esteem can be given in terms of three conditions: total or nearly total *acceptance* of the children by their parents, clearly defined and enforced *limits,* and the *respect* and latitude for individual action that exist within the defined limits."

Another factor that seems to be of crucial importance in raising children is the matter of fantasy versus reality. The most intractable cases seen in clinical practice were often children who had been handed a "cognitive map" that had no bearing on the realities of life. They were given versions of sex, birth, life, and death that bore no resemblance to the actual facts. Then, sooner or later, it became necessary to adjust to reality; to trade their fairy tales for some harsh and unromantic truths. Some found the transition from fantasy to reality difficult but possible; others simply could not bridge the gap. In the same way that an adopted child should learn about his true situation at three years of age and not fifteen (Lewin, 1948, p. 173), it is probably advisable to teach children the truth about life and reality in general right from the start.

There is persuasive evidence that modeling and imitation are undoubtedly among the most powerful influencing factors in the acquisition and maintenance of deviant behaviors, but they can also be employed as powerful agents for the establishment of prosocial adaptive behaviors (Bandura, 1969). Parents with courage, poise, and direction are more likely to transmit similar qualities (probably via imitation and identification) to their children. Conversely, parents with low self-worth, who expect to fail in life, who anticipate rejection, who feel unimportant, weak and passive, and whose inferiorities are made self-fulfilling by notions that they are unworthy of love and attention, tend to rob their children of vigor and leave them with very little hope or courage (Coopersmith, 1967). Therapeutic regimes which provide parents with intensive training in assertive behavior via modeling and role playing (see Chapter 6) can sometimes help to produce marked benefits among entire family units.

Learning Principles and Child Therapy

Wolberg (1967, p. 116) has stated that "it is better to ascribe the effects of behavior therapy to the disciplined use of learning principles than to the dubious application of learning theory." In simplest terms, problem behavior is usually due to the presence of "bad habits" or the absence of "good habits." Thus, the goal of therapy is to eliminate maladaptive responses and to facilitate adaptive behavior. Empirically, we may note that a chronic thumb-sucker may be induced to alter his behavior if a reward (e.g., a smile, or some candy, or the statement "good boy") frequently follows the cessation of the undesirable response or if punishment (e.g., a slap, or an electric shock, or the removal of candy) often follows its onset. This adds up to a simple principle of learning involving knowledge about the pragmatic effects of reward and punishment. Some learning *theorists* may contend that reward and punishment are "central mechanisms" which have an effect because of cognitive processes such as various expectancies and perceptual sets. Others would argue that "peripheral mechanisms" such as habits and responses are quite sufficient for understanding the impact of positive and negative stimuli. Polemical disputes of this kind seem to have died down among clinicians who realize that they take us far afield from what will prove therapeutically enriching. Resistance to the use of direct-learning principles comes from other quarters which the following incidents will describe.

Resistance to the Application of Learning Principles

Refusal to encourage or permit the widespread use of direct-learning principles often comes from a priori assumptions that deleterious effects will ensue. Thus, the nursery school supervisor of a destructive five-year-old boy refused to implement a simple design for operant retraining. She reasoned that since Don, the only child of an elderly couple, was described as "gentle and loving" at home, his parents were probably oversuppressive, and that school provided the only outlet for his pent-up aggressions. When an interview with Don's mother indicated that neither of his parents was a strict disciplinarian, the supervisor reluctantly conceded that the child's behavior was possibly provoked by specific events in the school situation. Less than fifteen minutes' observation of Don's behavior at school revealed the following incidents: (1) While the other children hung out their paintings to dry, Don tore up his own artistic effort, whereupon the teacher chided him (i.e., provided reinforcement via attention). (2) Don then proceeded to pull down the other children's paintings, and was again upbraided by the teacher (additional reward by attention). (3) He then threw rocks at a group of children and earned the approval of some of his peers who cheered him on. (4) A scuffle ensued in which he and another child kicked and punched each other. Don came off second best, whereupon he wept and was comforted by his teacher who offered him candy.

On the positive side, it was observed that Don enjoyed community singing and seemed inordinately fond of ice cream. The suggestion that the child should be informed that his participation in singsongs and his rations of ice cream would henceforth be contingent upon non-aggressive behavior was deferred in favor of symbolic play therapy with dolls. After six months of one hour per week of play therapy, they concluded that Don's aggressive acting out was an unconscious defense against castration. By this time, his belligerence at school had increased and Don was considered "seriously disturbed" by the nursery school personnel. The simple retraining regime proposed originally was finally implemented. In general, the teachers were told to try and ignore his destructive maneuvers (unless physical harm to himself or another child was likely) and to reward with approval all friendly social responses. It was explained to Don that three aggressive responses would cause him to forfeit his daily share of ice cream, and if there were five hostile outbursts in a morning he would also be banned from community singing and would have to sit alone in the supervisor's office.

On the next five school days, Don was deprived of both ice cream and community singing. On the sixth school day, he forfeited only his ice cream. Thereafter, aggressive and hostile responses vanished from his repertoire; one of the teachers observed that even when provoked Don failed to retaliate. This was obviously considered a negative and undesirable consequence of the operant training program. He was accordingly told that whenever he launched unprovoked attacks on other children and/or their property, he would forfeit his share of ice cream or be sent to the office. However, he was told that it was eminently desirable and necessary for him to defend himself when provoked or attacked by others (a generally expedient principle of interpersonal relationships).

A follow-up after eighteen months (when Don had completed his first elementary school grade) revealed that he was a healthy and somewhat boisterous child, well-liked by his peers and considered well-adjusted by his teacher.

This relatively straightforward case which followed the dictates of common sense could be made into a complex psychological treatise by considering the role of relationship variables, expectancies, positive and negative reinforcement, and so forth. It is presented to illustrate how, even in simple cases, putative dynamics (castration anxiety) can so often be given precedence over variables which are crucial and observable and readily manipulable. Yet some authorities condemn these direct retraining procedures completely. For instance Bettelheim (1967, p. 410) reviles operant procedures as coercive and dehumanizing processes which treat people as objects, strip away their defenses, and reduce "autistic children ... to the level of Pavlovian dogs." Further he states: "To create conditioned responses in the patient deprives him just as effectively of the human freedom to make choices, as does the destruction of part of his brain [p. 411]." Bettelheim's account is replete with non sequiturs which miss the point that conditioning procedures may be applied in a noncoercive context of human dignity, empathy, authenticity, and warmth. Just as a surgeon will assault and tear open one's flesh to save lives and alleviate suffering, an operant conditioner may use electric shock to prevent the head banging of autistic children who are bashing their heads to the point of damaging their brains, or biting off their own fingers. As we shall see below, some cases are just too desperate to "begin slowly to respond to treatment efforts based on psychoanalytically oriented hypotheses ... after years of frustrated attempts [Bettelheim, 1967, p. 412]."

All in all, the case of Don illustrates the immediate effectiveness of a simple operant retraining schedule which, far from treating Don like an animal, made good use of language and other distinctively human characteristics (e.g., the child was given prior and subsequent verbal information about the prearranged reinforcement contingencies). The critical question is whether or not these direct learning principles have a place in the treatment of seriously disturbed children.

The Application of Learning Principles to Seriously Disturbed Children

Few children are more socially unresponsive than those schizophrenic or autistic cases who are absorbed in stereotyped, repetitive self-stimulation (including self-destructive behavior). These children consistently react as if they are blind and deaf, so that the presence of other people in no way interrupts their persistent screeching, rocking, head banging, and similar self-absorbing activities (Lovaas, Freitas, Nelson, & Whalen, 1967). Whether one accepts Ferster's (1961) hypothesis that the development of such deviant behavior is purely environmental, or whether one subscribes to Rimland's (1964) hypothesis of autism as a biologically based illness, there is clear evidence that operant training techniques can lead to significant and beneficial changes (e.g., Davison, 1964; Ferster & DeMyer, 1962; Wolf, Risley, & Mees, 1964; Lovaas, Freitag, Gold, & Kassorla, 1965). In several instances throughout this book it was pointed out that a given *behavior-change* technique can be compatible with many different *etiological* notions. Davison (1967) has observed that Rimland's (1964) physiological concerns are actually in keeping with many psychological methods of treatment employed by operant conditioners.

　　To cite a typical operant procedure, Hingtgen, Sanders, and DeMyer (1965) trained several severely disturbed children to press a lever to obtain rewards such as candy. Gradually, the necessary behavior for reinforcement was shaped to include active cooperation with another child: both had to press the same lever alternately in order to obtain candy. As a consequence, hitherto unresponsive and uncommunicative children eventually engaged in mutual positive physical contact, exchanged appropriate facial expressions, and evinced other "healthy" interpersonal responses.

One of the principal advantages of these programmed strategies is that they make it possible to determine which particular aspects of a complex interaction have specific and predictable effects. Thus, if a regressed schizophrenic child who seldom walks but usually crawls is ignored when crawling and is given candy and/or attention when walking, one can predict that he will soon remain on his feet and off his knees. Experiments of this kind are often met by the following objections: "What proof have you that your rewards were the agents of change? Perhaps the child was just ready to stop crawling and start walking. Maybe the child just needed extra love and attention per se to develop enough ego strength to stop crawling, and thus the mechanics of your operant retraining (e.g., careful timing between a response such as walking, and its predetermined consequence, such as receiving immediate attention) were irrelevant." These assumptions are easily tested. If change is due to "ego strength" brought about by noncontingent love and attention, it should follow that continued love and attention (e.g., when the child is crawling) should serve to further the child's ego strength and thus perpetuate more adaptive walking responses rather than re-evoke regressed patterns of crawling. However, a test of this kind by Harris, Johnston, Kelley, and Wolf (1964) suggested that reinforcement contingencies were the determining factors of behavior change. Walking behavior in a three-year-old was established by means of positive social reinforcement; reversal of reinforcement contingencies weakened the behavior (i.e. rewards for *not* walking produced crawling behavior) ; and the reinstatement of social reinforcement when the child stopped crawling finally reestablished the walking response. Similarly, Hart, Allen, Buell, Harris, and Wolf (1965) treated a four-year-old who cried excessively. When the child's crying was ignored, except, of course, in instances of actual pain (i.e., respondent as opposed to operant crying) it took only ten days for this behavior to decline almost to zero. At this point, the teachers were instructed to reverse the contingencies so that attention again followed crying behavior. Rapidly, the frequency of crying was reinstated, thereby confirming the assumption that the behavior was under control of the contingencies being manipulated. Finally, the "therapeutic contingencies" were reapplied, and the frequency of crying returned to near zero. Reversal studies of this kind are not uncommon with animals (Skinner, 1953; Sidman, 1962) and in this sense, these reversal studies with children emphasize a parallel between the laboratory and the clinic. One of the main advantages in using these straightforward therapeutic methods is the fact that non-professionals can rapidly learn to apply them (Davison, 1964; O'Leary, O'Leary, & Becker, 1967; Wahler, Winkel, Peterson, & Morrison, 1965).

Other Specific Problems

The range of children's clinical problems to which learning principles have been successfully applied is extremely vast. A few examples (out of several hundred) are outlined below in order to demonstrate some of the more common problems which have been successfully handled by means of learning principles: Azrin and Lindsley (1965) illustrated how reinforcement programs can induce cooperation between children; Baer (1962) demonstrated the laboratory control of thumb-sucking; Barrett (1965) used reward principles with institutionalized retarded children; Brown and Elliott (1965) studied the control of aggression in a nursery school; and Fessant (1963) applied programmed learning to deaf children. Operant techniques have been applied to toilet training not only with normal children (Madsen, 1965) but with equal effectiveness with an autistic child (Marshall, 1966) and with severe retardates (Giles & Wolf, 1966). In addition, Neale (1963) has reported specifically on behavior therapy and encopresis in children, and Lovibond (1964) has examined several conditioning paradigms for treating enuresis. Operant programs were devised for developing speech in schizophrenic and autistic children (Lovaas, 1966) and were even successful in shaping vocalizations in a mute child (Kerr, Meyerson & Michael, 1965). Hawkins, Peterson, Schweid, and Bijou (1966) applied behavior therapy in the home to overcome problem parent-child relationships; Patterson, Jones and Wright (1965) devised a behavior modification technique for the hyperactive child as did Pihl (1967); Tate and Baroff (1966) used aversive control of self-injurious behavior in a psychotic boy; Whitlock (1966) extended laboratory principles to reading problems; and Wolf, Birnbrauer, Williams, and Lawler (1965) extinguished vomiting in a retarded child.

In a case reported by Davison (1968) it was shown how mediating responses may be used to free a child from negative environmental contingencies. An eleven-year-old boy was sent for therapy by his distraught parents who found him rebellious and unmanageable. The household was described as reaching near-continuous chaos. A detailed inquiry revealed that the boy was most obedient when he anticipated severe punishment from an irate father. He was inclined to overstep all reasonable limits whenever his father appeared relatively complacent. In order to decrease the frequency of his father's reactive hostility, the boy was taught to *imagine* a confrontation with his angry father as soon as he was about to engage in behavior which was likely to create problems. It was hoped that if the boy "created" this aversive contingency, he might thereby prevent the occurrence of an *actual* aversive event. This technique was quite effective and fostered considerable self-control in the boy and led to less friction in the home. Of course, as in most therapeutic interactions, other variables (e.g., his desire to please the therapist) also seemed to play a role.

The work of Patterson (Patterson et al., 1967; Patterson, Ray, & Shaw, 1968; Patterson & Reid, 1969) is particularly important as he and his coworkers tend to intervene directly in the families and in the schools of deviant children. By literally moving into the home, base-line information is first obtained, whereupon parents, siblings, peers, and teachers are then trained to alter the behavior of the disturbed or deviant children. There is, in fact, a consistent trend toward placing parents in therapeutic roles vis-à-vis their disturbed children (e.g., Hawkins et al., 1966; Wahler et al., 1965; Zeilberger, Sampen, & Sloane, 1968). As Garmezy (1970) has shown in his well-balanced review of psychological vulnerability and susceptibility to emotional suffering among children and adolescents, some problem children (such as those prone to "acting out") do not tend to "outgrow" their difficulties but are inclined to develop into problem adults. The need for effective intervention can hardly be overstated.

Learning Principles and Anxiety Reduction in Children

The various demonstrations by Mary Cover Jones (1924a; 1924b) provided the first systematic and comprehensive accounts of conditioning treatments for children's anxiety reactions. Her techniques were essentially those of counterconditioning but included several other strategies such as "elimination through disuse," "verbal appeal," "negative adaptation," "the method of repression," "the method of distraction," and "the method of social imitation." In recent years, *counter-conditioning* and *social imitation* have been shown to be particularly effective (Bandura, 1969).

Lazarus (1959) described several counterconditioning procedures for the treatment of children's phobias. In one case combined use was made of operant and respondent strategies. The child who was afraid of traveling in moving vehicles was given chocolate as a reinforcer for the operant behavior of talking about cars, then sitting in cars, and finally for riding in cars. In the same manner, various conditioned stimuli, such as toy cars, were paired with the pleasant unconditioned stimuli of eating chocolate which became conditioned to vehicle stimuli.

Bandura (1965; 1969) has explored various psychotherapeutic applications of *modeling and social imitation.* In a recent controlled experiment, Bandura, Grusec, and Menlove (1967) illustrated the "vicarious extinction" of avoidance responses in children. It was reasoned that emotional reactions such as an unadaptive avoidance of dogs could be eliminated by exposing the fearful child to a nonfearful model who enjoyed playing with a dog. Bandura and his coworkers found that children became significantly less fearful after seeing a peer model engaging in approach behavior without adverse consequences. Appropriate control groups ruled out various nonspecific factors such as contact with the experimenter, placebo effects, etc. In a subsequent study (Bandura & Menlove, 1968) it was found that children who were fearful of dogs were willing to perform potentially threatening interactions with dogs after seeing a "set of graded films depicting a variety of models interacting nonanxiously with numerous dogs varying in size and fearsomeness."

Lazarus, Davison, and Polefka (1965) also applied *classical and operant strategies* in overcoming a school phobia in a nine-year-old boy. The first phase of therapy consisted mainly of his gradual in vivo exposure to various aspects of the school situation, accompanied by a well-liked therapist. As the boy grew less fearful, it seemed that the therapist's noncontingent warmth and attention (useful if not essential for reducing high levels of anxiety) were now merely making the child dependent on the therapist. The second phase of therapy therefore consisted of making all rewards (including the therapist's presence) contingent upon approximations to the eventual goal of normal school attendance. The therapist's presence soon became less and less important to the child.

Lazarus and Abramovitz (1962) used *emotive imagery* in overcoming children's fears. The children imagined stronger and stronger phobic stimuli woven into progressively more enjoyable fantasies. One case cited by Lazarus and Abramovitz involved a fantasy modeling procedure:

> An eight-year-old girl was referred for treatment because of persistent nocturnal enuresis and a fear of going to school. Her fear of the school situation was apparently engendered by a series of emotional upsets in class. In order to avoid going to school, the child resorted to a variety of devices including temper tantrums, alleged pains, and illnesses, and on one occasion she was caught playing truant and intemperately upbraided by her father. Professional assistance was finally sought when it was found that her younger sister was evincing the same behaviour.
>
> When the routine psychological investigations had been completed, emotive imagery was introduced with the aid of Noddy, a fiction character introduced by the English authoress of many children's books, Enid Blyton. Noddy provided a hierarchy of assertive challenges centered around the school situation. The essence of this procedure was to create imagined situations where Noddy played the role of a truant and responded fearfully to the school setting. The patient would then protect him, either by active reassurance or by "setting a good example."
>
> Only four sessions were required to eliminate her school phobia. Her enuresis, which had received no specific therapeutic attention, was far less frequent and disappeared entirely within two months. The child has continued to improve despite some additional upsets at the hands of an unsympathetic teacher. [pp. 191–195].

I recently combined emotive imagery with fantasy imitation in treating an eight-year-old boy who was too afraid to visit the dentist. The sequence consisted of having the child picture himself accompanying Batman and Robin on various adventures and then imagining his heroes visiting the dentist while he observed them receiving dental attention. He was asked to picture this scene at least five times daily for one week. Next, he was to imagine himself in the dentist's chair while Batman and Robin stood by and observed him. He also practiced this image several times a day for one week. He visited the dentist the following week, and according to his mother he sat through four fillings without flinching.

The Treatment of Negative Self-states

Finally, it is germane to consider the contributions of behavioral methods to less specific clinical problems. Questions may be raised concerning the role of behavior therapy with children who are experiencing debilitating guilt, a sense of inadequacy, low self-esteem, etc., through being unwanted, rejected, or disliked by their parents. Such cases seem to require changes in feeling, attitude, and similar behaviors, that encompass the focal child and other members of the family. Complimentary implementation of different techniques and approaches appears to be most effective in these cases. The following case history should underscore these general remarks:

The Case of Fred. Fred, 7½ years of age, was seen by a medical practitioner because of persistent enuresis. The doctor, in turn, found the child to be extremely anxious and advised psychotherapy. The mother was interviewed and seemed unduly tense herself. It transpired that Fred was her son from a previous marriage and that his stepfather appeared to be expressing his antipathy towards Fred's biological father by imposing unfair sanctions upon the child. The child's tendency to cower suggested that physical punishment was frequently administered— a fact which later became evident. He was often punished for wetting his bed and was once whipped by his stepfather for allegedly "tampering" with his three-year-old half-sister. Two interviews with the child's mother elicited the aforementioned facts as well as evidence of the family's general psychological naïveté and ambivalence at all levels. The marriage was shaky due to the mother's "frigidity"; the stepfather, a frustrated accountant, worked as a bank teller having failed his final accountancy examination three times due to "poor concentration"; and the mother expressed guilt at having divorced Fred's father for committing adultery. "Perhaps I should have found it in my heart to forgive him and then Fred might have been better off."

The stepfather and mother had to be cajoled into a joint interview. After some general comments, I outlined my clinical impressions and proposed a treatment program. I tactfully expressed the opinion that Fred served as a scapegoat for their individual and mutual frustrations, and that most of their problems had predated Fred's birth and their marriage. I also emphasized that the mother's sexual anxieties played a major role in destroying her first marriage and were currently undermining her present marriage. In terms of dyadic transactions, I assumed that the stepfather had married a frigid woman because he was probably unsure of his own sexual prowess. It was clear that his work failures had further undermined his self-esteem and masculinity. All in all, apart from general admonitions to show Fred much love and no harshness, it was decided temporarily to shelve his bed-wetting and to concentrate on (1) the mother's sexual inadequacies, (2) the father's concentration difficulties, and (3) any other specific problems which arose during the course of therapy.

The parents were seen together twice weekly. Sessions were more or less equally divided into three sections: (1) general discussions concerning Fred, their marriage, the mother's previous marriage, and general issues ranging from morality to the formation of basic friendships, (2) systematic desensitization to more and more intimate sexual encounters (see Chapter 7), and (3) discussions of learning principles such as "active participation" and "distributed practice" in augmenting recall and concentration, and their implementation in encouraging the stepfather to resume his accountancy courses.

Therapy was unspectacular but very fruitful. A behavior analysis after eight months revealed a distinct sexual improvement and a better overall marriage. In addition, assertive training had enabled the stepfather to confront Fred's biological father about providing more adequate financial support for his child. A variety of subtle changes led to better rapport between stepfather and son and enabled the mother to accept her children on equal terms and to dispense equitable positive reinforcements. The stepfather, upon being promoted to chief teller, considered his newfound status commensurate with his abilities and abandoned his studies in accountancy. At this stage, Fred could be described as anything but cowering or anxious, but he still wet his bed at least five out of seven nights. A nocturnal enuresis alarm was installed (Lovibond, 1964) and was discontinued after 3½ months. All was well for about four months, when Fred again began wetting his bed. Specific reasons were sought but not found. Booster treatment with the enuresis alarm was administered for one month. A recent follow-up (two years later) revealed that Fred even weathered the birth of a brother without relapsing and that all other gains had been maintained.

Some Advantages of Learning Principles and Behavioral Methods

Learning principles, by their sensitivity to and sophisticated analysis of stimulus dimensions in the environments in which children live, experience, and behave, have opened up multiple settings for work with children's problems. Professionals who devote themselves to the task of understanding children's development and behavior, and to problems in these areas, should be sensitive to the relevance of experimental psychology in expanding their capacity for making meaningful interventions.

Scholarly reviews of conditioning and learning in relation to children's clinical problems date back to Seham (1932) and Gesell (1938) who listed fifty-seven references. Some enterprising archaeologist might well discover learning principles and behavior therapy techniques hidden among the hieroglyphics of an ancient Egyptian sarcophagus. Indeed, as Wolpe and Lazarus (1966, p. 1) point out, "empirical behavior therapy is probably as old as civilization." What then is novel, unique, or original about the current application of learning principles and behavioral methods? The *newness* lies in the systematic grouping of age-old data in parsimonious, basic, and congruent categories. This has led to clear operational definitions and to the development of lawful relations between behavior and the variables which control it (Yates, 1970; Krasner & Ullmann, 1965; Ullmann & Krasner, 1969). Cumulative records of behavior and computer analyses of data have further helped to yield more objective and precise information about the prediction and control of behavior. The field of application has extended to schools, clinics, penal institutions, and mental hospitals—as well as to methods of group and individual psychotherapy. In general, the trend has been to steer away from particular theories of behavior, and to focus attention on the functional analysis of behavior (i.e., an experimental and essentially empirical *modus operandi*). In this regard the book by Ferster and Perrott (1968) which describes precise and systematic procedures for conducting a behavioral analysis is probably without peer.

A rich technology of efficient therapeutic methods and techniques has resulted from studies of operant and reflex behavior. Those who apply these learning principles to clinical problems have been freed from the restraints of nondirective, passive-reflective procedures. Where necessary, they can now replace *symbols* (words, insights, ideas, dreams, and interpretations) with *action* (behavior rehearsal, relaxation, assertive training, systematic habituation, and rewards). Again, where necessary, they can combine the two. Woody (1969) in a book devoted to problem children in the schools, discusses assertive responses and behavior rehearsal, relaxation and desensitization, object and recognition rewards, social modeling and shaping behaviors, and positive reinforcement combined with punishment in the treatment of children.

Yet one must take care not to overstate the claims of scientific respectability and therapeutic efficacy for behavioral techniques. There are crucial gaps in our knowledge concerning the relation of learning principles to many aspects of emotional suffering. It is worth emphasizing that although the past two decades have witnessed an information explosion in the behavioral sciences, the field of psychological therapy is still "an area in which what is being done lags far behind what might be done [Sanford, 1948]." A comprehensive behavioral, humanistic, and personalistic approach can do much to expedite significant progress in the development of effective psychotherapy.

CHAPTER 11
OTHER
EFFECTIVE
TECHNIQUES

The Need for Techniques

Psychotherapy as a generic term covers a multitude of processes which include, among many others, tutoring, guiding, reeducating, information-giving, modeling and habit-training. Wolberg's (1967) comprehensive therapeutic coverage entitled *The Technique of Psychotherapy* lists more than three dozen techniques and processes which, apart from psychoanalysis and its numerous offshoots, includes suggestion, persuasion, conditioning, the use of dance and poetry, somatic intervention, relaxation, role playing, family therapy, as well as philosophical approaches such as Zen Buddhism and existentialism. Some people maintain that these activities should not all be lumped together and called psychotherapy. Patterson (1969) for instance, defines psychotherapy as "a method of behavior change in which the core conditions (or the relationship) are the sufficient conditions for change to occur." According to this definition, the "pure" psychotherapist would not treat the many paralyzing disorders which produce sheer torture for the afflicted, and the vast number of cases for whom "it is insufficient for us to sit back and reflect empathy, no matter how accurate; warmth, no matter how non-possessive; or any other facilitative conditions, no matter how genuine or concrete (Lazarus, 1969).

In a clever satirical article, Haley (1969) emphasized "The Five B's Which Guarantee Dynamic Failure": *Be* passive; *Be* inactive; *Be* reflective; *Be* silent; *Beware*. The personalistic emphasis of this book implies that one should be on the alert for those individuals who constitute the exceptions to the various rules which arise. Thus, perhaps a minority of people may in fact need their therapist to remain passive, inactive, reflective, silent and noncommittal. This is probably particularly true for certain college students who have to resolve their own "identity crises" with no more than the assistance of a concerned listener. The truly effective therapist, however, will usually have to provide much more than core facilitative conditions by working very actively at correcting faulty habits and numerous misconceptions in his patients. Furthermore, an assumption that is basic to social behavior theory is that "different problems require different treatment and that specific treatments can be designed to fit them [Mischel, 1968, pp. 235–236]." Yet as Bachrach and Quigley (1966) have pointed out, "It is undoubtedly true that the field of behavior therapy, with its worthy social goals, its theoretical simplicity (deceptive though it may be), and its empirical success (under certain circumstances), will attract many psychotechnicians. It is, therefore, a field in danger of being ruined by amateurs [p. 510]."

The main factor which gave rise to the proliferation of more and more techniques since Freud abandoned hypnosis (a grave error!) and introduced free association, was the general discontent with methods that aim only to promote insight or self-knowledge. The achievement of profound insights will frequently fail to eliminate tics, phobias, compulsions, or perversions, whereas operant conditioning, desensitization, or even straightforward hypnotic suggestion may often quell these "symptoms" with neither relapse nor substitution. Should we then abandon the quest for self-knowledge in favor of conditioning techniques? Indeed, if one's goal is to overcome enuresis, or to teach an autistic child to speak, or to instigate prosocial behaviors among schizophrenic inmates, the clinical and research evidence suggests that it would be foolhardy to bypass direct behavioral approaches (Lovibond, 1963; Lovaas, 1966; Schaefer & Martin, 1969). While even here, more attention to the patient's interpersonal relationships may well enhance the effects of specific reconditioning, it is obvious that instruction or training in a specific area will probably lead to improved performance in that area. Stutterers will usually find fluency exercises more helpful than introspection for their speech (Gray & England, 1969); phobic patients will usually respond better to desensitization than to psychoanalysis (Glick, 1969); social skills are more readily acquired through behavior rehearsal (modeling and role playing) than through advice or nondirective interviews (Lazarus, 1966a). Since it is not always so easy to determine when limited problems of function or dysfunction become entangled with farreaching problems of meaning, therapists should try to determine what they are dealing with before plunging ahead with deconditioning or reconditioning techniques. The basic question to be asked is whether one is dealing with a *problem* or a *symptom*. To desensitize a phobic patient, for instance, without first establishing whether his phobia is a straightforward avoidance reaction, or a psychotic manifestation, or a symbolic retreat, or a face-saving or attention-seeking device, or a weapon in family or marital strife violates the cardinal rule—"diagnosis before therapy." It may seem ridiculous to keep asserting the obvious. After all, what self-respecting therapist would apply desensitization (or any other technique) without first conducting a thorough evaluation of the patient's problem? The answer, regrettably, is all too many (see Lazarus & Serber, 1968).

Even when techniques are painstakingly applied after a thorough behavior analysis certain voids may nevertheless remain. Perry London (1964) has pointed out the hiatus between meaning and function in a most compelling and poignant passage:

> And perhaps as many times, there must be men who, freed of all their symptomatic woes, discover then a truer misery, until now buried underneath a host of petty ills. Preoccupied no more with pedantries, with headaches, phobias, or vile thoughts, a nauseating emptiness appears to them ahead, a nameless terror

of a nameless end. Can this still be a symptom, and if so, still violable by some concrete Act, by formulation of a habit or association with some pleasantness-arousing stimulus pulled from a bag of therapeutic tricks? May not men leap from cliffs for other reasons than those for which dogs salivate to bells? Are there not meanings, goals, and fears, and aspirations which, subject to words, to understanding and appraisal, dictate some pains and balms alike rooting themselves more firmly as they settle into consciousness and intertwine with all man's myriad thoughts of self? [pp. 38–39]"

In dealing with the behavioral manifestations of an *existential neurosis* (Maddi, 1967), it becomes clear that the quality of a man's life cannot always be inferred from his behaviors, and that there is no simple 1-to-1 relationship between a person's behavior and his experience of subjective meaningfulness in life. Problems of meaning take us too far beyond behavior therapy to remain within the scope of this book. To quote London (1964, p. 39) again: "Whether life has meaning or not, there are men who think it does, or can or should; for these, perhaps the search alone or lack of it brings repair or suffering."

The Nature of Techniques

It has been argued that the very acts of listening and of understanding and interviewing constitute *techniques* of therapy (e.g., Harms & Schreiber, 1963). Adhering to the dictionary meaning of the word "technique" (which implies the specific ordering of technical details) one can speak of various techniques of interviewing, but an interview per se is too vague to be considered a therapeutic technique. In the present context, the term *technique* will denote the use of procedures which go beyond the therapeutic relationship and the ordinary "clinical interview." This is not to deny that the effectiveness of a given technique may often be dependent upon the therapeutic relationship, or even constitute an extension of it.

Some writers confuse "techniques" with "processes." For instance, when Sloane (1969) alludes to a number of techniques which differ from "interpretation" to "counterconditioning," he tends to distort the clinical and theoretical issues involved. Counterconditioning is not a technique but a descriptive process for the procedure whereby a "conflicting response is conditioned to a CS that is not simultaneously being reinforced [English and English, 1958, p. 108]." The technique of desensitization may be viewed as one of the many counterconditioning processes.

Face Saving

Often, the use of a technique offers the patient a face-saving device. For instance, about ten years ago, a man consulted me with a fairly common problem. He claimed to be happily married to a delightful person with whom he had four children, but had nevertheless become involved with his secretary—a situation which was beginning to threaten his marriage. Attempts to discontinue his extramarital relationship were usually truncated by his secretary's tearful recriminations. He had consulted a hypnotist before seeing me but found that he was not "hypnotizable."

I decided to apply a simple "anxiety-relief" procedure. He was instructed to think about his mistress and to recollect especially intimate and erotic moments with her, at which point I delivered a fairly unpleasant electric shock to his right hand. He was to endure the shock for as long as possible and to say his wife's name when he wished me to turn off the electricity. We repeated this about twenty times during that session. I asked him to bring a photograph of his mistress to the next session so that we could "negatively condition" him to the relevant visual cues. He prevailed upon me to perform the visual conditioning the very next day.

He produced a photograph of his mistress and one of his wife. I proceeded to shock him whenever he looked at the picture of his mistress and to switch off the current as soon as he looked at his wife's photograph. This sequence was also repeated about twenty to thirty times within a half-hour.

I did not hear from him again, but I did receive an exceedingly impolite phone call from his irate mistress. Evidently, he had informed her that he had consulted me with a view to determining whether or not to divorce his wife, whereupon I allegedly attached him to an elaborate electrical conditioning apparatus which had brainwashed him—against his will and better judgment—to remain married to his wife. Furthermore, the conditioning had made it impossible for him to respond erotically to anyone but his own wife. As heavily committed as I was to conditioning theory in those days, even I was aware that the behavior change in question may have rested on factors other than conditioning!

Techniques as Shorthand Communication Levers

Many patients are prone to distort, magnify, and exaggerate anticipatory events which cause them undue concern. One may skillfully show them the irrational manner in which they repeatedly build up extreme anxiety; or one may interpret the psychodynamic implications which underlie these tendencies. Either path may seldom produce a noticeable decrease in, or control over such behavior. Yet a simple semantic device may often prove exceedingly helpful. I point out to my patients who complain of anticipatory anxiety that they invariably respond according to a *what if* principle. "What if so and so happens?" "What if so and so doesn't happen?" I instruct them to place a *so* in front of each "what if." The change from "what if," to "so what if," is frequently both far-reaching and profound.

While sitting in on cases with Milton Erickson one day, I observed him attempting to persuade a most obstinate man to pursue a different line of reasoning regarding his marital relationship. The patient was adamant that he had considered all the alternatives and refused to listen to Erickson's arguments. Dr. Erickson accused the man of being rigid and inflexible and added that he was able to think along one dimension only. The patient contested this observation and observed that he was anything but rigid or unidimensional in his thought patterns, whereupon Erickson said, "I'll prove my point to you." He then simply wrote "710" on a piece of paper and asked the man to provide him with every conceivable combination. The patient soon provided eleven combinations (107, 701, 170, 071, 017, 71, 17, 10, 07, 01, 70). Dr. Erickson emphasized that he had asked for *every possible combination,* to which the patient responded by insisting that he had exhausted every possibility. Erickson then accused him of making the same error as he did with his marriage by refusing to look at it from a different angle and thus perceive an entirely new world of discourse. He then turned the page upside down so that the numbers "710" now formed the word

"OIL." The patient became noticeably more receptive to Erickson's point of view and began examining the alternate conceptions to which he had been deaf before Erickson's "number-letter technique."

Any active clinician will undoubtedly have dozens of his own devices, diagrams, tricks, narratives, and methods of driving home a point, or of providing the patient with effective tools. Frequently, the right technique (meaning the one which fits the personalistic needs of the individual) will make the critical difference between failure and success. There are, of course, literally hundreds of different techniques in use, and it behooves clinicians to be familiar with as many as possible. Obviously, one need not subscribe to the theoretical system which gave rise to individual techniques in order to apply them effectively.

No attempt will be made to offer even a small representative sample of all the techniques on the market. The number is simply too great. In addition to the techniques already described, I shall list a few more methods which have tended to yield gratifying results when used in the right way with the right people. This is in keeping with Strupp and Bergin's (1969) emphasis upon clinical and research *specificity*. One might also mention that techniques per se can hardly counterbalance the harmful effects of low-empathy therapists who often seem inclined to do damage to their patients (Bergin, 1963, 1966; Truax & Carkhuff, 1967). The sharp focus upon techniques is in no way intended to support the alarming growth of dehumanizing influences. Indeed, *humanism*, which as Ullmann and Krasner (1969, p. 599) point out has been defined as "any system or mode of thought or action in which human interests, values, and dignity predominate," is the one fixed variable in our otherwise fluid and personalistic emphasis.

Additional Methods

Hypnosis

It is useful to learn five or six different methods of trance induction so that one can slip effortlessly and smoothly from one into another, thus maximizing the chances of inducing medium to deep states of hypnosis in those individuals who seem likely to benefit from it. Depending on the needs of each case, much can be accomplished with hypnosis. While phenomena such as age regression and time distortion, or the projection of vivid images and fantasies can be achieved without hypnosis (Barber 1962, 1964), it is usually easier to employ these techniques after using some trance-inducing patter. Besides, there is evidence that patients are more likely to accept therapeutic advice and suggestions while somewhat sleepy or drowsy than when wide-awake (Platonov, 1959).

Most of the techniques in this book can be applied with or without first inducing hypnosis, depending upon the therapist's appraisal of the situation. This is not the place to provide instructions on trance induction (there are already many books on the subject) and it should be noted that the best way to learn hypnosis is to observe one or two competent hypnotists in action.

A Case of Autohypnosis. People who respond favorably to posthypnotic suggestion can often be taught various techniques of autohypnosis (Salter, 1955) and thus inoculate themselves with numerous positive suggestions. A rather unusual case which I treated several years ago by means of autohypnosis is worth citing:

> Mrs. M. the illegitimate daughter of a prostitute spent her first three years in an atmosphere of disruption and decay. She was reared in the basement of a Parisian brothel until social welfare workers intervened and removed her to an orphanage. Her adolescent years were spent in London and, shortly before the outbreak of war, she returned to the Continent and married a rich industrialist. Her husband was killed in action and during the war she witnessed numerous atrocities and was allegedly raped by German soldiers. After the war she experienced a mental breakdown and underwent almost 5 years of psychoanalysis with a Viennese analyst. She claimed that this treatment was mildly successful in rendering her less prone to sexual recriminations, but what she termed her "panic attacks" remained unaltered.
>
> She described herself as living in an almost perpetual state of anxiety, but at about weekly intervals she would experience a sensation of mild panic which became progressively more intense in the span of only a few minutes until this feeling became so unbearable that she would scream with sheer terror, throw herself on the floor, and attempt to render herself unconscious. The intense panic would gradually subside after 4 or 5 minutes.
>
> A detailed neurological examination apparently ruled out the presence of epilepsy or other cerebral pathology. She reported

that her psychoanalyst had linked her "panic attacks" with previous real or imagined sexual traumata.

In 1952 she became the mistress of an English barrister and moved to London until 1955, when she became estranged from her lover. She stated that while in London she underwent about 20 insulin coma treatments which led to an exacerbation of her condition. She came to South Africa towards the end of 1955 and consulted a psychiatrist who allegedly suggested a leucotomy.

The present writer treated her during July, 1956. She was seen 15 times over a period of 4 weeks. After the initial diagnostic sessions (during which we unsuccessfully attempted to trace any specific factors which might have preceded her panic states) she was given concurrent training in relaxation and hypnotic procedures. Repeated posthypnotic suggestions to the effect that she would no longer experience her attacks of panic had no ameliorating effect whatsoever. She was experiencing these attacks at 5–7 day intervals and became depressed and suicidal when the ordinary hypnotic therapy failed.

Autohypnotic techniques were then administered and the patient was soon able to put herself into a fairly deep hypnotic trance by saying the words "deeply asleep" 5 times. She was instructed to employ autohypnosis as soon as she felt an oncoming attack of panic and to suggest to herself that, on awakening from her trance, she would feel completely calm and relaxed. This proved highly successful and she was thus able to circumvent her panic states. She reported that the entire autohypnotic sequence took less than a minute. At first, this method merely succeeded in reducing the intensity of her panic states, but as she became more proficient at autohypnosis, she managed to block these attacks completely.

A follow-up enquiry, after 22 months, revealed that she was generally less anxiety-ridden and that her attacks had diminished in frequency to less than once in 2 months. She still successfully used the autohypnotic procedure when necessary [Lazarus, 1958a].

Hypnotic Anxiety Relief. A method which has proved exceedingly effective with several people is outlined below:

The patient relaxes on a comfortable reclining chair or on a well-upholstered couch or bed, and is given repeated suggestions to feel more and more relaxed, pleasantly warm and heavy, drowsy and sleepy, calm and peaceful. Ever more deep and satisfying levels of calm and serenity are suggested over and over. This procedure continues for about ten to fifteen minutes, or until it is obvious (from psychophysical measurement or direct observation) that the patient is profoundly relaxed and calm. The patient is then requested to think the words "calmly relaxed" over and over, and to associate these verbal cues with the ongoing physiological and psychological states of tranquillity. He is then informed that in tension or anxiety-producing situations, he will find the words "calmly relaxed" capable of relieving his anxieties if uttered subvocally several times.

The "As If" Procedure

Patients often bemoan incidents in their past where significant others neglected or abused them. Rationally, one may emphasize that these events are in the past and should be forgiven and forgotten, but this frequently fails to have effect. In many instances, however, it has proved useful to take people "back in time" (under hypnosis or simply while relaxing with their eyes closed) and then to have them imagine the absence of the negative or traumatic incidents, or a sequence of positive interactions which they may have wished for at the time. Thus, for instance, a person who constantly complains about his ill treatment at the hands of an older sibling, now deceased and out of reach for an assertive confrontation, can go back in time and fantasy the opposite— his older brother being exceedingly kind, supportive, and considerate. Repetition of this fantasy can lead the patient to feel *as if* he had in fact been treated kindly by his brother.

Ahsen (1968) working from an entirely different theoretical standpoint, described the case of a thirty-five-year-old teacher who had suffered from constipation and anal fissures for a period of eight years. He was raised by puritanical parents in the absence of physical love and affection. When asked to state a pet name his mother may have used when in a loving mood toward him, he said, "She has never loved me, but once or twice she called me 'my little sonny.'" Ahsen then asked the patient to visualize the following sequence:

> He sees himself as very young. There is the old, old house where he used to live in his infancy. There is that old room where his mother used to sleep. There is also that old bed, where the mother used to lie. She is lying there. He as a child is lying with

her in that old bed. Mother is fondling him. She is calling him "my little sonny" and is kissing and hugging him. He is feeling those kisses and embraces all over his body. He is feeling wonderful.

The patient through encouragement and persuasion was able to project the whole scene vividly. When the imagery had become lucid and stable, he was instructed to repeat it during the next fortnight at home.

As a result of this image-exercise the patient started having regular motions from the next day. By another few days the anal fissure also subsided. He was feeling happy and contented. A follow-up carried over the next eight months showed no recurrence of symptoms [pp. 346–347].

The applications of "eidetic imagery" within a therapeutic context are very wide ranging. For instance, Ahsen (1968) reports rapid therapeutic effects from applying many images involving the expression of "love" and "hate." A patient conflicted by undue ambivalence toward, say, his mother, can imagine himself going back (or forward) in time and killing the "bad mother" (i.e., erasing her negative qualities) while loving the "good mother." This may be accompanied by directed muscular activity, such as kicking or punching a canvas bag when thinking about the "bad mother" (cf. Lazarus, 1965).

Time Projection

Time projection techniques can be used with or without hypnosis. In essence, the method enables people to imagine themselves a few days to several years into the future, while perceiving themselves functioning happily and effectively at that future date. I have used this procedure mainly with depressed patients (Lazarus, 1968), but it is by no means limited to this condition. For instance, a young man who lacked self-confidence in social situations was hypnotized and instructed to picture himself three months into the future where he would see himself brimming with confidence while handling his social interactions with assurance and aplomb. He was asked to practice positive imagery several times a day in between sessions. A diligent pupil, he reported imagining a film of himself having a range of successful personal and social encounters which, he claimed, tended to close the credibility gap between reality and fantasy with each projected rehearsal. His rapid gains in overt self-assurance were confirmed by his friends and acquaintances.

The rationale for the use of time projection with depressed individuals is that since "depression may be regarded as a function of inadequate or insufficient reinforcers ... once the patient can imagine himself sufficiently freed from his oppressive inertia to engage in some enjoyable (or formerly enjoyable) activity, a lifting of depressive affect is often apparent [Lazarus, 1968]."

A Case History Using Time Projection with a Depressed Patient.
A middle-aged woman was deeply depressed following the death of a good friend. She consulted a psychiatrist who prescribed drugs and explored her guilt feelings and overdependency, all to no avail. The patient spent most of her time in bed. An operant conditioner was of the opinion that her withdrawn behavior was being maintained and supported by positive reinforcement in the form of concern and sympathy from friends and relatives. There was no evidence to support this contention. It seemed to me that following the shock and grief which accompanied her good friend's demise, she had entered a self-perpetuating state of mourning, resulting in a weakened behavioral repertoire and a chronic nonreinforcing state of affairs which rendered her refractory to most positive stimuli. I offered to apply a time projection sequence hoping thereby to shatter her web of inertia.

A reinforcement survey schedule (Cautela & Kastenbaum, 1967) revealed that she derived some pleasure from eating ice cream and taking hot showers, and when not depressed she enjoyed listening to classical music, gardening, window shopping, reading about famous people, going to movies, dining in restaurants, playing bridge, and buying new clothes.

As the bulk of the initial interview was taken up with background information and administering the reinforcement schedule, I tried to expedite matters by inducing a light hypnotic trance in the patient, and suggesting that she would feel less depressed and engage in a number of rewarding activities before her next visit. She arrived for her second visit feeling no better, having been "forced to remain in bed" as she felt "so weak." The time projection sequence was then administered more or less as follows:

A light hypnotic trance was induced and the patient was asked to concentrate on each of her positive reinforcers in turn. "Imagine yourself eating a dish of delicious ice cream. Enjoy it to the full. See the creamy texture; dig your spoon in; bring it toward your mouth; smell and taste the delicious flavor; feel the smooth texture with your tongue. Relax and really enjoy it." Next, to enhance her ongoing positive feelings, she was asked to imagine herself enjoying a hot shower. Thereafter, the crucial *anticipation* of positive reinforcement was introduced in the following way: "Think about the enjoyable things you can do tomorrow. How about a bit of gardening, followed by a hot shower, after which you can play one of your favorite Mozart recordings, while indulging in another dish of ice cream." (At this point the patient interrupted the sequence and joked that I would replace her depression with a problem of obesity. She then remarked, "My God! That's the first time I've laughed since Myrna's death.")

We continued the time projection sequence by advancing, in imagination, day by day, and filling each day with a variety of "non-fattening reinforcers." She was required to immerse herself as realistically as possible in each activitiy until she could feel all the accompanying pleasures and the full enjoyment of each pursuit. Toward the end of the session we had advanced seven days into the future. The important *retrospective contemplation phase* was then carried out. "Now look back over the past week that you have just lived through. In retrospect it's been a pretty busy and rewarding time. Try to capture a good feeling about it all. It's been an enjoyable week. Now we can let that week become two weeks and two weeks soon becomes one month as we advance further into the future. . . ."

At the next visit (a week later) the patient reported that she had done "pretty much what we had covered in imagination" although she had to "push myself fairly hard in the beginning . . . but it's getting easier all the time." At her request, we then extended the time projection sequence several years into the future. This patient was followed up two years later and indicated that apart from "normal downs," she had experienced no undue misery or depression.

Thought Control

Many patients suffer from persistent and intrusive trains of thought that are unrealistic and upsetting. One of my patients, for instance, constantly brooded about the possibility of a fire breaking out at one of his stores although there were no objective fire hazards and he was fully insured. There are numerous individuals who worry incessantly about "low-probability catastrophies." An analytical chemist would torment himself quite unrealistically over the possibility that he may have come in contact with harmful or radioactive chemicals during his day's work. Another of my patients was obsessed with the idea that something might lodge in his windpipe and suffocate him to death. Eating became an overwhelming ordeal for him.

People who become anxious due to insistent negative thoughts that are out of proportion to the realities involved are often helped by a simple thought-stopping procedure that was advocated by Bain (1928). They are simply asked to shut their eyes and to dwell on their futile thoughts in the presence of the therapist. Suddenly the therapist shouts, "Stop!" and then draws the patient's attention to the fact that the thoughts actually do stop. This is repeated several times, and the patient is then asked to interrupt his own negative thoughts by saying "Stop" subvocally. He is urged to interrupt the returning thoughts again and again. Often patients report that this method causes the thoughts to become noticeably weaker and considerably easier to exclude.

Some people find it better to shout or to think the word "Stop!" and immediately to concentrate on something else. Others find it more effective to carry a small hand-shocking device and to give themselves a fairly unpleasant electrical impulse upon saying "Stop!" Other people find expletives such as "Go to hell!" "Screw you!" "Get out of my head!" more effective than "Stop!" Other people prefer to shout "Stop!" and immediately thereafter to picture a very large stop sign or a series of neon lights spelling out STOP!

The "Blow-up" Technique

The "blow-up" procedure is in a sense the antithesis of the thought-stopping method described above, yet its final effect is also that of controlling or eliminating obsessional thinking. People who do not find the "Stop!" technique effective often respond positively to the "blow-up" technique.

For instance, I had a twenty-two-year-old male patient with several debilitating obsessive-compulsive reactions. One of his most distressing habits was a tendency to keep checking the men's room at a theatre or movie for a possible outbreak of fire. Typically, at intermission, or before taking his seat in the movie, he would visit the men's room, smoke a cigarette, and then go inside the theatre. Soon he would feel a mounting panic. He would ask himself, "I wonder whether I accidentally started a fire in the men's room?" He would leave his seat and rush back to the men's room and carefully check to be sure that no fire had in fact broken out. When back at his seat again he would feel that he may have failed to detect the fire, and he would soon develop an overwhelming urge to rush back and make doubly sure. This was repeated about fifteen to twenty times during the average movie, thereby proving a source of annoyance and embarrassment.

He first tried ridding himself of these obsessional thoughts by internally or subvocally screaming "Stop!" over and over, supplemented by self-delivered electric shocks from a small portable faradic device. He would nevertheless experience a mounting tension which would soon "force" him to rush back to the men's room.

I then gave him the following instructions: "When the urge to check comes over you, do not leave your seat. Instead, I want you to imagine that a fire has indeed broken out. First, picture the toilet paper and then the toilet seats catching fire and spreading to the doors, then going along the floor, so that eventually the entire men's room is ablaze. Then, as you sit in your seat, imagine the crackling flames spreading outside the men's room into the lobby. The carpets quickly catch fire and soon the entire movie house or theatre is a roaring inferno. This blaze is like no other. It cannot be stopped. Still sitting in your seat, imagine the entire neighborhood on fire. Firemen battle the blaze unsuccessfully as all neighboring areas catch fire until the entire city is devoured. And still the flames keep spreading. One city after another is demolished in this voracious chain reaction until the entire country is ablaze. The flames even spread across the oceans until the entire world is on fire. Eventually the whole universe is one raging inferno."

The patient practiced this sequence when he next attended a movie and reported that after an initial acute feeling of panic, he became calm, somewhat amused, and "realized how ridiculous it was to keep checking." He then applied the same method to other obsessive-compulsive areas and reported, "When I get a frightening idea I immediately blow it up. . . . It's really great. . . . It works!"

The "blow-up technique" has a good deal in common with Stampfl's (1967) *implosive procedure*, but it is probably more similar to the method of *paradoxical intention* (Frankl, 1960; Gerz, 1962). Many phobic and obsessive-compulsive problems seem to disappear when the therapist deliberately prescribes the troublesome symptom (Haley, 1963). An integral element in Frankl's paradoxical intention procedure is the deliberate evocation of humor. A patient who fears that he may perspire is enjoined to show his audience what perspiration is really like, to perspire in gushes of drenching torrents of sweat which will moisturize everything within touching distance. The patient with anticipatory anxiety about fainting is told to become the world's best "passer-out" and is encouraged to start fainting immediately. Gerz (1962, p. 375) points out that "when the patient tries to pass out and finds he cannot, he starts to laugh." The therapeutic impact lies in the fact that when people encourage their anticipatory anxieties to erupt, they nearly always find the opposite reaction coming to the fore—their worst fears subside and when the method is used several times, their dreads eventually disappear. There are many theoretical explanations which can be offered to account for these observed changes. It would seem to me that cybernetic concepts applied to psychotherapy and behavior change can provide many fertile and meaningful explanations (e.g., Phillips & Wiener, 1966). However, in keeping with the tenor of this book, our main concern is with *what* works rather than *how* it works.

Within the same general area of encouraging the patient to permit his affective states to expand and develop (instead of suppressing or avoiding negative affect), Gendlin (1969) has described an interesting bodily method or introspective technique called *experiential focusing*. The patient, while quietly relaxed, is placed in a contemplative mood and gently coaxed into examining his spontaneous thoughts and feelings until one special *feeling* emerges at the focus of his full experiential attention. After several minutes of intense focusing the method ends with the patient taking "what is fresh, or new, in the feel of it *now*," and also allowing "the words and pictures to change until they feel just right in capturing your feelings." The primary impact of Gendlin's focusing technique is that it immediately shifts the emphasis from talking and thinking about problems to their felt bodily expressions. The net result is often an immediate desensitization.

Exaggerated Role Taking

A procedure similar to Kelly's (1955) fixed-role therapy has proved effective with several inhibited people. In essence, one instructs these individuals to adopt prescribed roles which are very different from their customary behavior.

For example, a timid housewife who found her husband's wealthy parents and her sister-in-law extremely patronizing and condescending toward her, inevitably became tense and unhappy prior to, during, and after their weekly visits. Her husband was unsympathetic to her plight and insisted that it was "all in her head." She was instructed, when next visited by her in-laws, to pretend that she had in fact descended from royalty and that she was a princess incognito. Throughout their entire social exchange, she was to act in a manner befitting to someone of her royal lineage. The patient was advised to keep saying to herself, "I am a princess; you are a commoner." This exaggerated role tended to mitigate those behaviors which formerly made her vulnerable to real or imagined slights from her husband's family. People with a reasonable dramatic flair often find this technique useful in dealing with specific interpersonal situations which ordinarily place them at an emotional disadvantage.

Differential Relaxation

Many tense or agitated individuals with somatic or so-called "psychosomatic" complaints derive immense benefit from relaxation training. In some people the autonomic effects of deep relaxation are the opposite of those which characterize anxiety. During relaxation, respiration usually becomes slower, pulse rate and blood pressure decrease, and a noticeable calming effect ensues. People who enjoy the relaxation process should be encouraged to practice total relaxation for ten to fifteen minutes at least twice a day (i.e., "letting go of all your muscles and relaxing deeper and deeper, further and further beyond the furthest point"). Then they are taught "differential relaxation," which is the ability to relax those muscles which are not in use during various activities. Thus, while driving a car, one is able to relax one's stomach muscles, chest, back, and (if the car has automatic transmission) one's left leg. While walking, it is possible to relax one's shoulders, arms, chest, and upper back. Patients may also profit from learning to *do* things (e.g., write, talk, walk, sit) in a relaxed manner. In training people to maintain some degree of relaxation nearly all the time, one of the best procedures is role playing or behavior rehearsal. The therapist asks the patient to perform various activities and points out his areas of tension.

It is often best to start with a fairly bland semihypnotic general relaxation sequence (see Appendix C) and then to modify the instructions or suggestions according to the patient's feedback. I usually record the General Relaxation Instructions on tape and lend it to those patients who have ready access to a recorder. Those who do not have a recorder may be handed a printed sheet of relaxation instructions and told to ask a friend or relative to read it to them in a slow, quiet tone. In either event, whenever the patient reports enjoyable feelings or sensations, these should be inserted into the person's individual sequence. For instance, the patient who reports, "I felt a safe feeling, as if I had been wrapped in cotton," should be told, toward the end of his next training session, "Now feel that safe feeling; feel that you are comfortably and protectively wrapped in cotton."

Although, contrary to Jacobson (1964), relaxation is hardly a panacea, relaxation procedures are often extremely useful in combating many of the effects of tension and, as such, deserve a respected place in every therapist's technical repertoire.

Aversion Therapy

The literature on aversion therapy is almost as voluminous as that on desensitization procedures. Aversive stimulation in therapy is usually limited to those disorders in which the patient frequently engages in undesirable or unacceptable behavior (e.g., excessive drinking, drug taking, overeating, smoking, homosexuality, fetishism, transvestism, and other compulsive behaviors). The aim is to eliminate responses which are considered injurious to the individual himself or to others. By introducing a painful, punishing, or unpleasant stimulus in temporal contiguity with the unacceptable or undesirable behavior, it is hoped that some permanent connection will be established between the unwanted responses and the unpleasant stimulation. The punishing stimulus is delivered immediately after the undesirable response so that unpleasant stimulation becomes an immediate consequence of the undesirable behavior, and autonomic reactions and associations are presumably changed from "positive" to "negative." In many instances, successful aversion therapy may be said to bring about a greater degree of "self-control."

Although entire books have been devoted to the subject of aversion therapy and aversive stimulation (e.g., Rachman & Teasdale, 1969; Jones, 1969), these procedures have come to play a less and less important role in my own practice over the past few years. In my experience, the construction of positively reinforcing conditions (such as decreasing heterosexual anxiety and building a repertoire of adequate lovemaking techniques in homosexuals) usually has longer-lasting benefit than the introduction of aversive stimulation. Obviously, aversive stimulation can be used in conjunction with the development of new prosocial responses, and it goes without saying that combined regimes are usually more effective than either procedure alone. In a dual program involving aversive stimulation and positive retraining, it is unnecessary to hurt people or rob them of their human dignity. Aversion therapy is usually a harrowing experience. Some studies have used *suffocation* produced by the injection of a curare-like drug which causes respiratory paralysis for between 30 and 150 seconds (Campbell, Sanderson, & Laverty, 1964; Sanderson, Campbell, & Laverty, 1964). The systematic use of powerful emetic drugs goes back many years (Voegtlin & Lemere, 1942) and despite their unesthetic, arduous, and extremely unpleasant (if not dangerous) side effects, many sexual deviates, alcoholics, and drug addicts have been subjected to "chemical aversion" (e.g., Raymond, 1964). Rachman (1965) has argued in favor of electrical aversive stimulation, although here also, the nature of the treatment is often exceedingly unpleasant and punitive if not harrowing.

There are three principal ways of employing aversive stimuli as treatment rather than torture:

1. Broad-spectrum therapy which employs several retraining procedures may call for unpleasant (rather than painful) stimuli at certain crucial stages (e.g., Lazarus, 1965a).

2. By employing appropriate cues to reinforcers, the strength of the aversive agent need not be excessive (Lazarus, 1968e; Wilson &

Davison, 1969). *This entails matching stimuli to appropriate modalities.*

3. The use of *aversive imagery* can often circumvent the need for unpleasant or painful physical stimuli (Lazarus, 1958; Cautela, 1967).
   Points 2 and 3 require elaboration.

Matching Stimuli to Sensory Modalities. My clinical impressions have led me to believe that in treating alcoholics, the administration of painful electric shocks to the sight, smell, and taste of alcohol, is not as effective as the inhalation of an ammonia compound in temporal contiguity with the ingestion of a favorite alcoholic beverage. The same is true for compulsive eaters, who usually seem to curb their overindulgence when using an olfactory-gustatory stimulus such as "smelling salts" rather than faradic shock when eating forbidden foods. Faradic shock seems appropriate when treating tactile stimuli, as would be the case in a hand-washing compulsion. As Wilson and Davison (1969) point out, behavior therapy should consider not only the *functional* nature of stimuli and responses, but also *topographical* considerations.

The Use of Aversive Imagery. One of the first reports of aversive imagery within a behavioral context was a case concerning a compulsive architect whose needlessly repetitive checking slowed down his work efficiency and productivity (Lazarus, 1958).

The patient was hypnotized and given, more or less, the following instructions while in a deep hypnotic trance: "You feel calm and relaxed, deeply relaxed and peaceful. Now I want you to imagine yourself at work. You still feel calm and relaxed. Now imagine yourself drawing a plan and checking as you go along. You're quite relaxed. You check it once. Everything is correct. You make sure and go over it again. You are still calm and relaxed. You begin to check it a third time, but now suddenly you feel anxious. You feel uneasy and tense. Rapidly the tension mounts. (The patient was writhing and breathing very heavily at this stage.) You leave the plan. You do not check it again. Now you start a new drawing. Picture the new situation. As soon as you start the new activity you are once again calm and relaxed. You feel calm and peaceful. . . ."

After about ten sessions the patient reported that he was turning out much more work, and that although he was still slightly compulsive, it no longer interfered with his work.

Cautela (1967) has extended the use of aversive imagery under the term *covert sensitization*. The patient, while relaxing with his eyes closed, is asked to visualize the pleasurable object (e.g., cigarettes, liquor, candy, homosexual companion) and upon picturing himself about to indulge, he is told to imagine that he begins to feel sick and, in imagination, begins to vomit all over the floor, and all over the cigarettes (or food or drink). He is further to imagine vomiting all over his companions and himself. Next he is asked to visualize the entire scene again by himself and to try and feel the sensations of nausea.

The relief scenes involve decisions to avoid the negative stimuli (i.e., he decides not to have a drink, or not to eat candy, and so forth), and he feels the clean fresh air, or pictures himself enjoying a clean and invigorating shower. When employing the technique, patients are advised to remember that nausea and vomiting will cease as soon as they turn away from the undesirable object or situation.

Upon examining many of the techniques described in this chapter and elsewhere throughout this book, the reader will probably observe how many methods hinge on the use of imagery. At present I am testing out several novel applications of emotive imagery and at the same time examining the value of exercises for training people to increase their powers of mental imagery. These methods, however, are still entirely experimental and have not been used with sufficient patients to warrant being included in this book.

Concluding Comments

Certain individuals will undoubtedly be inclined to emphasize the areas of overlap between the personalistic-behavioral procedures spelled out in this book and other approaches to psychotherapy. It can only be hoped that significant points of departure between some of the notions in this book and other systems of psychotherapy will not elude the reader.

The person who reads this book in search of a gimmick will doubtless be disappointed. He may discover several novel and effective procedures for particular individuals, but all these methods are intended for application by flexible and astute clinicians.

The personalistic emphasis focuses upon the individual case rather than upon averages derived from statistical analyses of relatively large groups of patients. Very little attention is devoted to broad descriptive or diagnostic labels such as phobics, homosexuals, sociopaths, schizophrenics, etc. The emphasis is upon the phobic or homosexual or so-called "sociopathic" individual. My colleagues and trainees often ask general questions which betray their nonpersonalistic attitudes: "I have a homosexual patient; how should I cure him?" "What is the best method for use with phobias?" "How do you overcome anxiety?" While it is true that data based on extensive group studies of patient populations can tell us that X percent of cases are likely to respond better to one method than to another, we are still unsure what will help a given individual in the group. Thus, while Yates (1970) correctly pointed to statistics showing the superiority of conditioning methods in the treatment of enuresis, he incorrectly alluded to the fact that this weakened the argument that the mother-child relationship was often responsible for the origin and maintenance of the problem. In many individual cases I have found that children sabotage or directly refuse to cooperate with a conditioning program until interpersonal factors have been ironed out. Statistically speaking, this may only be true of 15 to 20 percent of the patient population, but it matters greatly when the child under consideration happens to be one of these unusual cases. In other words, as Lazarus and Davison (1971) have pointed out, "the application of a general principle in a particular case would seem to depend not only on a familiarity with the principle but also on an accurate assessment of the given case."

The essence of meaningful clinical research has been clearly identified by Strupp and Bergin (1969) as the need to discover "how technique and therapist variables interact to influence client behavior under specifiable conditions." Hopefully some enterprising researcher will glean sufficient impressions from this book to design and carry out the necessary studies to shed further light on the active ingredients of therapeutic processes.

APPENDIX A
LIFE
HISTORY
QUESTIONNAIRE

Purpose of This Questionnaire:

The purpose of this questionnaire is to obtain a comprehensive picture of your background. In scientific work, records are necessary, since they permit a more thorough dealing with one's problems. By completing these questions as fully and as accurately as you can, you will facilitate your therapeutic program. You are requested to answer these routine questions in your own time instead of using up your actual consulting time.

It is understandable that you might be concerned about what happens to the information about you, because much or all of this information is highly personal. Case records are strictly confidential. *No Outsider Is Permitted to See Your Case Record without Your Permission.*

If you do not desire to answer any questions, merely write "Do not care to answer."

Date: _____

1. *General:*

Name: _____

Address _____

_____

Telephone Numbers: _____   _____

Age: _____ Occupation: _____

By whom were you referred? _____

With whom are you now living? (List people.) _____

_____

Do you live in a house, hotel, room, apartment, etc.? _____

Marital status: (Circle answer.)

Single; engaged; married; remarried; separated; divorced; widowed.

2. *Clinical:*

(a) State in your own words the nature of your main problems and their duration:

(b) Give a brief account of the history and development of your complaints (from onset to present):

(c) On the scale below please estimate the severity of your problem(s):

Mildly upsetting	Moderately severe	Very severe	Extremely severe	Totally incapacitating

(d) Whom have you previously consulted about your present problem(s)?

3. *Personal Data:*

(a) Date of birth: _____ Place of birth: _____

(b) Mother's condition during pregnancy (as far as you know:)

(c) *Underline* any of the following that applied during your childhood:

Night terrors   Bed wetting   Sleepwalking
Thumb-sucking   Nail-biting   Stammering
Fears   Happy childhood   Unhappy childhood
Any other:

(d) Health during childhood?

List illnesses:

(e) Health during adolescence?

List illnesses:

(f) What is your height? _____ your weight? _____

(g) Any surgical operations? (Please list them and give age at time.)

(h) When were you last examined by a doctor? _____

(i) Any accidents? _____

(j) List your five main fears:
   (1)
   (2)
   (3)
   (4)
   (5)

(k) *Underline* any of the following that apply to you:

Headaches	Dizziness	Fainting spells
Palpitations	Stomach trouble	No appetite
Bowel disturbances	Fatigue	Insomnia
Nightmares	Take sedatives	Alcoholism
Feel tense	Feel panicky	Tremors
Depressed	Suicidal ideas	Take drugs
Unable to relax	Sexual problems	Shy with people
Don't like weekends and vacations	Overambitious	Can't make decisions
	Inferiority feelings	Home conditions bad
Can't make friends	Memory problems	Unable to have a good time
Can't keep a job		Concentration difficulties
Financial problems		
Others:		

(l) *Underline* any of the following words which apply to you:
Worthless, useless, a "nobody," "life is empty."
Inadequate, stupid, incompetent, naive, "can't do anything right."
Guilty, evil, morally wrong, horrible thoughts, hostile, full of hate.
Anxious, agitated, cowardly, unassertive, panicky, aggressive.
Ugly, deformed, unattractive, repulsive.

Depressed, lonely, unloved, misunderstood, bored, restless.

Confused, unconfident, in conflict, full of regrets.

Worthwhile, sympathetic, intelligent, attractive, confident, considerate.

Others:

(m) Present interests, hobbies, and activities:

(n) How is most of your free time occupied?

(o) What is the last grade of schooling that you completed?

(p) Scholastic abilities; strengths and weaknesses:

(q) Were you ever bullied or severely teased?

(r) Do you make friends easily?

Do you keep them?

4. *Occupational Data:*

(a) What sort of work are you doing now?

(b) Kinds of jobs held in the past?

(c) Does your present work satisfy you? (If not, in what ways are you dissatisfied?)

(d) What do you earn? _____ How much does it cost you to live?

_____

(e) *Ambitions:*
Past:

Present:

5. *Sex Information:*

(a) Parental attitudes to sex (e.g., was there sex instruction or discussion in the home?)

(b) When and how did you derive your first knowledge of sex?

(c) When did you first become aware of your own sexual impulses?

(d) Did you ever experience any anxieties or guilt feelings arising out of sex or masturbation? If "yes" please explain.

(e) Any relevant details regarding your first or subsequent sexual experience:

(f) Is your present sex life satisfactory?
(If not, please explain.)

(g) Provide information about any significant heterosexual (and/or homosexual) reactions:

6. *Menstrual History:*

Age at first period? _____ Were you informed or did it come as a shock? _____

Are you regular? _____

Duration: _____

Do you have pain? _____

Date of last period: _____ Do your periods affect your moods?

_____

7. *Marital History:*

How long have you been married? _____

How long did you know your marriage partner before engagement?

_____

Husband's/wife's age:_____

Occupation of husband or wife: _____

Personality of husband or wife (in your own words):

In what areas is there compatibility?

In what areas is there incompatibility?

How do you get along with your in-laws? (This includes brothers- and sisters-in-law).

How many children have you?
Please list their sex and age(s).

Do any of your children present special problems?

Any relevant details regarding miscarriages or abortions?

Give details of any previous marriage(s):

8. *Family Data:*

(a) *Father:*

    Living or deceased? _____

    If deceased, your age at the time of his death? _____

    Cause of death? _____

    If alive, father's present age? _____

    Occupation: _____

    Health: _____

(b) *Mother:*

    Living or deceased? _____

    If deceased, your age at the time of her death? _____

Cause of death? _____

If alive, mother's present age? _____

Occupation: _____

Health: _____

(c) *Siblings:*

Number of brothers: _____ Brothers' ages: _____

Number of sisters: _____ Sisters' ages: _____

Relationship with siblings:

(a) Past:

(b) Present:

Give a description of your father's personality and his attitude toward you (past and present):

Give a description of your mother's personality and her attitude toward you (past and present):

In what ways were you punished by your parents as a child?

Give an impression of your home atmosphere (i.e., the home in which you grew up. Mention state of compatibility between parents and between parents and children).

Were you able to confide in your parents?

If you have a stepparent, give your age when parent remarried:

Give an outline of your religious training:

If you were not brought up by your parents, who did bring you up, and between what years?

Has anyone (parents, relatives, friends) ever interfered in your marriage, occupation, etc.?

Who are the most important people in your life?

Does any member of your family suffer from alcoholism, epilepsy, or anything which can be considered a "mental disorder?" Give details.

Are there any other members of the family about whom information regarding illness, etc., is relevant?

Recount any fearful or distressing experiences not previously mentioned:

List any situations that make you feel particularly anxious.

List the benefits you hope to derive from therapy.

List any situations which make you feel calm or relaxed.

Have you ever lost control (e.g., temper or crying or aggression?) If so, please describe.

Please add any information not tapped by this questionnaire that may aid your therapist in understanding and helping you.

Self-description:

Please complete the following:

I am _____.

I am _____.

I am _____.

I am _____.

I feel _____.

I feel _____.

I feel _____.

I feel _____.

I think _____.

I think _____.

I think _____.

I think _____.

I wish _____.

I wish _____.

I wish _____.

I wish _____.

Use the blank sides of these pages to give a word picture of yourself as would be described:

(a) By yourself

(b) By your spouse (if married)

(c) By your best friend

(d) By someone who dislikes you

APPENDIX B
PATIENT'S
THERAPY
SESSION
REPORT

This booklet contains a series of questions about the therapy session which you have just completed. These questions have been designed to make the description of your experiences in the session simple and quick. There are two types of questions.

One type of question is followed by a series of numbers on the right-hand side of the page. After you read each of the questions, you should circle the number "0" if your answer is "no"; circle the number "1" if your answer is "some"; etc.

The other questions have a series of numbered statements under them. You should read each of these statements and select the *one* which comes closest to describing your answer to that question. Then circle the number in front of your answer.

Once you have become familiar with the questions through regular use, answering them should take only a few minutes. Please feel free to write additional comments on a page when you want to say things not easily put into the categories provided.

Be Sure to Answer Each Question.

Identification _____

Date of Session _____

Reprinted by permission of David E. Orlinsky, Ph.D. and Kenneth I. Howard, Ph.D.

How Do You Feel about the Session Which You Have Just Completed?

(Circle the one answer which best applies.)

This Session Was:

1. Perfect

2. Excellent

3. Very good

4. Pretty good

5. Fair

6. Pretty poor

7. Very poor

What Subjects Did You Talk about During This Session?
(For each subject, circle the answer which best applies.)

During This Session I Talked About:

	No	Some	A Lot
My mother.	0	1	2
My father.	0	1	2
My brothers or sisters.	0	1	2
My childhood.	0	1	2
My adolescence.	0	1	2
Religious feelings, activities or experiences.	0	1	2
Work, career, or education.	0	1	2
Relations with others of the same sex.	0	1	2
Relations with the opposite sex.	0	1	2
Financial resources or problems with money.	0	1	2
Feelings about spouse or about being married.	0	1	2
Household responsibilities or activities.	0	1	2
Feelings about children or being a parent.	0	1	2
Body functions, symptoms, or appearance.	0	1	2
Strange or unusual ideas and experiences.	0	1	2
Hopes or fears about the future.	0	1	2
Dreams or fantasies.	0	1	2
Attitudes or feelings toward my therapist.	0	1	2

	No	*Some*	*A Lot*
Therapy: feelings and progress as a patient.	0	1	2
Other: _____		1	2

Be Sure That You Have Checked Every Item.

What Did You Want or Hope to Get out of This Session?

(For each item, circle the answer which best applies.)

This Session I Hoped or Wanted To:

	No	*Some*	*A Lot*
Get a chance to let go and get things off my chest.	0	1	2
Learn more about what to do in therapy, and what to expect from it.	0	1	2
Get help in talking about what is really troubling me.	0	1	2
Get relief from tensions or unpleasant feelings.	0	1	2
Understand the reasons behind my feelings and behavior.	0	1	2
Get some reassurance about how I'm doing.	0	1	2
Get confidence to try new things, to be a different kind of person.	0	1	2
Find out what my feelings really are, and what I really want.	0	1	2
Get advice on how to deal with my life and with other people.	0	1	2
Have my therapist respond to me on a person-to-person basis.	0	1	2
Get better self-control.	0	1	2
Get straight on which things I think and feel are real and which are mostly in my mind.	0	1	2
Work out a particular problem that's been bothering me.	0	1	2

	No	*Some*	*A Lot*
Get my therapist to say what he (she) really thinks.	0	1	2
Other: _____		1	2

Be Sure That You Have Checked Every Item.

What Problems or Feelings Were You Concerned about This Session?
(For each item, circle the answer which best applies.)

During This Session I Was Concerned About:

	No	*Some*	*A Lot*
Being dependent on others.	0	1	2
Meeting my obligations and responsibilities.	0	1	2
Being assertive or competitive.	0	1	2
Living up to my conscience: shameful or guilty feelings.	0	1	2
Being lonely or isolated.	0	1	2
Sexual feelings and experiences.	0	1	2
Expressing or exposing myself to others.	0	1	2
Loving; Being able to give of myself.	0	1	2
Angry feelings or behavior.	0	1	2
Who I am and what I want.	0	1	2
Fearful or panicky experiences.	0	1	2
Meaning little or nothing to others; being worthless or unlovable.	0	1	2
Other: _____		1	2

Be Sure That You Have Checked Every Item.

What Were Your Feelings During This Session?
(For each feeling, circle the answer which best applies.)

During This Session I Felt:

	No	Some	A Lot
Confident	0	1	2
Embarrassed	0	1	2
Relaxed	0	1	2
Withdrawn	0	1	2
Helpless	0	1	2
Determined	0	1	2
Grateful	0	1	2
Relieved	0	1	2
Tearful	0	1	2
Close	0	1	2
Impatient	0	1	2
Guilty	0	1	2
Strange	0	1	2
Inadequate	0	1	2
Likeable	0	1	2
Hurt	0	1	2
Depressed	0	1	2
Affectionate	0	1	2
Serious	0	1	2
Anxious	0	1	2
Angry	0	1	2
Pleased	0	1	2
Inhibited	0	1	2
Confused	0	1	2
Discouraged	0	1	2
Accepted	0	1	2

	No	*Some*	*A Lot*
Cautious	0	1	2
Frustrated	0	1	2
Hopeful	0	1	2
Tired	0	1	2
Ill	0	1	2
Thirsty	0	1	2
Sexually attracted	0	1	2
Other: _____		1	2

Be Sure That You Have Checked Every Item.

During This Session, How Much:

	Slightly or not at all	Some	Pretty much	Very much
Did you talk?	0	1	2	3
Were you able to focus on what was of real concern to you?	0	1	2	3
Did you take initiative in bringing up the subjects that were talked about?	0	1	2	3
Were you logical and organized in expressing yourself?	0	1	2	3
Were your emotions or feelings stirred up?	0	1	2	3
Did you talk about what you were feeling?	0	1	2	3
Were you angry or critical toward yourself?	0	1	2	3
Did you have difficulty thinking of things to talk about?	0	1	2	3

Be Sure That You Have Checked Every Item.

During This Session, How Much:

	Slightly or not at all	Some	Pretty much	Very much
Friendliness or respect did you show towards your therapist?	0	1	2	3
Were you free and spontaneous in expressing yourself?	0	1	2	3
Did you try to persuade your therapist to see things your way?	0	1	2	3
Were you attentive to what your therapist was trying to get across to you?	0	1	2	3
Did you tend to accept or agree with what your therapist said?	0	1	2	3
Did you have a sense of control over your feelings and behavior?	0	1	2	3
Were you negative or critical towards your therapist?	0	1	2	3
Were you satisfied or pleased with your own behavior?	0	1	2	3

Be Sure That You Have Checked Every Item.

How Did You Feel about Coming to Therapy This Session?
(Circle the answer which best applies.)

1. Eager; could hardly wait to get here.

2. Very much looked forward to coming.

3. Somewhat looked forward to coming.

4. Neutral about coming.

5. Somewhat reluctant to come.

6. Unwilling; felt I didn't want to come at all.

How Much Progress Do You Feel You Made in Dealing with Your Problems?
(Circle the answer which best applies.)

1. A great deal of progress.

2. Considerable progress.

3. Moderate progress.

4. Some progress.

5. Didn't get anywhere this session.

6. In some ways my problems seem to have gotten worse this session.

How Well Do You Feel That You Are Getting Along Emotionally and Psychologically at This Time?
(Circle the answer which best applies.)

I am getting along:

1. Very well; much the way I would like to.
2. Quite well; no important complaints.
3. Fairly well; have my ups and downs.
4. So-so; manage to keep going with some effort.
5. Fairly poorly; life gets pretty tough for me at times.
6. Quite poorly; can barely manage to deal with things.

To What Extent Are You Looking forward to Your Next Session?
(Circle the answer which best applies.)

1. Intensely; wish it were much sooner.
2. Very much; wish it were sooner.
3. Pretty much; will be pleased when the time comes.
4. Moderately; it is scheduled and I guess I'll be there.
5. Very little; I'm not too sure I will want to come.

What Do You Feel That You Got out of This Session?
(For each item, circle the answer which best applies.)

I Feel That I Got:

	No	*Some*	*A Lot*
A chance to let go and get things off my chest.	0	1	2
Hope: A feeling that things can work out for me.	0	1	2
Help in talking about what was really troubling me.	0	1	2
Relief from tensions or unpleasant feelings.	0	1	2
More understanding of the reasons behind my behavior and feelings.	0	1	2
Reassurance and encouragement about how I'm doing.	0	1	2
Confidence to try to do things differently.	0	1	2
More ability to feel my feelings, to know what I really want.	0	1	2
Ideas for better ways of dealing with people and problems.	0	1	2
More of a person-to-person relationship with my therapist.	0	1	2
Better self control over my moods and actions.	0	1	2
A more realistic evaluation of my thoughts and feelings.	0	1	2
Nothing in particular: I feel the same as I did before the session.	0	1	2
Other: _____		1	2

Be Sure That You Have Checked Every Item.

How Did Your Therapist Seem to Feel During This Session?
(For each item, circle the answer which best applies.)

My Therapist Seemed:

	No	Some	A Lot
Pleased	0	1	2
Thoughtful	0	1	2
Annoyed	0	1	2
Bored	0	1	2
Sympathetic	0	1	2
Cheerful	0	1	2
Frustrated	0	1	2
Involved	0	1	2
Playful	0	1	2
Demanding	0	1	2
Apprehensive	0	1	2
Effective	0	1	2
Perplexed	0	1	2
Detached	0	1	2
Attracted	0	1	2
Confident	0	1	2
Relaxed	0	1	2
Interested	0	1	2
Unsure	0	1	2
Optimistic	0	1	2
Distracted	0	1	2
Affectionate	0	1	2
Alert	0	1	2
Close	0	1	2
Tired	0	1	2
Other: _____		1	2

Be Sure That You Have Checked Every Item.

During This Session, How Much:

	Slightly or not at all	Some	Pretty much	Very much
Did your therapist talk?	0	1	2	3
Was your therapist attentive to what you were trying to get across?	0	1	2	3
Did your therapist tend to accept or agree with your ideas and point of view?	0	1	2	3
Was your therapist negative or critical towards you?	0	1	2	3
Did your therapist take initiative in bringing up things to talk about?	0	1	2	3
Did your therapist try to get you to change your point of view or way of doing things?	0	1	2	3
Was your therapist friendly and warm towards you?	0	1	2	3
Did your therapist show feeling?	0	1	2	3

Be Sure That You Have Checked Every Item.

How Well Did Your Therapist Seem to Understand What You Were Feeling and Thinking This Session?

(Circle the answer which best applies.)

My Therapist:

1. Understood exactly how I thought and felt.
2. Understood very well how I thought and felt.
3. Understood pretty well, but there were some things he (she) didn't seem to grasp.
4. Didn't understand too well how I thought and felt.
5. Misunderstood how I thought and felt.

How Helpful Do You Feel Your Therapist Was to You This Session?

(Circle the answer which best applies.)

1. Completely helpful.
2. Very helpful.
3. Pretty helpful.
4. Somewhat helpful.
5. Slightly helpful.
6. Not at all helpful.

Additional Comments:

APPENDIX C
GENERAL
RELAXATION
INSRUCTIONS

Begin by getting as comfortable as you can. Settle back comfortably. Just try to let go of all the tension in your body. Now take in a deep breath. Breathe right in and hold it (five-second pause). And now exhale. Just let the air out quite automatically and feel a calmer feeling beginning to develop. Now just carry on breathing normally and just concentrate on feeling heavy all over in a pleasant way. Study your own body heaviness. This should give you a calm and reassuring feeling all over (ten-second pause). Now let us work on tension and relaxation contrasts. Try to tense every muscle in your body. Every muscle: your jaws, tighten your eyes, your shoulder muscles, your arms, chest, back, stomach, legs, every part just tensing and tensing. Feel the tension all over your body—tighter and tighter—tensing everywhere, and now let it go, just stop tensing and relax. Try to feel this wave of calm that comes over you as you stop tensing like that. A definite wave of calm (ten-second pause).

Now I want you to notice the contrast between the slight tensions that are there when your eyes are open and the disappearance of these surface tensions as you close your eyes. So while relaxing the rest of your body just open your eyes and feel the surface tensions which will disappear when you close your eyes. Now close your eyes and feel the greater degree of relaxation with your eyes closed (ten-second pause) all right, let us get back to the breathing. Keep your eyes closed and take in a deep, deep breath and hold it. Now relax the rest of your body as well as you can and notice the tension from holding your breath. Study the tension. Now let out your breath and feel the deepening relaxation— just go with it beautifully relaxing now. Breathe normally and just feel the relaxation flowing into your forehead and scalp. Think of each part as I call it out—just relaxing—just letting go, easing up, eyes and nose, facial muscles. You might feel a tingling sensation as the relaxation flows in. You might have a warm sensation. Whatever you feel I want you to notice it and enjoy it to the full as the relaxation now spreads very beautifully into the face, into the lips, jaws, tongue, and mouth so that your lips are slightly parted as the jaw muscles relax further and further. The throat and neck relaxing (five-second pause), shoulders and upper back relaxing, further and further, feel the relaxation flowing into your arms and to the very tips of your fingers (five-second pause). Feel the relaxation in your chest as you breathe regularly and easily. The relaxation spreads even under your armpits and down your sides, right into the stomach area. The relaxation becomes more and more obvious as you do nothing but just give way to the pleasant serene emotions which fill you as you let go more and more. Feel the relaxation—stomach and lower back all the way through in a warm, penetrating, wavy, calm and down your hips, buttocks, and thighs to the very, very tips of your toes. The waves of relaxation just travel down your calves to your ankles and toes. Feel relaxed from head to toe. Each time you practice this you should find a deeper level of relaxation being achieved—a deeper serenity and calm, a good calm feeling.

Now to increase the feelings of relaxation at this point what I want you to do is just keep on relaxing and each time you exhale, each time you breathe out for the next minute, I want you to think the word *relax* to yourself. Just think the word *relax* as you breathe out. Now just do that for the next minute (one-minute pause). Okay, just feel that deeper relaxation and carry on relaxing. You should feel a deeper, deeper feeling of relaxation. To even further increase the benefits, I want you to feel the emotional calm, those tranquil and serene feelings which tend to cover you all over inside and out, a feeling of safe security, a calm indifference—these are the feelings which relaxation will enable you to capture more and more effectively each time you practice a relaxation sequence. Relaxation will let you arrive at feeling a quiet inner confidence—a good feeling about yourself (five-second pause). Now once more feel the heavy sensations that accompany relaxation as your muscles switch off so that you feel in good contact with your environment, nicely together, the heavy good feeling of feeling yourself calm and secure and very, very tranquil and serene.

Now we can deepen the relaxation still further by just using some very special stimulus words. Let's use the words *calm* and *serene*. What I would like you to do is to think these words to yourself twenty times or so. Don't bother to count. Approximately twenty or thirty times just say to yourself *calm* and *serene* and then feel the deepening—ever, ever deepening—waves of relaxation as you feel so much more calm and serene. Now you just do that; take your time, think of the words and feel the sensations over and over (pause of about one minute). Good.

Now I am going to count backward from 10 to 1. At the count of 5 I would like you to open your eyes, and then by the time I reach 1, just kind of stretch and yawn and then you can switch off the recorder and just go back and relax on your own. Okay, now counting backward: 10, 9, 8, 7, 6, 5, open your eyes 4, 3, 2, and 1. Now just stretch and kind of yawn and then slowly get up and switch off the recorder and then you can go back and carry on relaxing as long as you wish.

NOTE: For further reference consult A. Lazarus, "Daily Living: Coping with Tensions and Anxieties" (a series of cassette recordings incorporating three relaxation instructions) Chicago, Ill.: Instructional Dynamics Incorporated.

REFERENCES

Ahsen, A. *Basic concepts in eidetic psychotherapy.* New York: Eidetic Publishing House, 1968.

Alexander, F. The dynamics of psychotherapy in the light of learning theory. *American Journal of Psychiatry,* 1963, **120**, 440–448.

Arnold, M. *Emotion and personality.* New York: Columbia, 1960.

Ayllon, T. Intensive treatment of psychotic behavior by stimulus satiation and food reinforcement. *Behaviour research and therapy,* 1963, **1**, 53–62.

Ayllon, T., & Azrin, N. H. The measurement and reinforcement of behavior of psychotics. *Journal of the Experimental Analysis of Behavior,* 1965, **8**, 357–383.

Azrin, N. H., & Lindsley, O. R. The reinforcement of cooperation between children. In L. P. Ullmann & L. Krasner (Eds.), *Case studies in behavior modification.* New York: Holt, 1965. Pp. 330–333.

Bach, G. R., & Wyden, P. *The intimate enemy.* New York: Morrow, 1969.

Bachrach, A. J., & Quigley, W. A. Direct methods of treatment. In I. A. Berg & L. A. Pennington (Eds.), *Introduction to clinical psychology.* (3rd ed.) New York: Ronald, 1966. p. 510.

Baer, D. M. Laboratory control of thumbsucking by withdrawal and representation of reinforcement. *Journal of the Experimental Analysis of Behavior,* 1962, **5**, 525–528.

Bain, J. A. *Thought control in everyday life.* New York: Funk & Wagnalls, 1928.

Bambeck, J. J. *Kritische Analyse behavioristischer Lerntheorien hinsichtlich ihrer ideologischen Fundamente.* Unpublished doctoral dissertation, Salzburg University, 1968.

Bandura, A., & Walters, R. H. *Social learning and personality development.* New York: Holt, 1963.

Bandura, A. Behavior modification through modeling procedures. In L. Krasner & L. P. Ullmann (Eds.), *Research in behavior modification.* New York: Holt, 1965. Pp. 310–340.

Bandura, A., Grusec, J. E., & Menlove, F. L. Vicarious extinction of avoidance behavior. *Journal of personality and Social Psychology,* 1967, **5**, 16–23.

Bandura, A. Modeling approaches to the modification of phobic disorders. In R. Porter, (Ed.), *The role of learning in psychotherapy.* Boston: Little, Brown, 1968, Pp. 201–217.

Bandura, A., & Menlove, F. L. Factors determining vicarious extinction of avoidance behavior through symbolic modeling. *Journal of Personality and*

Social Psychology, 1968, **8**, 99–108.

Bandura, A. *Principles of behavior modification.* New York: Holt, 1969.

Barber, T. X. Hypnotic age regression: A critical review. *Psychosomatic Medicine*, 1962, **24**, 286–299.

Barber, T. X. Hypnotizability, suggestibility, and personality: V. A. critical review of research findings. *Psychological Reports*, 1964, **14**, 299–320.

Barnard, J. W., & Orlando, R. *Behavior modification: A bibliography.* Nashville: IMRID Papers and Reports, IV, **3**, 1967.

Barrett, B. H. Acquisition of differentiation and discrimination in institutionalized retarded children. *American Journal of Orthopsychiatry*, 1965, **35**, 862–885.

Beck, A. T. *Depression: Clinical, experimental and theoretical aspects.* New York: Harper & Row, 1967.

Bergin, A. E. The effects of psychotherapy; negative results revisited. *Journal of Counseling Psychology*, 1963, **10**, 244–250.

Bergin, A. E. Some implications of psychotherapy research for therapeutic practice. *Journal of Abnormal Psychology*, 1966, **71**, 235–246.

Bergin, A. E. & Garfield. *Handbook of psychotherapy and behavior change.* New York: Wiley, 1971.

Bergler, E., & Kroger, W. S. The dynamic significance of vaginal lubrication to frigidity. *Western Journal of Surgery*, 1953, **61**, 711–719.

Berne, E. *Games people play.* New York: Grove Press, 1964.

Bettelheim, B. *The empty fortress: Infantile autism and the birth of the self.* New York: Free Press, 1967.

Boulding, K. E. Am I a man or a mouse—or both? In A. Montague (Ed.), *Man and aggression.* London: Oxford University Press, 1968, Pp. 83–90.

Bousfield, W. A., & Orbison, W. D. Ontogenesis of emotional behavior. *Psychological Review*, 1952, **59**, 1–7.

Brady, J. P. Brevital-relaxation treatment of frigidity. *Behaviour Research and Therapy*, 1966, **4**, 71–78.

Breger, L., & McGaugh, J. L. Critique and reformulation of "learning-theory" approaches to psychotherapy and neurosis. *Psychological Bulletin*, 1965, **63**, 338–358.

Brown, P., & Elliott, R. Control of aggression in a nursery school class. *Journal of Experimental Child Psychology*, 1965, **2**, 103–107.

Cameron, D. E. *Psychotherapy in action.* New York: Grune & Stratton, 1968.

Campbell, D., Sanderson, R. E., & Laverty, S. G. Characteristics of a conditioned response in human subjects during extinction trials following a single traumatic conditioning trial. *Journal of Abnormal and Social Psychology*, 1964, **68**, 627–639.

Carkhuff, R. R., & Berenson, B. G. *Beyond counseling and therapy*. New York: Holt, 1967.

Carlin, A. S., & Armstrong, H. E. Aversive conditioning: learning or dissonance reduction? *Journal of Consulting and Clinical Psychology*, 1968, **32**, 674–678.

Cautela, J. R. Covert sensitization. *Psychological Record*, 1967, **20**, 459–468.

Cautela, J. R., & Kastenbaum, R. A reinforcement survey schedule for use in therapy, training, and research. *Psychological Reports*, 1967, **20**, 1115–1130.

Conn, J. H. Hypnosynthesis: Psychobiologic principles in the practice of dynamic psychotherapy utilizing hypnotic procedures. *The International Journal of Clinical and Experimental Hypnosis*, 1968, **16**, 1–25.

Coopersmith, S. *The antecedents of self-esteem*. San Francisco: Freeman, 1967.

Davison, G. C. A social learning therapy programme with an autistic child. *Behaviour Research and Therapy*, 1964, **2**, 149–159.

Davison, G. C. An intensive, long-term social-learning treatment program with an accurately diagnosed autistic child. Proceedings of the 73rd annual convention of the American Psychological Association. Washington: APA, 1965. Pp. 203–204.

Davison, G. C. Some problems of logic and conceptualization in behavior therapy research and theory. Paper presented at the first annual meeting of the Association for the Advancement of Behavior Therapy, held at the 75th Annual Convention of the American Psychological Association. Washington, 1967.

Davison, G. C. Systematic desensitization as a counterconditioning process. *Journal of Abnormal Psychology*, 1968, **73**, 91–99.

Davison, G. C. Self-control in an unruly young adolescent through imaginal aversive contingency and "one-downsmanship." In J. D. Krumboltz & C. E. Thoresen (Eds.), *Behavioral counseling: Cases and techniques*, 1969, Pp. 319–327.

Dollard, J., & Miller, N. E. (Eds.), *Personality and psychotherapy: An analysis in terms of learning, thinking and culture*. New York: McGraw-Hill, 1950.

Ellis, A. *Sex without guilt*. New York: Grove Press, 1958.

Ellis, A. Frigidity. In A. Ellis & A. Abarbanel (Eds.), *The encyclopedia of sexual behavior*. New York: Hawthorn, 1961, Pp. 450–456.

Ellis, A. *Reason and emotion in psychotherapy*. New York: Lyle Stuart, 1962.

Ellis, A. *The American sexual tragedy.* New York: Grove Press, 1962 (a).

Ellis, A. *The case for sexual liberty.* Tucson: Seymour Press, 1965.

Ellis, A., & Harper, R. A. *A guide to rational living.* Englewood Cliffs: Prentice-Hall, 1961.

English, H. B., & English, A. C. *A comprehensive dictionary of psychological and psychoanalytical terms.* New York: Longmans, 1958.

Eysenck, H. J. *The dynamics of anxiety and hysteria.* London: Routledge, 1957.

Eysenck, H. J. Learning theory and behaviour therapy. *Journal of Mental Science,* 1959, **105**, 61–75.

Eysenck, H. J. (Ed.), *Behaviour therapy and the neuroses.* New York: Pergamon, 1960.

Eysenck, H. J. Behaviour therapy, extinction and relapse in neurosis. *British Journal of Psychiatry,* 1963, **109**, 12–18.

Eysenck, H. J. *Experiments in behaviour therapy.* New York: Pergamon, 1964.

Eysenck, H. J. The nature of behaviour therapy. In H. J. Eysenck (Ed.), *Experiments in behaviour therapy.* New York: Pergamon, 1964 (a) Pp. 1–15.

Eysenck, H. J. *Fact and fiction in psychology.* Baltimore: Penguin, 1965.

Eysenck, H. J. The contribution of clinical psychology to psychiatry. In J. G. Howels (Ed.), *Modern perspectives in world psychiatry.* Edinburgh: Oliver & Boyd, 1968, Pp. 353–390.

Eysenck, H. J., Rachman, S. *The causes and cures of neurosis.* London: Routledge, 1965.

Feldman, M. P., & MacCulloch, M. J. The application of anticipatory avoidance learning to the treatment of homosexuality. I: Theory, technique and preliminary results. *Behaviour Research and Therapy,* 1965, **2**, 165–183.

Ferster, C. B. Positive reinforcement and behavioral deficits of autistic children. *Child Development,* 1961, **32**, 437–456.

Ferster, C. B., & DeMyer, M. K. A method for the experimental analysis of the behavior of autistic children. *American Journal of Orthopsychiatry,* 1962, **32**, 89–98.

Ferster, C. B., & Perrot, M. C. *Behavior principles.* New York: Appleton-Century-Crofts, 1968.

Fessant, J. M. Application of programmed learning for deaf children to industrial arts. *American Annals of the Deaf,* 1963, **108**, 241–244.

Frank, J. D. *Persuasion and healing.* Baltimore: Johns Hopkins, 1961.

Frankl, V. E. Paradoxical intention: A logotherapeutic technique. *American Journal of Psychotherapy,* 1960, **14,** 520–535.

Franks, C. M. (Ed.), *Behavior therapy: Appraisal and status.* New York: McGraw-Hill, 1969.

Freud, S. Turnings in the ways of psychoanalytic therapy (1919). In Collected papers, 1924, **2,** 392–402.

Freud, S. Analysis of a phobia in a five-year-old boy (1909). In Collected papers, 1925, **3,** 149–289.

Freud, S. Three contributions to the theory of sex. In A. A. Brill (Ed.), *The basic writings of Sigmund Freud.* New York: Modern Library, 1938, Pp. 553–629.

Friedman, P. H. *The effects of modeling and roleplaying on assertive behavior.* Unpublished doctoral thesis, University of Wisconsin, 1968.

Fromme, A. *Understanding the sexual response in humans.* New York: Pocket Books, 1966.

Garmezy, N. Vulnerable children: Implications derived from studies of an internalizing-externalizing symptom dimension. In J. Zubin, and A. M. Freeman (Eds.), *Psychopathology of adolescence,* New York: Grune & Stratton, 1970.

Gelder, M. G., Marks, I. M., Wolff, H. H. & Clarke, M. Desensitization and psychotherapy in the treatment of phobic states: A controlled inquiry. *British Journal of Psychiatry,* 1967, **113,** 53–73.

Gendlin, E. T. Focusing. *Psychotherapy: Theory, Research and Practice,* 1969, **6,** 4–15.

Gerz, H. O. The treatment of the phobic and the obsessive-compulsive patient using paradoxical intention. *Journal of Neuropsychiatry,* 1962, **3,** 375–387.

Gesell, A. The conditioned reflex and the psychiatry of infancy. *American Journal of Orthopsychiatry,* 1938, **8,** 19–30.

Giles, D. K., & Wolf, M. M. Toilet training institutionalized, severe retardates: An application of operant behavior modification techniques. *American Journal of Mental Deficiency,* 1966, **70,** 766–780.

Glick, B. S. Conditioning: A partial success story. *International Journal of Psychiatry,* 1969, **7,** 504–507.

Goldiamond, I. Stuttering and fluency as manipulable operant response classes. In L. Krasner & L. P. Ullmann (Eds.), *Research in behavior modification.* New York: Holt, 1965. Pp. 106–156.

Goldstein, A. P. *Therapist-patient expectancies in psychotherapy.* New York: Pergamon, 1962.

Goldstein, A. P. *Psychotherapeutic attraction.* New York: Pergamon, 1970.

Goldstein, A. P., Heller, K., & Sechrest, L. B. *Psychotherapy and the psychology of behavior change.* New York: Wiley, 1966.

Gray, B. B. & England, G. (Eds.), *Stuttering and the conditioning therapies.* Calif.: Monterey Institute for Speech and Hearing, 1969.

Griffin, G. A., & Harlow, H. F. Effects of three months of total sensory deprivation on social adjustment and learning in the rhesus monkey. *Child Development,* 1966, **37**, 533–547.

Guthrie, E. R. *The psychology of learning.* New York: Harper, 1935.

Guthrie, E. R. *The psychology of human conflict.* New York: Harper, 1938.

Haley, J. *Strategies of psychotherapy.* New York: Grune & Stratton, 1963.

Haley, J. The art of being a failure as a therapist. *American Journal of Orthopsychiatry,* 1969, **39**, 691–695.

Hammer, E. F. (Ed.), *Use of interpretation in treatment.* New York: Grune & Stratton, 1968.

Harlow, H. F. Mice, monkeys, men and motives. *Psychological Review,* 1953, **60**, 23–32.

Harlow, H. F. Social deprivation in monkeys. *Scientific American,* 1962, **207**, 136–146.

Harms, E. & Schreiber, P. (Eds.), *Handbook of counseling techniques.* New York: Pergamon, 1963.

Harper, R. A. *Psychoanalysis and psychotherapy: 36 systems.* Englewood Cliffs: Prentice-Hall, 1959.

Harris, F., Johnston, M., Kelley, S., & Wolf, M. M. Effects of positive social reinforcement on regressed crawling of a nursery school child. *Journal of Educational Psychology,* 1964, **55**, 35–41.

Hart, B. M., Allen, K. E., Buell, J. S., Harris, F. R., & Wolf, M. M. Effects of social reinforcement on operant crying. In L. P. Ullmann & L. Krasner (Eds.), *Case studies in behavior modification.* New York: Holt, 1965. Pp. 320–325.

Hastings, D. W. *Impotence and frigidity.* Boston: Little, Brown, 1963.

Hawkins, R. P., Peterson, R. F. Schweid, E., & Bijou, S. W. Behavior therapy in the home: Amelioration of problem parent-child relations with the parent in a therapeutic role. *Journal of Experimental Child Psychology,* 1966, **4**, 99–107.

Hayakawa, S. I. *Language in thought and action.* New York: Harcourt, Brace & World, 1964.

Hebb, D. O. Concerning imagery. *Psychological Review,* 1968, **75**, 466–477.

Hewett, F. M. Teaching reading to an autistic boy through operant conditioning. *The Reading Teacher*, 1964, **1**, 613–618.

Hilgard, E. R., & Bower, G. H. *Theories of learning.* New York: Appleton-Century-Crofts, 1966.

Hingtgen, J. N., Sanders, B. J., & DeMyer, M. K. Shaping cooperative responses in early childhood schizophrenics. In L. P. Ullmann & L. Krasner (Eds.), *Case studies in behavior modification.* New York: Holt, 1965. Pp. 130–138.

Hoch, P. H. Aims and limitations of psychotherapy. *American Journal of Psychiatry*, 1955, **112**, 321–327.

Hogan, R. A. The implosive technique. *Behaviour Research and Therapy*, 1968, **6**, 423–431.

Howard, F. E. & Patry, F. L. *Mental health.* New York: Harper, 1935.

Jackson, D. D. The study of the family. *Family Process*, 1965, **4**, 1–20.

Jacobson, E. *Anxiety and tension control: A psychobiologic approach.* Philadelphia: Lippincott, 1964.

Jaffe, S. L., & Scherl, D. J. Acute psychosis precipitated by T-group experiences. *Archives of General Psychiatry*, 1969, **21**, 443–448.

Jersild, A. T., & Holmes, F. B. Methods of overcoming children's fears. *Journal of Psychology*, 1935, **1**, 75–104.

Jones, H. G. The application of conditioning and learning techniques to the treatment of a psychiatric patient. *Journal of Abnormal and Social Psychology*, 1956, **52**, 414–420.

Jones, M. C. The elimination of children's fears. *Journal of Experimental Psychology*, 1924, **7**, 382–390.

Jones, M. C. A laboratory study of fear: The case of Peter. *Pedagogical Seminary*, 1924 (a), **31**, 308–315.

Jones, M. R. (Ed.), *Aversive stimulation.* Coral Gables: University of Miami Press, 1969.

Jourard, S. M. *The transparent self.* Princeton: Van Nostrand, 1964.

Kant, F. *Frigidity: Dynamics and treatment.* Springfield, Ill.: Charles C Thomas, 1969.

Kelly, G. A. *The psychology of personal constructs.* New York: Norton, 1955.

Kerr, N., Meyerson, L., & Michael, J. A procedure for shaping vocalizations in a mute child. In L. P. Ullmann & L. Krasner (Eds.), *Case studies in behavior modification.* New York: Holt, 1965. Pp. 366–370.

Kinsey, A. C., Pomeroy, W. B., Martin, C. E., & Gebhard, P. H. *Sexual behavior in the human male.* Philadelphia: Saunders, 1948.

Krasner, L. Studies of the conditioning of verbal behavior. *Psychological Bulletin,* 1958, **55,** 148–170.

Krasner, L. & Ullmann, L. P. (Eds.), *Research in behavior modification.* New York: Holt, 1965.

Kretschmer, E. *Kretschmer's textbook of medical psychology* (E. B. Strauss trans.) London: Oxford University Press, 1934. (1st German edition 1922.)

Kronhausen, E. & Kronhausen, P. *The sexually responsive woman.* New York: Ballantine Books, 1964.

Kugelmass, I. N. Foreward. In S. Rachman, *Phobias: Their nature and control.* Springfield, Ill.: Charles C Thomas, 1968.

Lang, P. J. The mechanics of desensitization and the laboratory study of human fear. In C. M. Franks (Ed.), *Behavior therapy: Appraisal and status.* New York: McGraw-Hill, 1969.

Lang, P. J., Lazovik, A. D. & Reynolds, D. J. Desensitization, suggestibility, and pseudotherapy. *Journal of Abnormal Psychology,* 1965, **70,** 395–402.

Lazarus, A. A. New methods in psychotherapy: a case study. *South African Medical Journal,* 1958, **32,** 660–664.

Lazarus, A. A. Some clinical applications of autohypnosis. *South African Medical Proceedings,* 1958, **4,** 848–850. (a)

Lazarus, A. A. The elimination of children's phobias by deconditioning. *Medical Proceedings,* 1959, **5,** 261–265.

Lazarus, A. A. Group therapy of phobic disorders by systematic desensitization. *Journal of Abnormal and Social Psychology,* 1961, **63,** 505–510.

Lazarus, A. A. The results of behaviour therapy in 126 cases of severe neurosis. *Behaviour Research and Therapy,* 1963, **1,** 69–79.

Lazarus, A. A. Crucial procedural factors in desensitization therapy. *Behaviour Research and Therapy,* 1964, **2,** 65–70.

Lazarus, A. A. A preliminary report on the use of directed muscular activity in counter-conditioning. *Behaviour Research and Therapy,* 1965, **2,** 301–303.

Lazarus, A. A. Towards the understanding and effective treatment of alcoholism. *South African Medical Journal,* 1965, **39,** 736–741. (a)

Lazarus, A. A. Broad spectrum behavior therapy and the treatment of agoraphobia. *Behaviour Research and Therapy,* 1966, **4,** 95–97.

Lazarus, A. A. Behavior rehearsal vs. non-directive therapy vs. advice in effecting behavior change. *Behaviour Research and Therapy,* 1966, **4,** 209–212. (a)

Lazarus, A. A. In support of technical eclecticism. *Psychological Reports,* 1967, **21,** 415–416.

Lazarus, A. A. Learning theory and the treatment of depression. *Behaviour Research and Therapy*, 1968, **6**, 83–89.

Lazarus, A. A. Behavior therapy and graded structure. In R. Porter (Ed.), *The role of learning in psychotherapy*, Boston: Little, Brown, 1968. (a)

Lazarus, A. A. Variations in desensitization therapy. *Psychotherapy: Theory, Research and Practice*, 1968, **5**, 50–52. (b)

Lazarus, A. A. Behavior therapy and marriage counseling. *Journal of the American Society of Psychosomatic Dentistry and Medicine*, 1968, **15**, 49–56. (c)

Lazarus, A. A. Behavior therapy in groups. In G. M. Gazda (Ed.) *Basic approaches to group psychotherapy and group counseling*. Springfield, Ill.: Charles C Thomas, 1968. Pp. 149–175. (d)

Lazarus, A. A. Aversion therapy and sensory modalities: Clinical impressions. *Perceptual and Motor Skills*, 1968, **27**, 178. (e)

Lazarus, A. A. Broad-spectrum behavior therapy. *Newsletter of the Association for the Advancement of Behavior Therapy*, 1969, **4**, 5–6.

Lazarus, A. A. Relationship therapy: often necessary but usually insufficient. *The Counseling Psychologist*, 1969, **1**, 25–27. (a)

Lazarus, A. A. Group treatment for impotence and frigidity. *Sexology*, 1969, **36**, 22–25. (b)

Lazarus, A. A. The "inner-circle" strategy: Identifying crucial problems. In J. D. Krumboltz & C. E. Thoresen (Eds.), *Behavioral counseling: Cases and techniques*. New York: Holt, 1969. Pp. 19–24. (c)

Lazarus, A. A. & Rachman, S. The use of systematic desensitization in psychotherapy. *South African Medical Journal*, 1957, **31**, 934–937.

Lazarus, A. A., & Abramovitz, A. The use of "emotive imagery" in the treatment of children's phobias. *Journal of Mental Science*, 1962, **108**, 191–195.

Lazarus, A. A., Davison, G. C., & Polefka, D. A. Classical and operant factors in the treatment of a school phobia. *Journal of Abnormal Psychology*, 1965, **70**, 225–229.

Lazarus, A. A. & Serber, M. Is systematic desensitization being misapplied? *Psychological Reports*, 1968, **23**, 215–218.

Lazarus, A. A. & Davison G. C. Clinical innovation in research and practice. In A. E. Bergin & S. L. Garfield (Eds.), Handbook of psychotherapy and behavior change. New York: Wiley, 1971.

Lazarus, R. S. *Psychological stress and the coping process*. New York: McGraw-Hill, 1966.

Lazovik, A. D. & Lang, P. J. A laboratory demonstration of systematic desensitization psychotherapy. *Journal of Psychological Studies*, 1960, **11**, 238–247.

Leitenberg, H., Agras, W. S., Barlow, D. H., & Oliveau, D. C. Contribution of selective positive reinforcement and therapeutic instructions to systematic desensitization therapy. *Journal of Abnormal Psychology*, 1969, **74**, 113–118.

Lewin, K. *Resolving social conflicts.* New York: Harper, 1948.

Lindsley, O. R. Operant conditioning methods applied to research in chronic schizophrenia. *Psychiatric Research Reports*, 1956, **5**, 118–153.

London, P. *The modes and morals of psychotherapy.* New York: Holt, 1964.

Lovaas, O. I. Program for establishment of speech in schizophrenic and autistic children. In J. Wing (Ed.), *Early childhood autism.* New York: Pergamon, 1966.

Lovaas, O. I., Freitag, G., Gold, V. J., & Kassorla, I. C. Experimental studies in childhood schizophrenia: 1. Analysis of self-destructive behavior. *Journal of Experimental Child Psychology*, 1965, **2**, 67–84.

Lovaas, O. I., Schaeffer, B., & Simmons, J. Q. Building social behavior in autistic children by use of electric shock. *Journal of Experimental Research in Personality*, 1965, **1**, 99–109.

Lovaas, O. I., Freitas, L., Nelson, K., & Whalen, C. The establishment of imitation and its use for the development of complex behavior in schizophrenic children. *Behaviour Research and Therapy*, 1967, **5**, 171–181.

Lovibond, S. H. The mechanism of conditioning treatment of enuresis. *Behaviour Research and Therapy*, 1963, **1**, 17–21.

Lovibond, S. H. *Conditioning and enuresis.* New York: Macmillan, 1964.

Maddi, S. R. The existential neurosis. *Journal of Abnormal Psychology*, 1967, **72**, 311–325.

Madsen, C. H. Positive reinforcement in the toilet training of a normal child: A case report. In L. P. Ullmann & L. Krasner (Eds.), *Case studies in behavior modification.* New York: Holt, 1965. Pp. 305–307.

Madsen, C. H. & Ullmann, L. P. Innovations in the desensitization of frigidity. *Behaviour Research and Therapy*, 1967, **5**, 67–68.

Maher, B. A. *Principles of psychopathology.* New York: McGraw-Hill, 1966.

Marks, I. M., Gelder, M. G., & Edwards, G. Hypnosis and desensitization for phobias: A controlled prospective trial. *British Journal of Psychiatry*, 1968, **114**, 1263–1274.

Marks, I. M. *Fears and phobias*, London: Academic Press, 1969.

Marquis, J. N. & Morgan, W. K. *A guidebook for systematic desensitization.* Palo Alto, Calif.: V. A. Hospital, 1969.

Marshall, G. R. Toilet training of an autistic eight-year-old through conditioning therapy: A case report. *Behaviour Research and Therapy*, 1966, **4**, 242–245.

Masters, W. H. & Johnson, V. E. *Human sexual response.* Boston: Little, Brown, 1966.

Masters, W. H. & Johnson, V. E. *Human sexual inadequacy.* Boston: Little, Brown, 1970.

McCary, J. L. *Human Sexuality.* Van Nostrand, Princeton, 1967.

Miller, N. E. Studies of fear as an acquirable drive: 1. Fear as motivation and fear-reduction as reinforcement in the learning of new responses. *Journal of Experimental Psychology*, 1948, **38**, 89–101.

Mischel W. *Personality and assessment*, New York: Wiley, 1968.

Moore, N. Behavior therapy in bronchial asthma: A controlled study. *Journal of Psychosomatic Research*, 1965, **9**, 257–276.

Mowrer, O. H. A stimulus response analysis of anxiety and its role as a reinforcing agent. *Psychological Review*, 1939, **46**, 553–565.

Murray, E. J. & Jacobson, L. I. The nature of learning in traditional and behavioral psychotherapy. In A. E. Bergin & S. L. Garfield (Eds.), *Handbook of psychotherapy and behavior change.* New York: Wiley, 1971.

Nagy, I. B. & Framo, J. L. (Eds.), *Intensive family therapy: Theoretical and practical aspects.* New York: Harper & Row, 1965.

Neale, D. H. Behavior therapy and encopresis in children. *Behaviour Research and Therapy*, 1963, **1**, 139–149.

O'Leary, K. D., O'Leary, S. G., & Becker, W. C. Modification of a deviant sibling interaction pattern in the home. *Behaviour Research and Therapy*, 1967, **5**, 113–120.

Orlinsky, D. E. & Howard, K. I. *Therapy session report, form P and form T.* Chicago: Institute for Juvenile Research, 1966.

Orlinsky, D. E. & Howard, K. I. The good therapy hour. *Archives of General Psychiatry*, 1967, **16**, 621–632.

Orlinsky, D. E. & Howard, K. I. Inside psychotherapy. *Psychology Today*, 1968, **2**, 50–53.

Orne, M. T. & Wender, P. H. Anticipatory socialization for psychotherapy: Method and rationale. *American Journal of Psychiatry*, 1968, **124**, 88–98.

Patterson, C. H. A current view of client-centered or relationship therapy. *The Counseling Psychologist*, 1969, **1**, 2–25.

Patterson, G. R., Jones, J. W., & Wright, M. A. A behavior modification technique for the hyperactive child. *Behaviour Research and Therapy*, 1965, **2**, 217–226.

Patterson, G. R., McNeal, S., Hawkins, N. & Phelps, R. Reprogramming the social environment. *Journal of Child Psychology and Psychiatry*, 1967, **8**, 181–195.

Patterson,G. R., Ray, R. S., & Shaw, D. A. Direct intervention in families of deviant children. *Oregon Research Institute Bulletin*, 1968, **8**, 1–62.

Patterson, G. R. & Reid, J. B. Reciprocity and coercion: Two facets of social systems. In C. Neuringer, & J. Michaels (Eds.), *Behavior modification for clinical psychology*. New York: McGraw-Hill, 1969, in press.

Paul, G. L. *Insight vs. desensitization in psychotherapy*. Stanford, Calif.: Stanford, 1966.

Paul, G. L. Outcome of systematic desensitization. In C. M. Franks (Ed.), *Behavior therapy: Appraisal and status*. New York: McGraw-Hill, 1969.

Perls, F., Hefferline, R. F., & Goodman, P. *Gestalt therapy*. New York: Julian Press, 1951.

Phillips, E. L. & Wiener, D. N. *Short-term psychotherapy and structured behavior change*. New York: McGraw-Hill, 1966.

Piaget, G. W. & Lazarus, A. A. The use of rehearsal-desensitization. *Psychotherapy: Theory, Research and Practice*. 1969, **6**, 264–266.

Pihl, R. O. Conditioning procedures with hyperactive children. *Neurology*, 1967, **17**, 421–423.

Platonov, K. I. *The word as a physiological and therapeutic factor*. Moscow: Foreign Languages Publishing House, 1959.

Rachman, S. The treatment of anxiety and phobic reactions by systematic desensitization psychotherapy. *Journal of Abnormal and Social Psychology*, 1959, **58**, 259–263.

Rachman, S. Aversion therapy: Chemical or electrical? *Behaviour Research and Therapy*, 1965, **2**, 289–300.

Rachman, S. *Phobias: Their nature and control*. Springfield, Ill.: Charles C Thomas, 1968.

Rachman, S., & Eysenck, H. J. Reply to a "critique and reformulation" of behavior therapy. *Psychological Bulletin*, 1966, **65**, 165–169.

Rachman, S. & Teasdale, J. *Aversion therapy and behaviour disorders: An analysis*. Coral Gables: University of Miami Press, 1969.

Raymond, M. The treatment of addiction by aversion conditioning with apomorphine. *Behaviour Research and Therapy*, 1964, **2**, 287–292.

Richardson, A. *Mental imagery*. New York: Springer, 1969.

Rimland, B. *Infantile autism*. New York: Appleton-Century-Crofts, 1964.

Rokeach, M. *The open and closed mind*. New York: Basic Books, 1960.

Rotter, J. B. *Social learning and clinical psychology*. Englewood Cliffs: Prentice-Hall, 1954.

Rubin, I. I. *The angry book.* London: Macmillan, 1969.

Russell, B. *Essays in skepticism.* New York: Philosophical Library, 1962.

Salter, A. *Conditioned reflex therapy.* New York: Farrar, Strauss, 1949.

Salter, A. *The case against psychoanalysis.* New York: Medical Publications Limited, 1953.

Salter, A. *What is hypnosis?* New York: Farrar, Strauss, 1955.

Sanderson, R., Campbell, D., & Laverty S. An investigation of a new aversive conditioning technique for alcoholism. In C. M. Franks (Ed.), *Conditioning techniques in clinical practice and research.* New York: Springer, 1964, Pp. 165–177.

Sanford, R. N. Psychotherapy and counseling: Introduction. *Journal of Consulting Psychology,* 1948, **12**, 65–67.

Sargant, W. *Battle for the mind.* London: Heinemann, 1957.

Schaefer, H. H. & Martin, P. L. *Behavioral Therapy.* New York: McGraw-Hill, 1969.

Schofield, W. *Psychotherapy: The purchase of friendship.* Englewood Cliffs: Prentice-Hall, 1964.

Segal, H. *Introduction to the work of Melanie Klein.* London: Heinemann, 1964.

Seham, M. The conditioned reflex in relation to functional disorders in children. *American Journal of Diseases of Children,* 1932, **43**, 163–186.

Semans, J. H. Premature ejaculation: A new approach. *Southern Medical Journal,* 1956, **49**, 353–361.

Sherman, A. R. Behavioral Approaches to the Treatment of Phobic Anxiety. Unpublished doctoral thesis, Yale University, 1969.

Sidman, M. Operant techniques. In A. J. Bachrach (Ed.), *Experimental foundations of clinical psychology.* New York: Basic Books, 1962. Pp. 170–210.

Skinner, B. F. *The behavior of organisms.* New York: Appleton, 1938.

Skinner, B. F. *Science and human behavior.* New York: Macmillan, 1953.

Sloane, R. B. The converging paths of behavior therapy and psychotherapy. *International Journal of Psychiatry,* 1969, **7**, 493–503.

Sloane, R. B. and Payne, R. W. Social rituals of psychotherapy. *Excerpta Medica International Congress Series* No. 150, 1966, 2799–2801.

Smith, D. D. *Mammalian learning and behavior.* Philadelphia: Saunders, 1965.

Solovey, G. & Milechnin, A. Concerning the criterion of recovery. *Journal of Clinical and Experimental Hypnosis,* 1958, **6**, 1–9.

Staats, A. W., & Staats, C. K. *Complex human behavior: A systematic extension of learning principles.* New York: Holt, 1963.

Staats, A. W., Staats, C. K., Heard, W. Q. & Finley, J. R. Operant conditioning of factor analytic personality traits. In A. W. Staats (Ed.), *Human learning.* New York: Holt, 1964. Pp. 416–425.

Stampfl, T. G. Implosive therapy: The theory. In Armtage, S. G. (Ed.), *Behavior modification techniques in the treatment of emotional disorders.* Battle Creek, Michigan: V.A. Publication, 1967. Pp. 12–21.

Stevenson, I. & Hain, J. D. On the different meanings of apparently similar symptoms, illustrated by varieties of barber shop phobias. *American Journal of Psychiatry*, 1967, **124**, 399–403.

Storrow, H. A., & Spanner, M. Does psychotherapy change patient's attitudes? *Journal of Nervous and Mental Disease*, 1962, **134**, 440–444.

Strean, H. S. A family therapist looks at "Little Hans." *Family Process*, 1967, **6**, 227–234.

Strupp, H. H. & Bergin, A. E. Critical evaluation of some empirical and conceptual bases for coordinated research in psychotherapy: A critical review of issues, trends and evidence. *International Journal of Psychiatry*, 1969, **7**, 116–168.

Tate, B. G. & Baroff, G. S. Aversive control of self-injurious behavior in a psychotic boy. *Behaviour Research and Therapy*, 1966, **4**, 281–287.

Taylor, J. G. *The behavioral basis of perception.* New Haven: Yale, 1962.

Thorpe, J. G., Schmidt, E., Brown, P. T. & Castell, D. Aversion—relief therapy: A new method for general application. *Behaviour Research and Therapy*, 1964, **2**, 71–82.

Truax, C. B. Reinforcement and non-reinforcement in Rogerian psychotherapy. *Journal of Abnormal and Social Psychology*, 1966, **71**, 1–9.

Truax, C. B. & Carkhuff, R. R. *Toward effective counseling and psychotherapy: Training and practice.* Chicago: Aldine, 1967.

Ullmann, L. P. & Krasner, L. (Eds.), *Case studies in behavior modification.* New York: Holt, 1965.

Ullmann, L. P. & Krasner, L. *A psychological approach to abnormal behavior.* Englewood Cliffs: Prentice-Hall, 1969.

Voegtlin, W. & Lemere, F. The treatment of alcohol addiction. *Quarterly Journal of Studies on Alcohol*, 1942, **2**, 717–803.

Wahler, R. G., Winkel, G. H., Peterson, R. E., & Morrison, D. C. Mothers as behavior therapists for their own children. *Behaviour Research and Therapy*, 1965, **3**, 113–124.

Walton, D. & Mather, M. D. The application of learning principles to the treatment of obsessive-compulsive states in the acute and chronic phases of illness. *Behaviour Research and Therapy*, 1963, **1**, 163–174.

Watson, J. B. & Rayner, R. Conditioned emotional reactions. *Journal of Experimental Psychology*, 1920, **3**, 1–14.

Watzlawick, P., Beavin, J. H., & Jackson, D. D. *Pragmatics of human communication.* New York: Norton, 1967.

Weitzman, B. Behavior therapy and psychotherapy. *Psychological Review*, 1967, **74**, 300–317.

Whitlock, C., Sr. Note on reading acquisition: An extension of laboratory principles. *Journal Of Experimental Child Psychology*, 1966, **3**, 83–85.

Wiest, W. M. Some recent criticisms of behaviorism and learning theory with special reference to Breger and McGaugh and to Chomsky. *Psychological Bulletin*, 1967, **67**, 214–225.

Wike, E. L. (Ed.), *Secondary reinforcement: Selected experiments.* New York: Harper & Row, 1966.

Williams, T. A. *Dreads and besetting fears.* Boston: Little, Brown, 1923.

Wilson, G. T. & Davison, G. C. Aversion techniques in behavior therapy: Some theoretical and metatheoretical considerations. *Journal of Consulting and Clinical Psychology*, 1969, **33**, 327–329.

Wolberg, L. R. *Medical hypnosis.* New York: Grune & Stratton, 1948.

Wolberg, L. R. *The technique of psychotherapy.* (2nd ed.) New York: Grune & Stratton, 1967.

Wolf, M. M., Risley, T., & Mees, H. Application of operant conditioning procedures to the behavior problems of an autistic child. *Behaviour Research and Therapy*, 1964, **1**, 305–312.

Wolf, M. M., Birnbrauer, J. S., Williams, T., & Lawler, J. A note on apparent extinction of the vomiting behavior of a retarded child. In L. P. Ullmann & L. Krasner (Eds.), *Case studies in behavior modification.* New York: Holt, 1965. Pp. 364–366.

Wolpe, J. An approach to the problem of neurosis based on the conditioned response. Unpublished doctoral thesis, University of the Witwatersrand, Johannesburg, South Africa, 1948.

Wolpe, J. Reciprocal inhibition as the main basis of psychotherapeutic effects. *Archives of Neurology and Psychiatry*, 1954, **72**, 205–226.

Wolpe, J. Learning versus lesions as the basis of neurotic behavior. *American Journal of Psychiatry*, 1956, **112**, 542–544.

Wolpe, J. *Psychotherapy by reciprocal inhibition.* Stanford, Calif.: 1958.

Wolpe, J. The systematic desensitization treatment of neuroses. *Journal of Nervous and Mental Disease*, 1961, **132**, 189–203.

Wolpe, J. Psychotherapy: The nonscientific heritage and the new science. *Behaviour Research and Therapy*, 1963, **1**, 23–28.

Wolpe, J. Behavior therapy in complex neurotic states. *British Journal of Psychiatry*, 1964, **110**, 28–34.

Wolpe, J. New therapeutic methods based on a conditioned response theory of neurosis. *Zeitschrift Fur Psychologie*, 1964, **169**, 173–196. (a)

Wolpe, J. Parallels between animal and human neuroses. In J. Zubin, & H. F. Hunt (Eds.), *Comparative psychopathology*. New York: Grune & Stratton, 1967.

Wolpe, J. From the president. *Newsletter of the Association for Advancement of Behavior Therapy*, 1968, **3**, 1–2. (a)

Wolpe, J. Learning therapies. In J. G. Howels (Ed.), *Modern perspectives in world psychiatry*. Edinburgh: Oliver & Boyd, 1968. Pp. 557–576. (b)

Wolpe, J. *The practice of behavior therapy*. New York: Pergamon, 1969.

Wolpe, J. For phobia: A hair of the hound. *Psychology Today*, 1969, **3**, 34–37. (a)

Wolpe, J. & Lazarus, A. A. *Behavior therapy techniques*. New York: Pergamon, 1966.

Wolpe, J. & Rachman, S. Psychoanalytic evidence: A critique based on Freud's case of Little Hans. *Journal of Nervous and Mental Disease*, 1960, **130**, 135–148.

Woody, R. H. *Behavioral problem children in the schools: Recognition, diagnosis, and behavioral modification*. New York: Appleton-Century-Crofts, 1969.

Yates, A. J. The application of learning theory to the treatment of tics. *Journal of Abnormal and Social Psychology*, 1958, **56**, 175–182.

Yates, A. J. *Behavior therapy*. New York: Wiley, 1970.

Zeilberger, J., Sampen, S. & Sloane, H. Modification of a child's problem behaviors in the home with the mother as therapist. *Journal of Applied Behavior Analysis*, 1968, **1**, 47–53.

INDEXES

NAME INDEX

SUBJECT INDEX